WAR AT SEA

ESSAYS ON NAVAL WARFARE, 1776–1945

MARK CARLSON, CL, ACS

SUNBURY PRESS

Mechanicsburg, PA USA

Published by Sunbury Press, Inc.
Mechanicsburg, PA USA

SUNBURY
P R E S S

www.sunburypress.com

For information about special discounts for bulk purchases, please contact Sunbury Press Orders Dept. at (855) 338-8359 or orders@sunburypress.com.

To request one of our authors for speaking engagements or book signings, please contact Sunbury Press Publicity Dept. at publicity@sunburypress.com.

FIRST SUNBURY PRESS EDITION: April 2023

Set in Adobe Garamond Pro | Interior design by Crystal Devine | Cover by Lawrence Knorr | Edited by Sarah Peachey.

Publisher's Cataloging-in-Publication Data
Names: Carlson, Mark, author.
Title: War at sea : essays on naval warfare, 1776 – 1945 / Mark Carlson.
Description: First trade paperback edition. | Mechanicsburg, PA : Sunbury Press, 2023.
Summary: *War at Sea* covers the most dynamic era in naval history, from the American Revolution to the end of the Second World War. More than twenty published essays relate the age of fighting sail to the era of steamships, from wooden hulls to the dawn of ironclads, from the first submarines to the apogee of the aircraft carrier, and from frigates to the death of the battleship. Naval historian Mark Carlson tells the remarkable saga of war at sea in a way never before written.
Identifiers: ISBN : 979-8-88819-073-9 (paperback) | ISBN : 979-8-88819-074-6 (ePub).
Subjects: HISTORY / Maritime History & Piracy | HISTORY / Military / Naval | HISTORY / Military / United States.

Product of the United States of America
0 1 1 2 3 5 8 13 21 34 55

Continue the Enlightenment!

This work is dedicated to the men who went down to the sea in ships to protect and fight for their nation, past, present, and future. The sailors who left their shores far behind to risk death in the cold and uncaring sea have earned a place in history and in the hearts of their countrymen.

Ex communi periculo fraternitas

From common peril, brotherhood

CONTENTS

INTRODUCTION

Most people fascinated by naval warfare were first exposed to the subject through movies. Like a lot of red-blooded American boys, I loved watching war movies. I grew up with *Sink the Bismarck!* and *Task Force* with Gary Cooper, *The Enemy Below* with Robert Mitchum, and *PT 109. Tora! Tora! Tora!* has been a favorite for fifty years. Even though most of the films used large, highly detailed models in the absence of real ships, watching them depict the battles of Trafalgar, Denmark Strait, the River Plate, and Midway have brought a measure of reality to those historic events. When I saw a film about a naval battle, I was often intrigued enough to do some reading. In the era before the internet and Wikipedia, that meant going to the public library. As the years passed, my fascination with the age of fighting sail, battleships, and mighty carrier fleets, slugging it out on the ocean, grew to encompass my imagination.

For my entire adult life, I have been fascinated by military history. Books, documentaries, articles, and college courses added to my interest and knowledge. There was no going back, even when I was going back in time.

I first began writing articles on military history in 2009. At that time my focus was on aviation, a long-time passion for me. But over the past few years, I began expanding into naval history. It was not a difficult move, as many of my articles concerned the aircraft carrier war in the Pacific. From there, it was a short step to battleships, cruisers, destroyers, and even submarines. From sail to steam, from wooden hulls to ironclads, from the ancient world to the nuclear age, from broadside cannons to turrets, and from the Norman Conquest to the sinking of the *Yamato*, I have been fascinated by naval warfare.

I am fortunate to live in San Diego, where many veterans of World War II have settled. When I needed personal sources, my network of friends and associates helped me find men and women who had participated in, witnessed, or had personal knowledge of the event I was researching. Talking to these veterans has provided deep and moving insight into what it was like to be part of the Battle of Santa Cruz or the Pearl Harbor attack. Unfortunately, we have lost so many of the people who had been there and done that. In their absence, it is up to the historian and writer to dig the grains of truth out of the chaff of legend and fabrication. I often say that history is never "chiseled into stone." It is an ever-shifting horizon where the winds of time erase some information while exposing what has been long buried. That is one of the most rewarding things about history. We will always be learning more.

Captain Alfred Thayer Mahan's landmark book, *The Influence of Sea Power upon History*, has been read by many, if not most, students of war on the waters. The Spanish Armada and Trafalgar have been examined and dissected by scholars down to the last ounce of gunpowder, but even hundreds of years later, the subject never fails to fascinate. Today we have the great advantage of quickly aaccessing resources that were once only available to those who patiently dug into old files, dispatches, and documents in dusty archives. While that is still the best way to uncover long-lost tidbits of history, I am glad to make use of the books, articles, and internet archives to find what I am looking for.

What I most enjoy is digging into an event or era and finding a new way of looking at it. This book is a collection of published and unpublished essays covering many events in world naval history, from the American Revolution to the end of the Second World War.

They were published in *Naval History, Aviation History, Military History, Military Heritage, World War II History, World War II Quarterly*, and others. I expanded a few from the original published versions. With most articles limited to three thousand words, it is often difficult to include as much detail as I would like. But here I can go for broke.

Some of the most famous battles are included, along with other obscure events.

Was the German battleship *Bismarck* really the most powerful warship in the world? What was the cause of the problems with the American

Mark 14 torpedo in the first years of the Pacific War? How did the iron-clad warship come to be? What critical role did the escort carriers play in the eventual victory? How close did Admiral Horatio Nelson come to missing the French fleet in 1798? How did a single American battleship, racing around the Horn in 1898, affect United States foreign policy in the next century? What were the Q-ships of the Royal Navy? When did the last warship under sail put to sea? All these and many other moments in naval history are examined in this book.

Each chapter ends with a transition to the following essay. This is by no means a complete history of naval warfare, but I hope you will agree it has some interesting moments. I take my work seriously. What I write is intended to add to the historical record, but I hope it will also be informative and even entertaining to anyone interested in naval history.

Mark Carlson
San Diego, July 2022

THE DAY THE ROYAL NAVY LOST THE AMERICAN REVOLUTION

Published in Naval Institute Press, *Naval History*, Fall, 2022

The age of fighting sail began in the early sixteenth century during the reign of King Henry VIII. He was the first monarch to see the advantage of a navy with large, powerfully armed warships. His greatest ship was 1547's *Henry Grace à Dieu*, popularly known as *Great Harry*, a 1,000-ton, four-masted ship with forty-two cannons and 132 swivel guns. Heavily ornamented with gold leaf and high castles at the bow and stern, the ship was more suited for close-in boarding than long-range dueling. But she was the first of what would one day be the Royal Navy. Others, such as the more famous *Mary Rose* and the lavishly-gilded *Sovereign of the Seas*, soon raised the bar of size, tonnage, and firepower. But it was not until the early eighteenth century that a fully organized and equipped navy would project England's mastery of the seas.

The "ship of the line" was the most destructive engine of military power in the eighteenth century. Serving virtually the same role as nuclear weapons in today's world, the huge sailing warships, mounting from seventy to more than a hundred heavy cannons, dominated the seas for more than two hundred years. These ships, the largest of which could fire a half-ton broadside of iron death in a single devastating blast, had no equals except among themselves.

They were the largest wooden vessels ever built, requiring up to sixty-five acres of old-growth oak and pine forests to provide the 3,500 tons of wood for their immense hulls and towering masts. With a crew of more than seven hundred officers and men, the ships of the line carried 120 tons of shot and 35 tons of powder for their heavy guns.

But despite their immense power and influence, they were as vulnerable as any weapon when used improperly or, worse, confronted with radical new tactics. Thus it was in 1781 when the Royal Navy, whose supremacy of the seas had been virtually unbroken since the mid-seventeenth century, was challenged and defeated by a French fleet off the coast of North America. To add insult to that ignominy, the naval debacle led directly to the victory of George Washington over General Cornwallis at Yorktown.

"Nothing equals the beautiful order of the English at sea. Never was a line drawn straighter than that of their ships; thus, they bring all their fire to bear upon those who draw near them."

An admiring French admiral wrote those words in 1666 when the Royal Navy was beginning its ascendancy in projecting the expansion of the British Empire.

The core belief of the Admiralty was in the sheer power of the line of battle formed by several huge ships of the line bombarding an enemy fleet into splinters. The ships of the line were the very backbone of the navy.

During the 1588 battle with the Spanish Armada, warships acted independently, each captain moving against an enemy and delivering broadsides. This usually led to total confusion for a fleet commander and, with no reliable means of communication between ships, often brought less of a victory than might have been achieved with a coordinated plan.

By the time of Oliver Cromwell, a supporter of an organized navy, the concept of concentrating a fleet's firepower by following a single line under the command of a fleet admiral had become the Royal Navy's standard formation. With all the large ships following in a single line, separated by a cable's length or about two hundred yards, the full might of all the ships could be concentrated on an enemy fleet. The doctrine was printed in the Royal Navy's bible, *Fighting Instructions*, in 1663.

The use of signal flags greatly improved ship-to-ship communications, and a system of lanterns did the same at night. By the early 1700s, the Royal Navy had standardized how ships were rated. Below is a list of rates, beginning with the most powerful:

First Rate: 220 feet   850 crew   100 or more guns
Second Rate: 195 feet   700 crew   90 to 95 guns
Third Rate: 190 feet   400 crew   64 to 80 guns
Fourth Rate: 170 feet   350 crew   50 to 65 guns
Fifth Rate: 150 feet   300 crew   38 to 44 guns
Sixth Rate: 125 feet   200 crew   28 to 38 guns

Only the first three rates served in the line of battle. The fifth raters, the frigates, were the "cavalry" of the navy. For the next 120 years, no seafaring nation, including England's longtime adversaries, France and Spain, could successfully defeat a Royal Navy fleet or squadron in battle. By the time of the Seven Years' War of 1756 to 1763, the Admiralty, flushed with a string of victories by fleets using the tried and true line-ahead formation, had made it a punishable offense for any ship's captain or fleet admiral to divert from it. No captain was allowed to move independently under any circumstances, even when a golden opportunity presented itself.

There were three essential factors in eighteenth-century naval warfare. First, the weather, specifically the wind direction. While the ships of the line were the most advanced sailing vessels of their era, they were still dependent on the direction of the wind. The most favorable position for any fleet was the weather gauge, or upwind, of an enemy. With the wind behind them, a fleet could close with or refuse battle. With the maximum speed of the ship of the line being between 6 and 8 knots, simply moving a fleet into position could take several hours, during which the opposing force would be doing the same. Nothing happened fast in an eighteenth-century naval battle. The second element was the number of guns—the more, the better. Lastly, and most importantly, the skill of the fleet commander and his captains. But by the early 1780s, the skill of British admirals was of little use against the French Navy; in fact, experience was a liability instead of a benefit.

After losing several battles in the Seven Years' War, the French Navy began a serious study of how it might gain an advantage over the larger

British Navy. King Louis XVI, believing it was the "First Service of the Realm," provided large sums to renovate and improve his fleet. Beginning in 1765, the French designed and built dozens of large, powerfully armed, fast warships. New training academies were established for shipwrights, sailors, and gunners, resulting in a higher standard of gunnery and sail handling. Entire forests were cut down and transported to dozens of new dockyards along the southern and western coasts.

By 1775, France possessed the most advanced navy in the world. More than ten thousand trained gunners manned sixty-four ships of the line and over fifty frigates.

While this did not go unnoticed in England, the fossilized Admiralty saw no reason to spend huge amounts of money to improve its own fleet, neither in strength, tactics, nor efficiency. Every new ship was constructed under what was known as the "Rule of King's Thumb," meaning without any refinement or change.

It had been a popular dictum in the Royal Navy that "Just lay a Frenchman close alongside and you will defeat him every time." This was certainly true, but only if the Frenchman was unwise enough to come within close range of the British guns. While British gunners were trained to fire into enemy hulls with the heavy 32-pound and 64-pound cannons, intended to stove in and crush ribs and deliver structural damage, the better-trained French gunners aimed higher. Even with heavy cannons firing solid shot as large as a man's head, it could take dozens of broadsides to do significant damage to stout oak timbers. But the masts, yardarms, sails, and rigging, not to mention the men who handled them, were far more vulnerable. A single well-directed broadside of chain or bar shot could seriously impair a ship's ability to maneuver or maintain its position in the line of battle. In short, the French had learned not to destroy a ship's hull but rather its ability to navigate. With shredded sails and toppled masts, British ships couldn't catch the faster French ships, which would sail away at their leisure. The French now had a decided lead over the conceited Royal Navy.

By 1778, France possessed eighty modern and fast ships of the line. With Spain honoring the Bourbon Compact, another sixty powerful ships were added to the fleet to challenge Great Britain. While the Royal

Navy had about 140 big ships to go against the two fleets, only about half were in shape to fight.

The first ominous sign of looming disaster for the Royal Navy came on July 23, 1778, in the Battle of Ushant, off the coast of Brittany. Thirty British warships under the command of Admiral Augustus Keppel interposed themselves between the French coast and thirty-two French ships of the line that had come out of Brest to intercept a British convoy from the West Indies. The French force was commanded by Palliser Comte d'Orvilliers, one of the most experienced and innovative admirals in the French Navy. Keppel, having the weather gauge with the wind out of the southwest, decided to form his line ahead and wait until dawn to open fire on the enemy ships. He ordered his ships cleared for action in case the French tried an attack during the night. But instead, they managed to work their way around to the south, thereby gaining the weather gauge. When the sun came up on July 24, Keppel found he no longer had the advantage.

To make matters worse, Admiral d'Orvilliers did not form his own line of battle, instead choosing to use the wind to move in on Keppel's line. Then the French did something totally unheard of in naval warfare. Instead of sailing in a parallel line and delivering broadsides into their opponents' hulls, they aimed the cannon at the English masts, rigging, and sails. In a short time, Keppel's ships began to lose speed as their sails were shredded.

Soon d'Orvilliers made port while the British fleet was forced to return to England for repairs. The Battle of Ushant was technically not a French victory, but it was an English defeat. Keppel was forced to face an inquiry at the Admiralty.

For the first time, the vaunted Royal Navy faced an entirely new form of warfare. It wouldn't be the last.

By 1780 the American Revolution had turned from a series of land battles to one defined by the actions of the British and French Navies. While the land armies fought from the Canadian border to the Carolinas, it was a single sea battle that decided the final outcome of the war for

The Battle of Chesapeake Bay, also known as the Battle of the Capes, September 5, 1781.
Imperial War Museum

American Independence. When France allied with the American colonies
in 1778, she boasted a fleet of modern and fast ships of the line. The Royal
Navy had more large ships, but their design and how they were commanded fell far short of the French. This was how affairs stood during the
fall of 1781 when George Washington made one of the most important
decisions of the war. His army was facing the seven thousand redcoats
of Major General Earl Cornwallis encamped on the Yorktown Peninsula
along the western shore of Chesapeake Bay. With Washington were the
French troops of Major General Gilbert du Motier, the Marquis de Lafayette. If the revolutionary army could be reinforced by more troops,
artillery, cavalry, and supplies, there was a good chance that the combined
armies could surround and defeat the British. At that time, the bulk of the
French fleet was in the West Indies, where Rear Admiral Francois Joseph
Paul de Grasse was making plans to retake the islands seized by the British during the Seven Years' War. Writing via the French minister to the
colonies, Washington sent word to de Grasse to come as fast as possible.
He hoped the French fleet could bring the needed reinforcements to the
combined army while blocking the entrance to the Chesapeake Bay. This

Rear Admiral Francois Joseph Paul de Grasse, victor of
the Battle of the Capes.

would not only support his army but would deny the British any help
from their own fleet, anchored in New York at the time.

The French admiral responded by turning his fleet north through
the Bahamas Channel and working up the Florida coast. On the way, his
fleet suffered two identical losses. The 74-gun *Intrepide* and the 40-gun
Inconstante were lost to identical accidents. While a quartermaster doled
out portions of Tafia brandy, the French equivalent of grog, a candle was
knocked over and started a fire. To lose two powerful warships to such
avoidable mishaps was inexcusable, and de Grasse took steps to ensure
it never happened again. His force consisted of twenty-eight ships of
the line, carrying three regiments of infantry and 350 artillerymen. Ac-
companying the warships were fifteen merchantmen that de Grasse had

chartered with his own funds, each carrying a portion of the supplies, cannons, and ammunitions.

Rear Admiral Samuel Hood, the British commander in the Caribbean, learned of de Grasse's departure and rightly assumed the French were headed to support Washington and Lafayette. Aboard his 92-gun flagship *Barfleur*, Hood sailed from Antigua with fourteen ships of the line on August 10 and set a direct course toward Virginia. But de Grasse had taken a circuitous route before heading west. When Hood reached the entrance to the bay on August 25, he found no French fleet.

He continued north toward New York.

Four days later, the French warships and transports entered the huge bay. The transports moved north toward the rendezvous with the allied forces while the warships anchored in Lynnhaven Roads at Cape Henry along the southern coast of the bay. Cape Charles was twelve miles north at the Delmarva Peninsula's southern end. While the mouth of the bay was wide, the dredged ship channel was only three miles across.

Hood reached New York and met with Vice Admiral Thomas Graves, the senior British admiral in North America. At fifty-two years old, Graves was a respected and experienced commander who was confident he and his force could defeat the French fleet coming from the south. But he also had other prey in mind. Commodore Comte de Barras was bringing eight warships, loaded with heavy siege artillery, men, and munitions, from Rhode Island. He was to rendezvous with de Grasse. Knowing that the British Navy was hunting him, de Barras sailed far out to sea and south to the Carolinas before turning northwest.

With nineteen ships of the line, Graves, in his flagship, the 90-gun *London*, sailed south to Virginia. The fleet also carried two thousand fresh troops to reinforce Cornwallis, as well as four hundred New Yorkers, forcibly impressed into the Royal Navy. It was a clear indication of the poor state of the British fleet that Graves had to kidnap colonists, even those not loyal to the Crown, to serve in the fleet. In fact, the Royal Navy could not fully man its ships without impressing men into service. It was estimated by 1800 that more than 41,500 Americans had been forced into the Royal Navy.

Vice Admiral Thomas Graves, whose old line-ahead
tactics lost the American Colonies for Great Britain.

Graves and Hood reached the mouth of the bay on the late morning
of September 5. At first, his leading ships reported a few masts visible
just past Cape Henry, and Graves assumed they were Barras's ships. They
would be an easy target for the big British men of war. But when his
lookouts reported a veritable "forest of masts," it was obvious there were
far more than the eight ships they had expected. There were twenty-four
of de Grasse's ships of the line. Four French ships were out to sea on other
missions.

Admiral de Grasse found himself at a great disadvantage. The British
had the weather gauge, with the wind coming out of the northeast and
the tide coming in. Worse, the French warships had anchored on the lee
shore of Virginia with little room to maneuver. Yet that was not what
worried de Grasse. The fifteen transports that sailed up the Chesapeake

estuary were accompanied by some of his frigates and more than 1,300 of his men. His own flagship, the 104-gun *Ville de Paris*, was short almost two hundred men. Upon sighting the British warships bearing down on the entrance to the bay, de Grasse gave orders to clear for action. Immediately his captains responded to the signal by casting off anchor lines and buoying them, loosing sail, and loading the guns. But time was short. The only edge de Grasse had was in numbers. He had twenty-four ships to the British nineteen.

But what the French commander did not yet know was that he had one element in his favor. Vice Admiral Thomas Graves was an ardent follower of *Fighting Instructions*. He vowed to do exactly as the Royal Navy had been doing since 1663.

Graves had the French fleet and transports in his grasp. If he simply moved in among the French fleet, he could destroy them with near impunity. Yet true to the Admiralty's standing orders, he raised the signal to form a line ahead with his flagship, the *London*, in the vanguard.

Admiral de Grasse must have felt like cheering as he saw the perfect orchestration of the British men of war lining up to enter the bay through the channel. It was a splendid sight with all the sails set along the British line, hundreds of black gun muzzles bared like iron teeth, flags and signals flying, and white bones churning at their bows. Graves's ships executed the maneuver to perfection. It was magnificent and imposing.

But it was also useless. By the time Graves's *London* had entered the wide bay, de Grasse's ships had managed to clear Lynnhaven Roads and formed up in the open ocean.

With startling speed for an eighteenth-century naval battle, the advantage had gone to the French. Now Graves found himself inside the bay with de Grasse to his rear and widening the gap. If he had been a bit cleverer, he might have moved up the estuary where his ships could have destroyed the transports carrying troops and guns for Lafayette and Washington. But Graves saw only de Grasse over the muzzles of his cannon. With the signal for "line ahead" still flying, he ordered his fleet to turn about in place and pursue the fleeing French. With this order, each ship turned and headed east. The tide and wind were now against him. This took nearly an hour, during which de Grasse took up a northeast heading. Graves had to chase the French fleet, but instead of having his most powerful ships in the van, the weakest, the 74-gun *Shrewsbury* and the 64-gun *Intrepid*, were leading. The *London* was tenth in the line of battle.

In addition, Graves was facing a situation for which he and the vaunted *Fighting Instructions* had no answer. Admiral de Grasse's ships had managed to reach open waters off the coast but had not formed into a line of battle. The French ships were in small knots; the neat British line of battle was useless. By late afternoon de Grasse had formed his ships into a loose line intended to maintain control rather than be used in ship-to-ship battles.

With his "line ahead" signal still flying, Graves sent his leading ships at the French vanguard. But because of the wind and the ragged enemy formation, the *Shrewsbury* approached at an angle, so the two fleets formed a "V" pointed east.

This meant that only the lead British warships could engage the French. The following ships of the line were still too far away to begin firing.

Graves compounded the worsening situation by raising the signal to "bear down and engage the enemy more closely." While this signal by itself meant for each captain to order his ship to break out of the line and attack the nearest French ship, the "line ahead" signal was sacrosanct. In other words, the two signals contradicted each other. Confusion reigned in the British fleet. Far to the rear, Admiral Hood followed the *Fighting Instructions* dictum that the "line ahead" superseded every other order, while Rear Admiral Francis Samuel Drake chose to follow the second signal. Aboard the 70-gun *Princessa*, he led the lead ships at the French van. But this only created more havoc.

Almost immediately, the *Shrewsbury* received heavy damage from the leading French ship, the *Pluton*. After two French broadsides, twenty-seven of her crew were dead, including the captain. With her masts teetering and rigging shot apart and more than fifty of her crew wounded, the British ship veered away. Then the 64-gun *Intrepid* moved in and was battered by the bigger *Marseillais*. With twenty men killed and thirty-five wounded, the *Intrepid* also left the broken British line. The French gunners were proving the merit of their training. Every British ship that came near de Grasse's guns had its rigging and masts shredded by chain and bar shot.

Orange and yellow flashes strobed like lightning in the thick clouds of white smoke while the roar of cannon vied with the dull thud of impacting balls on solid oak hulls. Tall waterspouts erupted from the blue sea from cannonballs around and beyond the two fleets. The sea air was rent with the stink of gun smoke. Hundreds of men lay in pools of blood that ran across the scrubbed decks. Tarred rigging hung like torn black webs while shredded sails flapped in the wind.

The *Terrible* was so battered that Graves ordered her to be scuttled.

Graves's big guns did damage the French ships. Drake's *Princessa* delivered a withering broadside against the *RefMehl*, shattering planking, ribs, and bulwarks. Jagged splinters of wood tore across the desks, killing and dismembering men as they worked the guns and sails.

The first shots of the Battle of the Capes were fired just after noon, but it was not until nearly evening when Graves, at last, lowered his "line ahead" signal. This was the point where all his captains were free to steer independently at the French line and engage them in a series of ship-to-ship fights. But it was far too late to matter.

By now de Grasse was far out into the Atlantic with plenty of room to maneuver. What is more, his ships had suffered no crippling damage, while nearly every British ship had torn sails and toppled masts. As night fell, Graves was determined to catch and stop de Grasse from reinforcing Lafayette. The following morning, with temporary repairs made to his ships, Graves ordered Hood and Drake to resume the chase. But the wily de Grasse led the British far from the coast, using his fleet's better maneuverability to keep the lumbering British ships within view. It was cat and mouse for the next five days while de Grasse remained enticingly close. By the time the French turned back to the entrance to the bay, Commodore de Barras had entered and sent his transports north to deliver the siege artillery to Washington and Lafayette.

When de Grasse, at last, took up a blocking position between capes Henry and Charles, Graves was forced to accept defeat. His weakened fleet of eighteen battered ships was now facing thirty-three fully manned and ready men of war.

Consultations with Hood and Drake led Graves to order the fleet to return to New York for repairs and reinforcements. By October 20, with twenty-five ships of the line, Graves headed for the Chesapeake Bay to confront de Grasse again. The French did what they had intended. Washington and Lafayette had bombarded General Earl Cornwallis until, on October 19, the British surrendered.

While this was not the end of land fighting, the American victory was sealed at Yorktown.

As for Admiral Grave, he faced a court-martial in England not only for losing the battle but to explain how the line-ahead tactics had failed to beat the French. He was forced to defend himself against criticism of his handling of the fleet.

But the sacred cows of the Admiralty refused to accept that the line ahead was flawed and responsible for the loss in the Chesapeake Bay. They also refused to see any alternative to the old system, insisting that what had always worked in the past was still the best way to fight at sea.

It would take almost twenty years and a series of minor and major battles, and the audacity of men like Admirals George Bridges Rodney, Sir John Jervis, and, most notably, Lord Horatio Nelson, to cast the useless *Fighting Instructions* into the sea forever.

It isn't a stretch to say that the very existence of the United States owes itself to the refusal of the Royal Navy to see the writing on the wall in September of 1781.

It was a landlubber who had never gone to sea, an Edinburgh merchant named John Clerk, who devised the tactics and maneuvers that would again put the Royal Navy in the lead in naval combat. Future admirals like Jervis, Collingwood, Ball, Troubridge, and Nelson made excellent use of Clerk's ideas. Yet even with solid proof that the line-ahead formation was too cumbersome and easily outmaneuvered, the Royal Navy and many other fleets continued to use the basic concept for the next 160 years. Other than in the American Civil War, when nearly every naval battle was fought between single ships, fleets of warships still met to fight in neat lines during the Spanish-American War at Manila

Bay and Santiago, during the Russo-Japanese War at Tsushima, and at Dogger Bank, Heligoland Bight, and Jutland in the Great War. Even as late as 1942, fleets of Japanese and American surface ships slugged it out at Guadalcanal and Leyte Gulf. The advent of radar and naval aviation altered but did not eliminate how the big-gun warships fought one another in fleet actions until the last year of World War II. Only then did the world recognize that battleships were more suited to shore bombardments for amphibious operations than in useless ship-to-ship duels that did little more than coat the ocean's surface with oil and dead men.

Admiral Lord Horatio Nelson's reputation for success is well founded. But he did experience some failures and defeats. From his early years in command, the diminutive young officer had a gift for daring action and quick decisions. These qualities brought him to the attention of senior officers, particularly Admiral Sir John Jervis, soon to be Earl of St. Vincent. Nelson's greatest victory, the August 1798 Battle of the Nile, was as much a result of pure luck as his skill on the attack. The next essay involved the most frustrating month in the life of the man who would one day be known as Britain's greatest fighting admiral.

NELSON'S HUNT FOR NAPOLEON

Published in *Naval History*, December 2020

Admiral Lord Horatio Nelson. Today, more than two centuries after his death, the name still evokes awe and respect among naval and military historians. Even though there have been dozens of contenders for the title, Nelson is still considered England's greatest fighting admiral. Standing only five feet, seven inches tall and hardly denting the scales at 130 pounds, how could this one-armed, one-eyed, frail man who was often ill from malaria and even seasickness command great fleets in battle, outwit and defeat experienced French, Danish, and Spanish admirals, and earn the eternal respect of an entire nation? Nelson was a brilliant and innovative tactician, a popular leader who fought alongside his captains and sailors in some of the most legendary battles in history.

He led from the front amid powder smoke and flying cannonballs. He made brilliant tactical decisions on the fly but was also known for careful planning. No one could dictate how a battle should be fought like Nelson.

But in the summer of 1798, Horatio Nelson embarked on an impetuous sea chase that could have resulted in the loss of Great Britain's most important colonial possession to the man who would soon change the course of history, Napoleon Bonaparte.

England and France went to war when the five-member French Revolutionary Directory impulsively declared war in February 1793. After conquering the Low Countries and securing a treaty with its old enemy Austria, France set its covetous eyes on the rest of Europe. Leading the

Admiral Horatio Nelson in 1799, while riding the fame of his victory at the Nile. *Imperial War Museum*

campaign was the new commander-in-chief of the French Army, a short, aggressive twenty-eight-year-old Corsican named Napoleon Bonaparte. His invasion and conquest of Northern Italy in 1796 secured his status as a formidable and successful army commander.

For the Directory, their ultimate goal was the invasion of Britain. In February 1798, they sent Bonaparte to Dunkirk to decide what could be done. After examining the French fleet at Brest, the young general reported that any invasion of England would be "the boldest and most difficult task imaginable" so long as Britannia ruled the waves.

Bonaparte was already thinking ahead. He proposed that until the Channel fleet was fully prepared, he should lead a fleet in the Mediterranean to seize Malta, invade Egypt, and threaten England's most valuable colony, India.

The capture of Egypt would close the shortest route to India and force England to take the long way around Africa to reach its rich colonial possessions in the Far East.

While Napoleon was easily the most influential member of the directory council governing France, he was not yet the sole ruler. His dark eyes were already on the throne. He would have to prove his mastery of the military and political art. The invasion of Egypt and the conquest of India would be the next step in his ultimate goal of undisputed rule.

In March 1798, the naval ports of Toulon and Genoa were a beehive of activity as the fleet was assembled, provisioned, and equipped. The invasion army consisted of 55,000 infantry, mounted cavalry, and artillery troops. This required 280 transports to carry it to Egypt.

In command of the French fleet was the loyal and patriotic Admiral François-Paul Brueys, who led from his splendid flagship *l'Orient*, a huge three-deck, 124-gun behemoth. His naval force consisted of nine 74-gun ships of the line, three more of eighty guns, and forty-four frigates. Considering the size of the transport fleet, fifty-seven French warships were a small force to protect them. Brueys requested additional warships from Brest, but the Directory refused on the grounds that the Brest fleet was diverting English attention from the Mediterranean.

This was not the same French Navy that had confounded and beaten the Royal Navy only two decades earlier. Officers were promoted solely on their noble status, regardless of experience or skill. With the French Revolution came the disintegration of the navy. Sailors organized soviets and voted on which orders to follow. Discipline and training suffered. The ships, once the terror of the seas, had been stripped of their crews and guns for the land revolt.

By 1792, the Directory realized the danger. They embarked on a war of conquest against Great Britain, Austria, Holland, and Prussia. By 1796, the ranks and officer corps of the navy were leavened with experienced officers and graduates of the academies. For the Egyptian campaign, Brueys's fleet chiefly consisted of repaired ships. It may have been a far cry from what de Grasse had known in 1781, but it was still a formidable force.

Brueys was no coward, but neither was he a fool. While his ships of the line were well armed, few had experienced gunners. He was anxious to avoid battle with the well-trained Royal Navy. His voyage to Egypt was fraught with risk no matter what the arrogant young general asserted.

Brueys's frigates would be herding 280 ships spread out over twenty square miles. The Mediterranean Sea covered more than 950,000 square miles, but there were many narrow passages and choke points his vast fleet would have to pass on the way to Egypt.

Bonaparte had chosen *l'Orient* for his own command ship. Loaded with fine food and spirits for his comfort, the huge ship also carried more than seven million francs in gold to finance the expedition.

Admiral Sir John Jervis commanded the Royal Navy's Mediterranean fleet, with Gibraltar as his home base. Jervis had expanded his area of responsibility by watching the Spanish naval base at Cadiz, considered a threat to England's last continental ally, defenseless Portugal. In the spring of 1798, Jervis received word from the Admiralty concerning an ominous naval build-up in the Mediterranean ports of Toulon and Genoa. He needed someone to command a squadron to approach Toulon and determine what the French were up to. He had just the man in mind. Rear Admiral Sir Horatio Nelson was already a hero in Great Britain, having been knighted and given flag rank after his audacious boarding and capture of two Spanish ships of the line at the Battle of Cape St. Vincent in February 1797. This cemented his growing reputation for boldness and innovative action. Already blind in one eye from a battle in 1795, Nelson had commanded a disastrous invasion of Santa Cruz de Tenerife in the Canary Islands in which over a hundred marines were killed. He lost his right arm when a musket ball shattered the elbow. But the injuries did not slow Nelson down; rather, they only added to his public notoriety.

Nelson was aboard HMS *Vanguard* as he joined Jervis in April 1798. Jervis told Nelson to take the 74-gun *Vanguard*, along with two other 74s—*Orion* and *Alexander*—plus three frigates into the Mediterranean. It was a major amphibious operation in the making. But the destination was the big question. It could be any of half a dozen ports or islands of tactical or strategic importance. Jervis and Nelson were certain Bonaparte's goal was Egypt, from which he could seize Suez and threaten India. This would be a catastrophe for Great Britain.

On May 8, the small squadron passed through the Pillars of Hercules and headed north. By May 20, under cloudy but calm skies, Nelson was seventy miles south of Toulon. Suddenly a savage gale tore out of the northwest and slammed into the ships. Mountainous seas fought against the six battered ships, but *Vanguard* caught the worst of it. By the following afternoon, all three of her masts had gone over the side, leaving the flagship wallowing helplessly. Nelson signaled *Alexander* to take *Vanguard* in tow, but little progress was made. At last the squadron managed to reach shelter off the coast of Sardinia. There, the carpenters and crew set to work jury-rigging masts and spars. But when the weather finally abated, Nelson was astounded to find his three frigates missing. The three frigate captains, having been separated from the ships of the line in the storm, logically assumed Nelson would return to Gibraltar.

This was no small matter. While the bulk of the navy consisted of the 74-gun ships of the line, the most essential ships were the smaller and more nimble frigates. Carrying only thirty-two to thirty-eight guns, they were never intended to fight in the line of battle. Instead, frigates were the eyes of the navy, scouting ahead of and around the fleet. They carried dispatches and often towed damaged and captured vessels.

Just when he needed them most, the frigates had left Nelson blind.

This played directly into Bonaparte's hands. The French invasion fleet had sailed one day before the storm struck the British squadron. Bonaparte's huge expeditionary fleet passed out of the Gulf of Genoa and headed south between Italy and Corsica.

Nelson was not only blind but had to figure out where the French had gone.

Just then, the brig *Mutine* arrived and informed Nelson that Jervis was sending him ten more 74s along with the 50-gun *Leander*. Nelson's force would be "a match for any hostile fleet in the Mediterranean." But Jervis, according to historian John Keegan in his book *Intelligence in War*, was apparently unaware that Nelson was bereft of frigates and did not send any.

New orders from the Admiralty told Nelson "to proceed in quest of the armament (French warships) of the enemy at Toulon and Genoa. On falling in with said armament, you are to use your utmost endeavors to take, sink, bur, or destroy it." This would prove far more difficult than the Admiralty, Jervis, or Nelson could have imagined.

On June 7, eleven ships of the line under Rear Admiral Thomas Troubridge hove into view. Three days later, the fleet set sail in pursuit of Napoleon Bonaparte. They took the most logical route south along the Italian coast. Nelson learned that the French fleet had passed through the Strait of Messina in early June. But he had no information beyond that. In fact, Bonaparte had already struck.

The strategic island of Malta, located seventy miles southeast of Sicily, had been in possession of the Knights Hospitaller, descendants of crusaders, since 1530. On June 9, the Maltese found their island ringed by a "forest of masts." The French first tried guile to enter the port, but the grand master of the Knights refused. His tiny army of unmotivated mercenaries and knights had no chance against Napoleon Bonaparte's forces. The island surrendered on June 12.

For the next week, Bonaparte busied himself with organizing a government and setting up a secure line of trade with France. After provisioning the fleet, Bonaparte ordered Brueys to raise anchor and head east toward Crete.

The French fleet was still at Malta when Nelson reached Sicily. He was slowed by the need to inspect every major port along the way in search of the enemy. On June 13, he learned that the French had been spotted off Sicily on June 4, headed east. Needing both information and frigates, Nelson requested three frigates from Naples. But the neutral Neapolitans refused, fearing French reprisal. It was at Naples that the British finally learned of the capture of Malta. But clearly the French fleet had not been assembled merely to take the tiny island.

To Nelson, this meant either Greece or, more likely, Egypt. He had few solid facts to work with, and even educated guesswork in such situations could lead to failure.

Such was the case on the morning of June 22 near the southern tip of Sicily, when the fleet stopped a small brig whose master told Nelson that the French had left Malta six days earlier, on June 16.

The audacious admiral's eagerness led to his first real blunder. Early that same morning, HMS *Leander* spotted four ships on the eastern horizon and reported them to the *Vanguard*. But Nelson, certain the French had a six-day head start, ignored the sighting. The French had to be at least a hundred miles away, headed southeast to Egypt.

This was a moment that might have changed history, but Nelson was wrong. Bonaparte's fleet left Malta late on June 18, only three days earlier. The four ships *Leander* saw that morning were, in fact, the trailing screen of Bonaparte's fleet, only thirty miles away. They were within the Royal Navy's grasp.

John Keegan stated that, at this point, Nelson, "uncharacteristically, consulted his captains as to what to do." Nelson normally did not consult but commanded. After hearing the opinions of four of his most experienced captains, he chose to head directly for Egypt, dismissing the evidence that the French were actually within reach. The fleet raised anchor and raced southeast.

But Nelson was still blind. According to Foreman and Phillips in *Napoleon's Lost Fleet*, "A fleet can never have enough frigates." Nelson had none. In his writings, Nelson lamented, "Were I to die at this moment, 'want of frigates!' would be stamped on my heart."

With no other choice, he spread his fourteen ships out in a line as far as practicable. On a clear day, a masthead lookout, perched about two hundred feet above the water, could see to the horizon about twelve miles away. Nelson's ships commanded a vista of a hundred miles across and twenty-four miles in depth. Signals were sent by flag hoist that could be discerned through a spyglass, but only on clear days. At night, lookouts had lanterns that could be seen from many miles distance. Signaling was accomplished by cannon fire and bells.

On the night of June 22, with a dank fog shrouding the invasion fleet, Admiral Brueys stood on the quarterdeck of the huge *l'Orient*. Far away to the south, over the rush of water past the hull, the creak of the rigging, and the flap of sails, he heard the distant muted booms of cannon fire. He was hearing Nelson's ships signaling to one another as they pushed hard to catch his fleet. Brueys had to have felt a mixture of relief and trepidation. If just one of the nearly three hundred transports showed a light, it could spell doom for his fleet.

On the morning of June 23, Nelson was already well past the French, leaving them in his wake. Sailing hard before a strong wind, he reached the Nile delta city of Alexandria on June 28. He reckoned that the French, limited to the speed of the slow transports, would have arrived in the ancient port at least a day before. All his ships were ready for action. But except for trading and merchant vessels, the port was empty. There was no sign of Bonaparte's invasion fleet or warships.

Horatio Nelson was an excellent commander, a clever tactician, and a brave fighter. He was at his best in heated combat with the roar of battle around him. While he was rarely indecisive, he sometimes questioned his own judgment. This was the case on June 28 as he surveyed Alexandria. Where had he erred? Did Bonaparte have another destination in mind? Nelson endlessly paced *Vanguard*'s quarterdeck. Yet he found no answers to the ultimate question: Where was the French fleet?

Inaction was not in Nelson's character. The British ships raised anchor and headed east, then north along the Turkish coast, still searching for any sign of the French.

Again Nelson's impetuous nature had led him astray. General Napoleon Bonaparte, resplendent in his gold-braided uniform, stood next to Admiral Brueys aboard the *l'Orient* as he entered Alexandria's harbor. He had arrived at his destination without encountering opposition.

Had Nelson lingered in Alexandria only twenty-five hours longer, he would have been waiting when Bonaparte's fleet arrived. Again fate had dealt a winning hand to the French. Brueys had escaped annihilation by a single day. It was only a temporary reprieve. The invasion began and Napoleon Bonaparte landed and drove his mighty army into Alexandria. After leaving several frigates in Alexandria harbor to proctect the transports, the bulk of the French fleet anchored in a sheltered bay twelve miles farther northeast.

Meanwhile, Nelson was fighting only with himself. As Captain Ball of the *Alexander* wrote, "His anxious and active mind wouldn't permit him to rest for a moment in the same place."

Finding the Levantine coast empty of French warships, Nelson turned west and skirted the southern coast of Crete. Then he compounded his error by heading back to Sicily. After beating against headwinds, his fleet anchored in Syracuse on July 20. Nelson was now swimming in self-doubt. How could his fleet, spread out and alert, have sailed the length of the Mediterranean twice, a total of 1,800 miles, and failed to find the huge invasion fleet?

After poring over charts and again conferring with his captains, Nelson told them he would sail for Cyprus. The French had to be somewhere down there.

The British fleet left Syracuse on July 25. On that very day, Napoleon's army, having defeated the Egyptian Mamluks at the Battle of the Pyramids, moved in to occupy Cairo. So far Lady Luck had favored the French commander's bold plan.

Then, at last, fate dealt Nelson a good hand. HMS *Culloden*, under Admiral Troubridge, had entered a port on the southern tip of Greece's Peloponnesian coast and captured a French wine brig that relayed shocking news. Napoleon had landed in Egypt a full month previously, only one day after Nelson had been there.

This news galvanized Nelson. He was vindicated in his insistence that Egypt had been Bonaparte's goal all along. Nelson was not one to question his good fortune. He sent two ships, *Alexander* and *Swiftsure*, to approach Alexandria and learn the disposition of the French fleet. They arrived on the morning of August 1 to find the French tricolor flag flying over the city and the harbor packed with hundreds of merchant ships and several frigates. But there was no sign of Brueys's ships of the line. Nelson then sent *Goliath* and *Zealous* to search eastward to the only port that could support deep-hulled warships. And there they were, in Aboukir Bay.

They found thirteen ships of the line and three frigates, with the *l'Orient* anchored in the center. The bay was semicircular, with the Rashid mouth of the Nile to the northeast and the fortified peninsula of Aboukir Point to the southwest. The thirteen French 74s were riding at anchor with about two hundred yards between ships. Brueys had only anchored his ships at the bow, leaving them to swing with the wind.

Brueys called a council of war with his captains. They had few options. The fleet was there to support Napoleon's land campaign. But now that the British had found them, battle was unavoidable. Brueys's ships were undermanned. At least a third of his crews were on shore, foraging for the food and water Napoleon failed to provide for the fleet.

As the leading British ship, the 74-gun HMS *Goliath*, rounded the tip of Aboukir Island, her captain, Thomas Foley, displaying the zeal and initiative of Nelson's "Band of Brothers," turned sharply to starboard directly at the leading French ships. Foley had spotted the key to victory. Where there was room for a French 74 to swing, there was room for a British 74 to move in. Passing the bow of the 74-gun *Guerrier*, *Goliath* turned sharply to port and slid into the landward side of the French line. At 5:30 P.M., Foley unleashed a deadly broadside on the French warships. *Zealous*, *Theseus*, *Orion*, and *Audacious* followed *Goliath* into the channel and began firing.

On board the *Vanguard*, sixth in the British line, Nelson raised his favorite signal, "engage the enemy more closely." He was doing what had never been permitted in the old Royal Navy—letting his captains take the initiative.

Brueys, anticipating that the British would attack from seaward, had ordered his gunners to load and ready the cannon on that side. The portside guns were not loaded or run out when the British ships came alongside. Even worse, the crews had piled stores and loose gear on the portside, making it virtually impossible to reach those guns. Every ship in the van of the French line was mauled by passing Royal Navy 74s. Each moved beyond the first ships and let go their sails and dropped anchor. While the first five British ships bombarded the port side of the French line, Nelson, aboard *Vanguard*, led six more 74s into the attack from seaward. The French fleet was caught between two lines of British ships. Nelson's ships delivered a furious and concentrated close-range cannonade. The outnumbered French gunners were blown apart by British cannonballs as they desperately tried to load and fire their guns. Nelson thrived on this type of battle: to lay his ships directly alongside the enemy and batter them to flaming splinters.

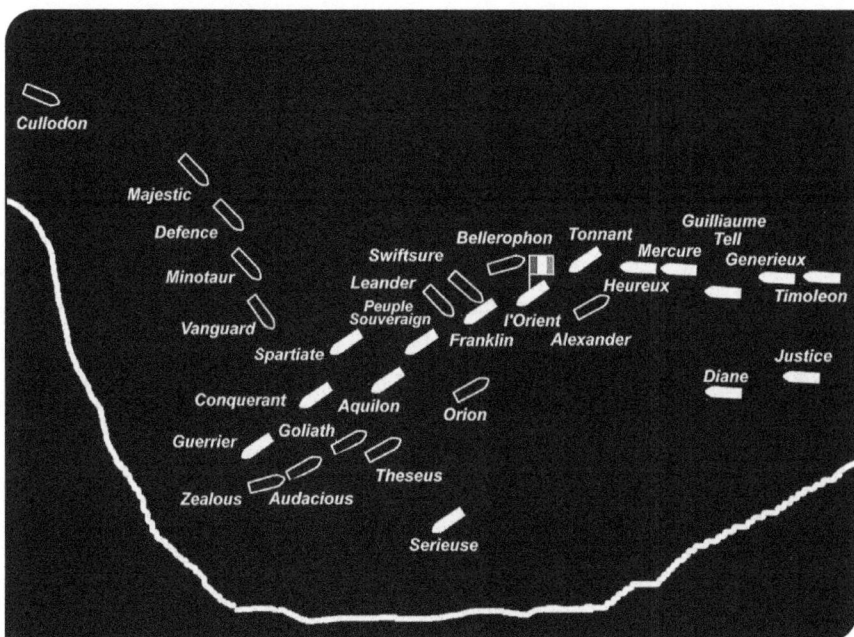

Nelson's ships batter the trapped French fleet at the Nile, August 1, 1798. *Imperial War Museum*

By 9:30 A.M., twelve British 74s had anchored along the French ships. As darkness fell, flashes of gunfire strobed in thick clouds of powder smoke. Some ships were so close that when the gunners fired a shot, they immediately threw a bucketful of seawater out of the gunport to prevent a fire on the other ship from igniting their own ship.

The huge *l'Orient*, in the French center, did well in the first hour. HMS *Bellerophon*, known to her crew as the "Billy Ruff'n" was horribly smashed by the bigger ship's guns. Her captain, Henry Darby, was forced to turn away. She would survive the battle, and in one of those curious quirks of history, the Billy Ruff'n would be the ship that would carry the dethroned Napoleon to England in 1815.

Then the *Swiftsure* anchored at *l'Orient*'s bows while the *Alexander* moved in under the flagship's unprotected stern. Together they began pouring shot into the bigger ship, inflicting terrible carnage. Among the casualties was Admiral Brueys, who lost both legs from a single shot. He was still giving orders when another British cannonball tore him in half.

The worst hit ships were in the French van at the southern end of the anchorage. The passing British 74s had pounded them. The heavy 32-pound shot tore into their bows and down the entire length of the decks, tearing up planking and bodies as they went. With the portside guns blocked by crates and gear, there was no way to fight back until they had been cleared for action.

One of the leading French ships, the *Conquerant*, manned by only four hundred men, just over half its normal complement, had lost 120 men in the first ten minutes of battle. She surrendered to a British captain who paled at the sight of so much blood pooled on the torn decking. The 74-gun *Spartiate*, the first to be hit, had lost two hundred men and two of her masts.

Nelson, directing the battle from the quarterdeck of his *Vanguard*, was struck in the head by a piece of langridge, the scrap metal the French used to cut up rigging and sails. His scalp was laid open for three inches over his good eye. He calmly waited his turn to be seen by the surgeon. To his flag captain, Berry, he said, "This is the twenty-fourth time I have been in action, and I feel it is nearly all over with me."

Late in the evening, the *l'Orient* caught fire from the *Alexander* at her stern. The fire quickly blazed out of control, turning the ship into a roaring inferno. Every ship in the vicinity cut its cables in an effort to escape. Captain Saumarez of the *Orion* ordered his gunports closed in anticipation of the impending explosion. At just after 10:00 P.M., the flames reached the powder magazines, and the vessel exploded in a titanic detonation that crested in a fireball hundreds of feet high. Burning spars, guns, masts, planks, and bodies rained down like meteors on the battling ships. Of the more than one thousand in her crew, only about sixty survived, pulled out of the water by British sailors. The shipwrecked Frenchmen received clothing, food, and medical care from their captors.

By the following morning Aboukir Bay was littered with floating wreckage and destroyed ships. Hundreds of dismembered and burned French bodies floated in the sea and washed ashore among the debris of their destroyed warships. The few remaining battered French ships fought valiantly all through August 2, but the outcome was inevitable. Out of sixteen French ships, only four frigates and one 74 escaped destruction or capture. It was Nelson's most stunning and complete victory. After the frustrating month-long chase around the Mediterranean, he had not only found the French fleet but had virtually annihilated it.

Napoleon's army was cut off from France. The Battle of the Nile was a disaster for the French general. Naturally, he blamed the dead Brueys. A year later, Napoleon Bonaparte abandoned his army and left them to their fate as he escaped back to France, his dreams of conquering India in ashes. In the end, luck and daring won the day for Nelson, but it had been very close to failure.

The Barbary Wars of 1802 to 1804 were one of the first tests of the new United States Navy. The corsairs of the Barbary Coast of North Africa practiced what would today be called "state-sponsored piracy and terrorism." Their fast, armed xebecs attacked and captured the ships of western nations for ransom unless their governments paid annual tributes. The United States, having gained its independence from Great Britain, was no longer protected by the huge Royal Navy. This was one of the catalysts for the formation of a navy. In 1803, the new frigates and sloops were sent to the Mediterranean to confront the Barbary states. But as with many first attempts at armed diplomacy, things went wrong. The next essay concerns one of the most legendary exploits of the new navy and one of its most famous officers.

"BOARD HER, BOYS!": *PHILADELPHIA* BURNING

Published in *Military History*, July 2019

When the American colonies declared their independence from Great Britain in 1776, it set into motion events that the signers of the Declaration of Independence had not considered. As long as the Americans were part of the British Empire, its unarmed merchant ships were under the protection of the mighty Royal Navy. By 1780, American ships carrying cotton, tobacco, wheat, and rice generated $79 million in trade between the New World and the Old. But this was endangered by the Barbary states along Africa's Atlantic and Mediterranean coasts.

Morocco, Tunis, Algiers, and Tripolitania were run by the Deys, Sultans, and Pshaws, who believed they had the right and might to commit armed piracy upon any foreign ships plying the seas. With swift, lateen-rigged Corsairs carrying cannons and heavily armed crews, the Barbary pirates routinely stopped, boarded, and seized unarmed merchant ships. They imprisoned their crews and cargo for ransom. The only way to deal with this was either by concentrated armed force, which was impractical and extremely expensive, or by the annual payment of tribute, agreed upon by treaty. Even Great Britain, with its globe-spanning navy, was inclined to pay tribute rather than deal with the expense of a protracted naval campaign.

Now American ships were no longer under the protection of the Royal Navy. Thus the Barbary pirates were free to attack and capture any American ships and crews unlucky enough to come under their greedy eyes. Starting in 1784, American ships were seized and their crews held in virtual slavery for exorbitant ransom. The Ambassador to France, Thomas Jefferson, eventually negotiated a treaty with the Barbary states for their release and the annual payment of $1,000,000 per year. For fifteen years, the pirates were mollified until 1801, when the Pshaw of Tripoli Youssef Karamanli chose to tear up the treaty and resumed attacks on American shipping. President Thomas Jefferson, never an advocate of a strong permanent military, was forced to accept that something had to be done. Fortunately, his predecessor George Washington had signed the 1793 Naval Act, which provided the amount of $688,888.88 for the building, launching, and manning of six new frigates for the United States Navy.

The new nation could not afford to build the big ships of the line used by France and Great Britain. For the cost of a single 90-gun three-decker, the new navy constructed six frigates of between 38 and 44 guns. Large and sturdy, the six vessels were fast, well-armed, and manned by a crew of motivated volunteer sailors, many of whom had served on Royal Navy warships. This was the infant nucleus of what would one day become the navy that defeated Japan 130 years later. Among the new ships were the *Constitution, United States, President, Constellation, Congress,* and *Chesapeake*. Many of these ships would go on to achieve fame in the War of 1812.

In 1802, Jefferson sent Commodore Richard Dale, in command of a three-ship squadron, to escort American ships and attempt to intimidate the bellicose Karamanli, but this proved inadequate. Next, Commodore Richard Morris received more ships, but he was not aggressive enough to handle the job. But in the summer of 1803, an irascible, hard-driving Yankee taskmaster named Edward Preble earned the job. He was to use his naval force to convoy American ships and blockade the ports of Tripoli and Algiers. For this he commanded a small fleet, the flagship of which was the soon-to-be-famous USS *Constitution*, as well as the brigs *Argus, Siren,* and the schooner *Enterprise*. Also included was the frigate *Philadelphia*.

Philadelphia was launched in her namesake city in 1799, her entire cost paid for by the citizens as a gift to the United States. At 1,240 tons, she was 130 feet long and carried 36 guns and a crew of 300 officers and men. Her captain was William Bainbridge, a stocky, red-haired former merchant officer from New Jersey. An excellent sailor, Bainbridge joined the navy in 1798. Although he tended to be aggressive on the quarter-deck and was respected for his bravery, he had the dubious distinction of being the only American Navy commander who had twice struck his colors to another nation. In this age of chivalry and honor, to lower a ship's colors, or national flag, was the ultimate disgrace. Even the total loss of a warship and crew was considered more honorable than striking its colors to an enemy.

On November 20, 1798, while in command of the schooner *Retaliation* in the so-called Quasi-War with France, he was forced to surrender to a larger French force. He was acquitted of any charges, but the sting of disgrace remained heavy on his mind. Then almost exactly a year later, he was in command of the new brig, USS *George Washington*, on one of the missions to pay the annual tribute to Algiers. The Dey of Algiers had asked to carry an envoy to Turkey, a request Bainbridge could not refuse. But then he was told to lower his colors and replace them with the Algerian flag. This he could not do, but when he was reminded that his ship was anchored directly under the guns of the Algerian forts, he was forced to accept the ignominy. While not the same as surrender, it was a stain on his and the nation's honor.

This was probably in the recesses of Bainbridge's mind as *Philadelphia* cruised along the North African coast on the morning of October 31, 1803. *Philadelphia* had been on blockade duty for weeks and, due to the Mediterranean's often capricious winds, had been forced far to the west of her station, the harbor of Tripoli. With favorable winds, Bainbridge had brought his powerful frigate toward Tripoli. One of his lookouts spotted a sail ahead, which was determined to be a small Arab trader headed for the city. Bainbridge hesitated briefly and then gave the orders to give chase. After two frustrating hours, *Philadelphia* had gained little on the foreign ship. Bainbridge fired several shots from his 18-pounder bow cannons but to no effect. The Arab ship gained entrance to the safe harbor. *Philadelphia* drew between eighteen and twenty-one feet of water. Bainbridge had three leadsmen take depth soundings as she rounded the headlands. With at least forty feet of water under his keel, Bainbridge continued the chase. The city and defenses of Tripoli were now only three miles distant. It was now 11 A.M. Reluctant to risk his ship in an unfamiliar harbor with uncharted reefs and shoals, Bainbridge broke off the chase. He ordered the helm to port, but it was already too late. At full speed, the 1,200-ton *Philadelphia* struck a hard shoal and drove herself onto it. Her bow was thrust more than five feet out of the water and the crew thrown to the decks.

Philadelphia was hard aground on a hostile coast within sight of enemy fortifications. The Tripolitanian Navy could discern the American frigate's plight. Sure enough, soon nine gunboats arrived and prowled around the big warship, careful to remain outside of the reach or aim of her guns. A grounded ship was helpless to a mobile force.

Bainbridge acted quickly. In an attempt to lighten the ship, he ordered that all the water casks be drained and nearly all the big cannons, each of which weighed at least two tons, thrown overboard. The anchors and cables were then cut loose, followed by the foremast. Even with the release of at least 800 tons of deadweight, *Philadelphia* would not float off the reef. The Tripolitanian gunboats began firing on the helpless ship. Unable to aim his few remaining guns, Bainbridge was faced with no alternative but surrender. He ordered all signal and code books destroyed and the magazine flooded. He attempted to sink the big frigate by having holes cut into the hull, but this did little good. As night fell, Bainbridge struck his colors for the third time. The gleeful and victorious Tripolitanians boarded and took the crew prisoner.

Preble, while at his base in Syracuse, learned of the seizure nearly three weeks later when a Royal Navy officer informed him. With one blow, Preble had lost one of his two frigates and a quarter of his guns. But worse, Karamanli now held more than three hundred Americans hostage. He could demand almost any ransom. To make matters worse, a few days after the grounding, a storm raised the water level in the harbor, and the frigate, considerably lightened by Bainbridge's desperate efforts, floated off. The Tripolitanians repaired the hull, recovered all the cannons, and towed her to an anchorage directly in front of the forts. Karamanli now had a virtually intact, powerful frigate to commission into his navy as a prize of war. All she needed was a crew and gunpowder, both readily obtainable. This was an unprecedented disaster for Preble and the United States.

"Would to God that the officers and crew of the *Philadelphia* had preferred death to slavery," Preble wrote to the Secretary of the Navy. But the problem still had to be solved somehow. Could *Philadelphia* be recaptured or destroyed? That was topmost on Preble's mind when a young, eager, bold officer entered the story.

This was twenty-four-year-old Lieutenant Stephen Decatur, as hot a firebrand as any man in the new navy. Born in Philadelphia, Decatur had already distinguished himself in action during the Quasi-War with France. Handsome, with wavy black hair and piercing dark eyes, he seemed to radiate confidence and audacity. As commander of the brig *Argus*, Decatur had arrived in the Mediterranean on November 1, carrying $32,000 worth of gold and silver for the fleet. He met Preble at Gibraltar, then took command of the 12-gun schooner *Enterprise*. Upon hearing of *Philadelphia*'s capture, Decatur and his crew visited Preble on board *Constitution* to discuss the navy's options. This was typical of Decatur, who tended to be in the right place at the right time throughout his naval career.

Decatur was told to take the nimble *Enterprise* close to Tripoli Harbor to scout the situation. What he saw proved that *Philadelphia* could not be recaptured. She was under the firm protection of the heavily gunned forts and gunboats. There was no way to board her with enough Americans to raise sail and maneuver her clear of the harbor before being turned into a floating wreck by the enemy batteries. It would be suicidal. After returning to Preble on *Constitution*, Decatur told the commodore that the only recourse was to destroy *Philadelphia*. Decatur must have had mixed feelings. He had seen *Philadelphia* built in his hometown, and his own father, Stephen Decatur, Sr., had been her first captain. But true to his patriotism and aggressive spirit, he suggested that he be allowed to take *Enterprise* into the harbor and board the *Philadelphia* with the aim of setting her afire. It was a daring proposition that must have made the crusty Preble smile. He too was a man of action. The plan was dangerous, but he knew something had to be done before Karamanli could make *Philadelphia* into the terror of the Mediterranean.

But a stroke of good fortune had already happened. The *Mastico*, a small Tripolitanian 4-gun ketch of 60 tons, was captured with her crew. An old vessel, she was indistinguishable from the hundreds of others that plied the blue waters of the Mediterranean. The small trading vessel would be the key to the destruction of *Philadelphia*. Preble had the small ketch commissioned as the USS *Intrepid*, the first of a long line of American warships to bear that name. During January 1804, under a cloak of secrecy, Decatur, Preble, and their officers worked out the details of the audacious raid. By the beginning of February, Preble was ready. He insisted that Decatur's crew all be volunteers. This proved no obstacle.

In the strong voice of confidence that would see him through two more wars, Decatur explained the situation to the crew of *Enterprise*. In moments he had more enthusiastic volunteers than he could use. Every single one of *Enterprise*'s crew of seventy officers and men joined him. This was typical of the young United States Navy, which, for all its inexperience, was composed of the best and most motivated sailors in the world.

Preble watched as *Intrepid*, accompanied by the brig *Siren*, sailed out of sight to the south on February 2. He hoped he was not sending Decatur and his brave crew to their deaths. But he had little choice. *Philadelphia* had to be burned. "It will undoubtedly cost many lives," he wrote, "but it has to be done."

After holding station off the coast for five days during a spell of rough weather, *Intrepid* and *Siren* approached the harbor. With her weather-beaten hull and faded lateen sails, *Intrepid* appeared badly in need of a refit. This was exactly what Decatur had counted on as he, along with his sixty eager volunteers, approached the eastern end of Tripoli Harbor on the afternoon of February 16. Decatur had recruited a Sicilian pilot who spoke the language of the region and knew Tripoli Harbor well. Some of *Siren*'s crew were supposed to join Decatur, but contrary winds prevented the two ships from coming together. Decatur, in his usual dramatic style, quoted *Henry V* by saying, "The fewer men, the greater share of honor."

A crescent moon hung low over Tripoli that evening as *Intrepid* left her escort behind. To the west were the spires and minarets of the city, dominated by Karamanli's palace and the hulking forts. More than 150 big guns guarded the harbor, along with the guns of scores of armed brigs, gunboats, and corsairs. *Philadelphia* was anchored in the center of the harbor. Even shorn of her foremast and bowsprit, she was still formidable. All her gunports were open, revealing the twenty-eight 18-pound cannons and sixteen 32-pound carronades. Decatur had no illusions that the guns were unloaded. The Tripolitanians would make maximum use of their newly increased firepower. There had to be at least two hundred men on board since that was the number needed to fight the cannons.

Most of the Americans were concealed below decks with kegs of gunpowder and incendiary devices. About a dozen were on deck, disguised as local sailors. At about 10 P.M., the wind died down, and *Intrepid*, almost a hundred yards off the big warship's port bow, was becalmed. A lookout on *Philadelphia* ordered her to sheer off. The Sicilian pilot called that he had lost his anchors and asked to tie up until morning. After a moment, the man on the frigate agreed. By then, *Intrepid*'s head was even with the bigger ship and only about twenty yards off her port side. A line was made fast to the ringbolt on the forechain. At this point, according to Decatur's detailed orders, the deck crew unobtrusively pulled on the lines, thus pulling the ketch close to the frigate.

The huge ship dwarfed the *Intrepid*, and the sight of long rows of black cannons was intimidating. After several minutes of pulling on the lines, the two ships were nearly touching. The Tripolitanians were helpful, unaware they were inviting a wolf into the fold. Each man on Decatur's crew had specific instructions as to his job upon boarding the ship. No one carried pistols or muskets. All fighting was to be done by hand with cutlasses and boarding axes to avoid alerting the fort batteries. The fight would have to be hand-to-hand against an enemy of an unknown number.

Suddenly, a cry of "*Americanos! Americanos!*" cut through the night, and Decatur knew the Tripolitanians had somehow been alerted. He immediately yelled, "Board her, boys!" Sixty men armed to the teeth swarmed over the rails and onto the frigate. They clambered through the gunports, up the ladders, and onto the rigging. It was perfect pandemonium as they screamed the name of the ship they had come to destroy. Even though the crew had boarded in extreme haste, the Americans quickly overwhelmed the enemy sailors. Only a few Tripolitanians resisted, and not a shot had been fired. In less than ten minutes, *Philadelphia* was back in American hands. True to his impetuous nature, Decatur must have considered trying to take her intact and bring her to Preble. But he knew this was folly. He had his orders. Time was now critical.

Somehow the alarm had been raised. Sentries on other ships and in the forts heard the commotion, and in minutes, the entire harbor was alerted to the attack. The Americans spread gunpowder over the decks, gun rooms, and storerooms. They had sperm oil candles and, upon the order from Decatur, set them alight. Instantly, long trails of orange flames climbed into the rigging, setting the tarred hemp and sails on fire. Below decks, the incendiaries engulfed the stores and cockpit, spreading in all directions. Once it was apparent that *Philadelphia* would be totally consumed, Decatur and his crew scrambled back down to *Intrepid*, where the mooring lines were cut loose. In the manner of a swashbuckler, Decatur was the last to leave, jumping to *Intrepid*'s rigging. The entire raid had taken twenty minutes, and not a single American life had been lost.

Then the situation became dire. The air sucked into the rising pyre of flames literally pulled *Intrepid* backward. The Americans used long oars to push the ketch away from the doomed vessel. The air was alive with embers and scraps of flaming sails. The inferno illuminated the entire harbor. *Philadelphia* was a towering mass of fire, from the waterline to the tops of her two masts. A few guns discharged, adding to the chaos. *Intrepid*, also brightly lit by the flames, sailed toward the safety of the harbor mouth. Some fort guns fired, but it was too late to stop the Americans. *Intrepid* met *Siren* and together the jubilant crews left the glow of the burning *Philadelphia* far behind. They reached Syracuse two days later, whereupon Decatur reported success to Commodore Preble. The navy's honor had been reclaimed.

Admiral Lord Nelson was at blockade station off Toulon on *Victory* when he heard of the Yankee feat. "It's the most bold and daring act of the age," he laughed. But Nelson, who was blessed with remarkable foresight, may well have recognized something more important. Seeing *Constitution* off Gibraltar one day, he observed, "In the handling of those big warships lies a nucleus of trouble for the navy of Great Britain." How right he was.

The Barbary Wars had yet to fully play out. In fact, in 1815, it would be Decatur himself, as commodore of a new large fleet, who would finally force the Barbary states to accede to American sea power and end the piracy. Yet it was the burning of *Philadelphia* that enshrined his name in the pantheon of American naval heroes.

The Barbary Wars and the subsequent War of 1812 were fought with ships powered by sail. Wind and currents, good sail handling, and quick decisions often influenced the outcome of a battle at sea. To be totally dependent on the wind was galling to the officers and sailors of the age of sail. But as the next essay will show, a new day was dawning over the seas of the world.

FROM SAIL TO STEAM: THE SLOW GENESIS OF A MODERN NAVY

It is difficult to know when the first crafts moved out to sea under the power of wind. It is safe to assume that it was at least two thousand years before Christ in the eastern Mediterranean. There are carvings and illustrations of small boats using sails on the Nile and Euphrates Rivers in 3,000 BC. But the primary means of travel by water was by pure human muscle power. The Persians, Greeks, and Phoenicians extensively used oars on the first navy ships. The large, light galleys, biremes, and triremes were the Classical Age's fastest and most effective warships.

While the Greek and Phoenician ships used sails, they were used only when the winds were favorable. They had little ability to sail across the wind, and their simple steering oars kept the ship on course. Yet what these ships did have in their favor was speed. With as many as ninety oarsmen to a side, moving in a steady rhythm, the triremes could slice through the water at nearly 8 knots in an attack. Every man had to pull and row in unison with the others. Petty officers with whips walked the center platform, looking for any rower not "pulling his weight." Archers on the narrow deck loosed arrows at enemies on other ships as the forward momentum drove the heavy bronze ram into the hull. These tactics lasted long after the Battle of Salamis in 480 BC and were superseded only after the Battle of Lepanto between the Turkish and Christian navies in 1571. Lepanto marked the end of the oar-driven galley and the dawn of the sail galleon of the Spanish Armada of 1588.

Yet sails wouldn't be practical for naval warfare until someone found a way to sail across or even into the prevailing wings. Merchant ships of the Mediterranean Sea had stout, rounded hulls for large cargo capacity

A modern reproduction of Drake's *Golden Hind*, a typical warship of the late
1500s. Note the square-rigged sails and single lateen on the mizzen mast.

and stability. They were slow, using the reliable square sail and steering
oar. They remained largely unchanged until the time of the Roman Empire. Then a change began turning up on ships in the form of the lateen
sail, which was standard on the Arab dhows that had plied the sea for
centuries. The lateen was triangular and hung from a long diagonal yard
suspended at the center by a short mast. With two of these sails, a dhow
could sail in nearly any direction, almost into the wind. This made it
possible to make more voyages and not wait until the wind was blowing
in the direction they wished to go.

Early in the Middle Ages, some square-rigged ships mounted a small
lateen sail on the stern mast. This allowed the vessel to sail closer to the
wind. More refinements, such as multiple tiers of sails and the sternpost
rudder, made the long and hazardous voyages to explore the New World
possible.

Up to this point, the navies of Europe—that is, Portugal, England,
Spain, Italy, France, Denmark, Holland, Germany, Norway, and Swe-
den—had adopted the square-rigged and lateen combination. Merchant
shipowners, eager to adopt any technology that would increase a ship's

speed, seaworthiness, and consequently its profitability, quickly added them to their ships. This led to the use of a spanker, a sort of "half lateen," suspended from the aft mast. The addition of triangular staysails on the stays between masts, and jibs between the foremast and bowsprit, gave ships the ability to sail in virtually any direction, no matter which way the wind blew. By the early seventeenth century, the East India Company's ships, which sailed to every corner of the globe, were the most efficient sailing vessels in the world. Since there was a direct connection between the merchant fleets and the ships that protected them, it was natural that naval vessels would use the same sail arrangements.

The ships of the line in use during the American Revolution and Napoleonic Wars were the largest and most efficient windships built up to that time. They could navigate the world and project their nation's influence with their rows of black cannons. Nothing on the seas could resist the might of a fleet of warships.

But even the largest and most powerful ship of the line was at the capricious mercy of the wind. Every ship at sea, whether merchant or naval, tried to gain the weather gauge; in other words, they tried to take maximum advantage of the wind speed and direction. A skilled captain could judge the wind by watching the sails and waves and make adjustments. Well-trimmed and handled ships could sail almost into the wind, even though they suffered in speed. But it was a great improvement over the ships of the Classical Era.

If the wind died altogether so did the ship's motion. Becalmed.

Then even the most experienced captains could do nothing but wait for a wind or lower boats to tow the ship to find a wind. Thus even the most advanced sailing vessels were reduced to something akin to what Odysseus had in Homer's time.

During the War of 1812, five British frigates chased the American frigate USS *Constitution* south of Long Island. While the American ship had a lead, the wind died out completely. Captain Isaac Hull, an excellent sailor, was familiar with the local waters. He lowered his longboats to tow the big ship out of enemy reach. The British ships quickly followed suit. Then Hull started kedging. By having the longboats carry a small anchor to the extent of a line and drop it, sailors on deck could literally "pull" the ship toward the anchor. Using two boats and two anchors, *Constitution* slowly drew away from her pursuers. This went on for a full day as the hunters and hunted exchanged long-ranging shots. Hull saw a line squall in the distance. He had his sails wetted to make them less porous. When the squall struck, the big American ship made full use of the light wind. By the afternoon of the second day, all that was visible of what would soon be the biggest thorn in the side of the Royal Navy was disappearing over the horizon. A week later, Hull and the *Constitution*, gaining the name "Old Ironsides," defeated the frigate HMS *Guerriere*, one of the ships that had pursued her.

As in nearly every marine technology case, the originator was a merchant ship owner. In 1818, the SS *Savannah* was launched in Georgia. Less than one hundred feet in length, *Savannah* was the world's first ship to use steam power to cross the Atlantic to Britain. With a single-cylinder 90-horsepower engine to drive twin paddlewheels, *Savannah* made her maiden voyage in May 1819. She couldn't carry enough coal for the entire voyage. Fortunately she had masts and sails. Her owners hoped the small ship would encourage investors for bigger and better ships. While *Savannah* was an unsuccessful venture, she proved that steam-powered oceangoing ships were possible.

The first naval ship driven by steam was *Comet* in 1822. With twin sidewheels, *Comet* was 125 feet long and displaced 240 tons. She was not a warship but a tug to tow other ships of the Royal Navy. The use of sidewheels would have made her too vulnerable to enemy fire. Yet the first steam-powered warships were indeed driven by paddlewheels.

As engines improved in power and reliability, they could sail for longer distances on a full load of coal. This made it necessary to increase the size and tonnage of both merchant and naval ships. They had to be large enough to carry the coal for a voyage—that is, in addition to cargo—or, in the case of a warship, guns and crews to man them. Isambard Kingdom Brunel, one of the era's most innovative engineers, realized that while a ship's tonnage rose by the cube, the resistance in the water was only squared. In other words, the larger a ship was, the more efficiently it could sail.

By the mid-1850s, coaling stations in most major ports around the world made steam navigation practical. This led to the early ocean liners, but even these still depended on sail as a safety measure. The navies of the world used the sails for long distances, while the steam engines were employed for maneuvering and better control in battle. All these ships still had broadside batteries along the hull. But the combination of sail and steam caused some conflicts.

When under sail, the coal and machinery were dead weight. When under steam, the masts, yards, rigging, and sails slowed the ship. They needed men to fight the guns, plus engineers and stokers for the boilers. More men were needed to work the sails. Consider that the 104-gun HMS *Victory* required more than eight hundred men, a large number for a vessel only 275 feet long. Eliminating sail altogether would cut a ship's complement in half. That would mean less berthing space, provisions, storage for spare sails, rigging and spars, and, most important to any navy budget, expense.

The slow removal of paddlewheels in the late 1840s improved matters. In addition to being bulky and vulnerable, paddlewheels were inefficient, wasting much of the engine's power. The invention of the screw propellor changed the equation. Propellors provided more thrust and were unlikely to be hit by enemy fire. A ship using a propellor did not have to concern itself with wind direction. Furthermore, the propellor made it possible for a ship to do something new: reverse direction. The early propellor designs were crude, but as the decades passed, naval engineers developed more efficient water screws. In April 1845, HMS *Rattler*, driven by propellor, and HMS *Alecto,* with paddlewheels, engaged in a series of tests. Joined at their sterns by a heavy hawser with both ships' engines at full power, *Rattler* pulled *Alecto* backward at 2.8 knots. It was a bold demonstration of the propellor over the paddlewheel.

The first United States naval vessel to carry a screw propeller was the USS *Princeton* of 1843. While still employing sails and masts, her excellent engines were designed by Swedish-born inventor John Ericsson, who would go on to fame as the designer of the ironclad *Monitor*. *Princeton* was an innovative ship. Her career was marred by a tragic accident when an Ericsson-designed smoothbore cannon exploded during a demonstration, killing several people, including the Secretary of the Navy. Although

John Ericsson, the brilliant but cantankerous designer of the
Princeton and *Monitor*.

Ericsson created the cannon, he did not cast it. That was taken over by
an ambitious and unqualified naval officer named Commodore Robert
Stockton, who foolishly used poor-quality iron for the casting, then fired
it with more powder than Ericsson advised.

But despite this, *Princeton* was a landmark warship.

When the Confederacy fired on Fort Sumter in 1861, most of the
world's large navies used steam and screws. But steam brought other
changes. In the past, the ship's wheel was always located at the very
stern so the captain and quartermaster could monitor the sails and
make helm and course changes. With the advent of paddlewheels, a
structure had to be built athwartships so the engineers could watch
over the pistons and axle that drove the paddlewheels. This evolved
into the midships bridge, a more effective way to conn the ship. With
the increased speed of steam, a captain had to be closer to the bow.

Eventually all ships were conned from the bridge, which soon migrated to the forward superstructure.

When the CSS *Virginia,* formerly the USS *Merrimac,* first slid into the waters at the Norfolk Navy Yard in early 1862, she heralded the dawn of a new era. While it is true that she was not the first ironclad warship, even in the Confederacy, the black ship had a place as one of a new breed of warship.

As for the Union ships blockading Hampton Roads, the USS *Congress* and USS *Cumberland* were sail frigates, while the USS *Minnesota* was a steam frigate with auxiliary sail. March 8, 1862, was a day with little wind over Hampton Roads. When the *Virginia* made her run to ram the *Cumberland,* the Union ship needed the aid of a steam-powered tug named the *Zouave* to move her so her rifled bores could be used against the ironclad. Being at anchor, *Cumberland* was at the mercy of the wind and tide. When *Virginia* rammed into her hull, the Union frigate could not escape but still managed to fire two full broadsides before sinking. The same was true of the *Congress,* which was hammered hard in a ship-to-ship duel until she too sank.

It was the fact that *Minnesota* had screw propulsion and that her boilers were always kept fired that she could slip her anchor chain and move away from the approaching ironclad. In the night, the Union ironclad *Monitor* arrived.

The Battle of Hampton Roads on March 9, 1862, has long since earned its place as one of the watershed moments in naval history. Many historians point to the *Virginia* and her Union adversary, the *Monitor,* as being the first ironclads to fight one another. This is true, but it is often overlooked that they were also the very first ships in history to fight under steam power. Neither had sails. In fact, the *Virginia*'s speed under the heavy casemate of iron steamed faster than it had in its earlier incarnation as the steam frigate *Merrimac.* Without the heavy top hamper of masts, yards, sails, and rigging, the ironclad moved with less resistance to wind. Although neither ironclad inflicted any crippling damage to the other, the world had changed that day. Steam was here to stay. Sail power was on the wane. It remained to be seen how fast the winds of change would affect the world's navies. But it would be a slow and unstable evolution. While France and England had already constructed ironclad ships, they were little more than steam and sail frigates with iron plating.

Not until the last years of the nineteenth century would sails be fully eliminated. By then, steam engines, which had matured from the old reciprocating piston designs, had given way for the revolutionary turbine engines designed by Charles Parsons in 1888. The Parsons steam turbine concept has been used in virtually every warship in the world's biggest navies ever since. But as with all generalizations, there are exceptions. In 1954, the first nuclear-powered submarine, the USS *Nautilus*, was put to sea. Yet even her futuristic atomic power only served one purpose—to drive steam turbines to turn the propellors. Some things never change.

It is an interesting side issue that, even as late as the Second World War, there were still coal-fired paddlewheelers in the service of the United States Navy. The navy converted two lake excursion ferries into USS *Sable* and USS *Wolverine* by adding a 500-foot-long wooden flight deck. The ships were based at the Navy Pier in Chicago and sailed every day to provide a landing and takeoff training platform.

USS *Wolverine*, one of two paddle-wheeler training aircraft carriers on Lake Michigan, 1943. *Official U.S. Navy Photo*

It was a brilliant solution to a difficult problem. They were never intended for combat, but they accepted the role that would otherwise have required the use of one of the precious carriers needed in the Pacific or Atlantic. Thousands of pilots who later fought in the skies over the Pacific earned their qualifications aboard either *Sable* or *Wolverine*. Although the old 7,200-ton ships could barely maintain 18 knots, the high winds off Lake Michigan gave the new pilots plenty of headwind to practice their first landings on a flight deck.

Well into the twentieth century, these throwbacks to a long-gone era served the national interest.

As we have seen, the idea of sails giving way to steam power took decades to evolve into the prime mover of the world's merchants and navies. But the other major change that progressed in less than a year was the transition from wooden ships to ironclads. To most landsmen in Europe and America, and even many seafarers, the idea of putting heavy iron on a ship seemed ludicrous. Iron would never float. Even wooden ships sank when water entered their hulls after storm or battle damage. How could an iron ship float? It was a simple matter of physics. As long as a ship weighs less than the amount of water it displaces, it will float, no matter what it is made of. Thank Archimedes for that little gem 2,266 years ago.

But putting iron on a ship had some merit. It could resist even the heaviest shot and possibly survive damage from rocks and shoals. The next essay will describe the history of the ironclad, focusing on the two most famous, the *Merrimac* and *Monitor*. Together they changed the world.

THE DAWN OF THE IRONCLAD

Few watershed moments in history define the end of one era and the beginning of another with such precision as the Battle of Hampton Roads on March 9, 1862. In three blazing and violent hours, the world's first fight between ironclad warships forever changed the course of naval warfare. It marked the transition from sail to steam, from wood to iron, from broadside to turreted armament, and from smoothbore to rifled cannon. Several other new inventions and machineries came to death blows that day, some of which started a trend in naval design and others that died without a trace.

It was also a moment when tactics began to change, but there was still a long way to go to convince the old guard of admirals and captains who refused to accept that a new day was dawning and that they needed to adapt or go down in defeat.

After wooden sailing ships began fighting in the sixteenth century, there had been little innovation beyond size, speed, and the number of guns. A sailor on the 42-gun *Victory* that fought the Spanish Armada in 1588 would have been impressed by the 104-gun HMS *Victory* of 1764, but it would have been familiar to him.

The advent of steam propulsion changed the dynamics of naval warfare in a way that demanded a serious change in tactics. But it was the coming of the ironclad at the end of the 1850s and the following decade that decisively changed how navies were built and operated.

England and France, always casting wary eyes across the Channel at each other, constructed ironclad warships in 1859 and 1860. HMS *Warrior* was a steam frigate carrying fourteen rifled and twenty-six smoothbore guns in the standard broadside configuration. Her hull was plated in 4.5 inches of iron sheets. France's *Gloire* of 1859 boasted thirty-six rifled cannons in a hull clad in 4.7-inch iron. While both ships were innovative and nearly equal in size, engine power, and armament, they were little more than steam and sail frigates with iron plating over wooden hulls. They were "ironclads" in the most literal sense, not true iron warships.

That distinction was reserved for the *Monitor* and only partially for the *Merrimac*. The birth of the two ironclads marks one of the most amazing parallels in history. In the space of six months, two nations—the United States and the Confederate States—each began a crash program to construct an impregnable "battery," as such vessels were known, resulting in two entirely unique warships that proved to be nearly equal. The CSS *Virginia*, constructed upon the burned hull of the steam frigate *Merrimac* (sometimes spelled *Merrimack*) was the first real ironclad warship ever launched, carrying ten rifled and smoothbore cannons. The *Monitor*, far smaller and carrying only two guns in a revolving turret, was the first all-iron ship ever built.

This essay will detail the concept, design, and construction of the two most famous ships of the Civil War.

CSS *VIRGINIA* NÉE USS *MERRIMAC*

Things happened quickly in the weeks after the shelling of Fort Sumter in April 1861. One of the Confederacy's most important objectives in Virginia was the Norfolk Navy Yard on the Elizabeth River inland from the Chesapeake Bay. The second-largest naval base after Boston, the yard had the finest granite drydock in the country. At Norfolk were a dozen warships, some of which were near relics, such as the famous frigate USS *United States*, the ship that, under Captain Stephen Decatur, had captured the British frigate *Macedonian* in the War of 1812. Also in the yard was the largest sail warship ever built in America, the 140-gun USS *Pennsylvania*. More than twenty-five years old, she had never fired her guns in anger. But the most important ship was the steam frigate USS *Merrimac*. The first of a class of steam warships named for rivers,

Merrimac was launched in 1855. At 275 feet in length and displacing 3,200 tons, the *Merrimac* carried forty guns in a broadside configuration. Her engines drove a screw propeller to move the ship at a respectable 12 knots. She also had three masts. But her engines were unreliable from the start, resulting in frequent breakdowns. On April 17, the day Virginia seceded from the Union, Secretary of the Navy Gideon Welles sent several officers to oversee the defense and, if necessary, destroy the base and its facilities. The *Merrimac* was to be repaired and removed if possible. Chief Engineer of the Navy Benjamin Isherwood, the designer of *Merrimac*'s engines, managed to get them in working order by April 20, but there was no time to assemble a crew and escape. Instead, Isherwood had his team spike the guns of the other ships and dump them overboard. Then he burned the *Merrimac*. The frigate burned to the waterline and sank at her berth.

The Confederacy captured the base and all its facilities, including the machine shops, foundries, rope walks, lumber yard, and the all-important drydock. All the cannons dumped into the water from the other ships were raised and sent to forts and artillery units all over the South. The sunken hull of the *Merrimac* would become the foundation of the new Rebel ironclad.

Ironclads were not a new concept, even in the new Confederacy. In 1592, Korea built a series of "Turtle Ships," wide oar-driven craft covered with a roof of spiked iron to repel a Japanese invasion. France and England had already launched steam frigates with iron plating, and the North had ordered a ship called the "Stevens Battery" in 1841, but it was never finished. France used three iron-plated floating batteries to shell Russian positions in Crimea in 1855.

The Confederate Secretary of the Navy Stephen R. Mallory was faced with the nearly impossible task of constructing a navy to challenge the Union from scratch. Knowing full well there was no time to build a wooden fleet, he had the idea of building a few ironclads. He heard of the French batteries, was involved in the congressional funding for the Stevens Battery, and understood the advantage of an ironclad ship. But the big question was: could the Confederacy, a new nation with virtually no industrial infrastructure, build something so advanced? Few

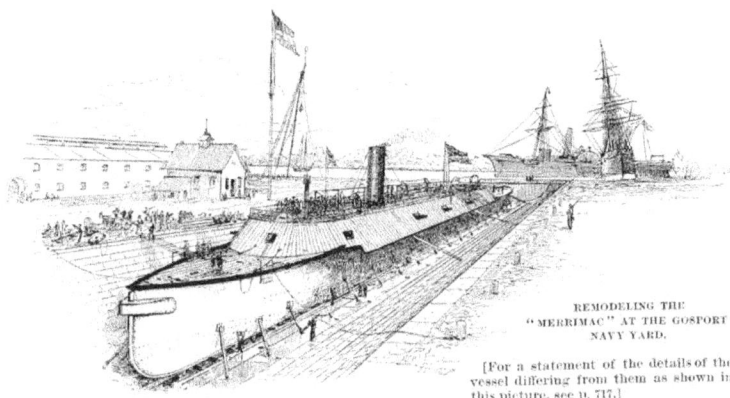

REMODELING THE
"MERRIMAC" AT THE GOSPORT
NAVY YARD.

[For a statement of the details of the
vessel differing from them as shown in
this picture, see p. 717.]

At the captured Norfolk Navy Yard, the hull of the *Merrimac* is converted into the CSS *Virginia*.

Americans, North or South, thought so. At the time, a standing joke in the Union held that a reporter, questioning a Confederate official, asked "Sir, is your navy iron-plated?" The official replied, "Our navy is hardly even contem-plated."

Even a small number of these impregnable floating batteries would be enough to face and destroy the Union blockades that were even then sailing to Southern ports.

But like many cabinet secretaries before and since, Mallory was at the mercy of a parsimonious Confederate Congress. Out of the 1861–1862 budget of $374 million, the infant navy received only $14.7 million. Even with such a meager amount, he thought of purchasing or leasing the ironclad British *Warrior* or French *Gloire* but was unsuccessful. The South needed a way to build a powerful ironclad as quickly as possible.

Then on May 30, the frustrated navy secretary received a telegram from Norfolk, possibly the most important message of the war. "We have the *Merrimac* up and are just pulling her into drydock."

Enter Lieutenant John Mercer Brooke, a naval officer who had resigned his commission from the United States Navy after Virginia seceded. A brilliant gunnery officer, he was ordered to report to the Commander of the Virginia forces, General Robert E. Lee, who ordered Brooke to scour the country and abroad to collect every pistol, gun, rifle, cannon, and mortar he could find. But Mallory then cabled Brooke to find as much plate iron as possible in every thickness from one to five inches. That would be a difficult job. In 1860, the total iron produced by the Southern states was 26,000 tons. During the same period, the North produced 450,000 tons. The Rebel ironclad would require at least 700 tons of rolled iron plates. Only one foundry was capable of the job—the huge Tredegar Iron Works in Richmond, which produced steam locomotives, iron rails, cannons, and a host of other iron and steel products.

By June 1861, Brooke had a preliminary design for the ship. He envisioned a shed or casement built upon a wooden frame of two-foot thick timbers. The casement would be sloped at an angle of 36 degrees to deflect incoming shot. The acute angle would double the apparent thickness of the plate, which had to be three layers of 1-inch thick iron. Brooke wanted 3-inch thick plates, but Tredegar couldn't provide them.

The *Merrimac's* hull was sound, with keel, ribs, and deck beams. It was copper-sheathed and held the recently repaired boilers and engine, as well as the rudder and propellor. Brooke intended to build a heavy deck and superstructure extending past the bow and stern and hanging like eaves over the port and starboard bulwarks. This, timbered in thick beams and covered in iron plates, would protect the wooden hull from enemy shot and increase the ship's buoyancy. On June 23, he presented the plans to Mallory. He in turn had them examined by a naval architect named John Porter.

Porter had submitted plans for an ironclad to the United States Navy in 1846 but never received a response. He examined the Brooke design and realized it was a close approximation of his own concept. Together, the two men merged their ideas, but the basic concept was almost all Brooke's.

Porter drew up the final plans, which were twenty-seven feet long. The *Merrimac's* power plant would be retained.

Once the work began, there was little doubt in Mallory's mind that a race would begin. While the South may have a lead, the industrial power of the North would be put into motion for a Union ironclad. Even on a guarded naval base, it would be impossible to conceal the huge project of refitting an entire ship. Word would get out.

Yet the idea of putting hundreds of tons of iron on a waterlogged hull seemed ludicrous to many, even in the Confederate Navy. One critic said that once the *Merrimac* was launched, it would have the distinction of being the first ship to sink twice. Few people could grasp the mathematics and physics of displacement and surface area, which Porter and Brooke believed would allow the ship to float.

There was considerable criticism from informed and uninformed sources that the *Merrimac* would turn over, couldn't be steered, and that the first broadside from another frigate would be fatal to her crew.

In August, the Confederate Congress released the amount of $172,500 for the work of building an ironclad. Tredegar Iron Works was paid 6.5 cents per pound of iron for the ship. Iron was secured from all over Virginia.

Mallory then tasked Brooke with testing the strength of three 1-inch plates against smoothbore cannon shot. A frame holding three layers of 1-inch plates backed by 27 inches of timbers and sloped at an angle of 36 degrees was set up for the tests. The first tests showed that the heavy ordnance used by most Union warships would pierce the iron. Brooke then used two layers of 2-inch plates. The next firing from 300 yards with an 8-inch cannonball shattered the outer plate and cracked the inner one but did not expose the wood. He changed the plans to incorporate the heavier casemate. Tredegar could produce the thicker plates but did not have a punch to drive rivet holes through 2 inches of iron. Fortunately the Union Navy had left a punch at Norfolk that could do the job.

On February 12, 1862, Tredegar rolled out the last plate. In all, the foundry had rolled 740 tons of iron for the *Merrimac*.

While Brooke oversaw this, Porter worked out how to fit and balance 800 tons of iron on a wooden hull. It had never been done in the history of the world. As stated by Richard Snow in his excellent book *Iron Dawn: The Monitor, the Merrimack and the Civil War Sea Battle that Changed History*, the construction of the superstructure of the *Merrimac* was closer to bridgebuilding than shipbuilding. Porter designed a timber trusswork 150 feet in length and 24 feet in beam. It was clad in 4 inches of clean white oak. Two more layers of oak and pine were added even before the iron was fitted. Fortunately, the Union Navy had left behind plenty of seasoned lumber for the job. Long threaded bolts, iron above the water-line and copper and bronze below, clamped the casemate together.

At this time Mallory gave Brooke an unusual job. He was to design a uniform for the new Confederate Navy. It was to be gray, which Brooke hated. But he did it, then, to his relief, was tasked with developing a rifled cannon for use in the new ironclad. This was much more to his liking, and he put his considerable talents and ingenuity to work.

Up to this point, every naval gun in the world had been a smooth-bore. John Dahlgren had designed the best and biggest guns, and eight of them would be mounted on the *Merrimac*, four to a side. Mallory wanted rifled cannons, which would have greater range, accuracy, and hitting power. Brooke came up with a superb gun with heavy iron bands of diminishing sizes from the breech to the bore. They required less iron and time to cast than the Dahlgrens. The heavy thickness would contain the massive charges of powder for the projectile.

The new gun fired a 100-pound shot a distance of five miles, an astonishing improvement over a smoothbore.

The Brooke Rifle, used by Confederate land and naval forces during the war, ranged from 7-inch to 11-inch. Two of the former would be mounted on the bow and stern pivots of the ironclad. This meant the Brooke Rifle could inflict damage long before any conventional smooth-bore. The pivot guns had three ports on the centerline and at 45-degree angles. *Merrimac* would have a four-gun broadside, with the guns stag-gered to allow the crews to work opposite each other.

Despite having the most advanced guns in the world, the *Merrimac* was also fitted with a weapon right out of antiquity. A yard-long, wedge-shaped iron ram was bolted to the bow, a throwback to the weapons the Greek Admiral Themistocles used to defeat the Persian fleet at Salamis in 480 BC. The mating of such an antiquated weapon to the *Merrimac* was oddly logical. Sailing ships could never use a ram since they couldn't move fast enough to do any damage. Also, a vessel would have to point its bow at its target, which meant its broadside cannons could not be used. With a propellor and iron plating to protect the ship, the Rebel ironclad was the first ship in more than two thousand years for which a ram was practical.

Mallory had a reason for having it fitted to his ironclad. With the South's chronic shortage of powder and ammunition, a ram would be a simple way to sink an enemy ship with one blow.

Her two horizontal beam engines had been repaired and improved by the engineer. With her four boilers, she rated 1,200 horsepower. It remained to be seen how fast she would be on the open water. Displacing more than 4,000 tons, she drew 22 feet of water, a deep draft for the Chesapeake Bay.

On February 13, seven months after work commenced, the drydock was flooded. Hundreds of interested onlookers and naval personnel watched with bated breath to see if the newest ship in the Confederate Navy would float or sink like an iron brick. Despite the gloomy predictions, she remained obstinately afloat. The official launch took place with little pomp and ceremony four days later. She was christened the Confederate States Ship *Virginia*, after the state of her birth. But no matter how much official weight was given to the name, most accounts and verbal utterances still called her the *Merrimac*.

The guns were already aboard, having begun arriving in November. There was a change from the original specifications. It was decided that two of the broadside guns should be Brooke Rifles, so in addition to the two 7-inch pivot guns would be two more 6.4-inch ones. Six 9-inch Dahlgrens filled out the armament. Altogether the guns weighed 11 tons.

As for the ammunition, Brooke felt that explosive shells would be most useful since their targets would be wooden-hulled ships. Unfortunately Tredegar couldn't cast enough shells in time. For the Dahlgrens, solid cannonballs were available from the Norfolk yard. These could also be heated on the firebox grates to make them red-hot, an effective means of damaging wooden ships.

The four rifles required a crew of twenty-six men, and the smoothbores each needed fourteen men. While the ship was undergoing her final fitting-out, they trained on the old USS *United States*. But the 24-pounder guns were a poor substitute for learning how to load and fire the much bigger guns on the *Merrimac*.

Her total crew and officers numbered 320 men. Many were landlubbers recruited from the Confederate Army. This seemingly strange choice had its merits. Real blue-water sailors would have no advantage on the mastless ironclad. They wouldn't have to know the skills of seamanship or knot tying. Men who could work the guns, fire the boilers, and maintain the engines would be satisfactory. Only the quartermaster, officers, and helmsman needed to be experienced sailors. The South was in a hurry to destroy the Union blockade. The first time the gunners would fire their big cannons would be when they faced Union ships.

When *Merrimac* was fully loaded with shot, powder, and 150 tons of coal and provisions for sea, she presented a strange and impressive image. Although the underwater hull was 275 feet long, the sloping casemate extended only 150 feet. The armored deck was sharp at the bow and squared off at the stern. Two anchors were suspended from hawseholes at the bow. No part of the hull was visible. Jutting from the casemate was a single cylindrical smokestack, painted black along with the rest of the ship. Boats were suspended from davits at either side of the stack. None of these were armored. A conical pilothouse poked up from the sloped forward end. The top of the casemate was about ten feet wide and had large gratings to provide ventilation and light for the gunners. Heavy iron swinging shutters covered the gunports to protect the gunners and prevent water from entering.

She was commissioned into the navy on March 7, the day before she first went into action.

All in all, the infant Confederate Navy had managed to conceive, design, construct, and launch a remarkable warship in just eight months. She was unique and possessed two of the three critical innovations in naval technology. The first was the elimination of sail for steam; the second was in being iron-plated. But the third innovation would be reserved for her adversary—the USS *Monitor*.

USS *MONITOR* NÉE ERICSSON BATTERY

Keeping the existence of the Confederate ironclad a secret was an exercise in futility. There were just too many eyes and ears around Norfolk. Word reached Secretary of the Navy Gideon Welles, whom Abraham Lincoln liked to call "Father Neptune," as soon as the *Merrimac* had been raised and put into the drydock. Welles had favored a Union ironclad from the start, but he had no idea how to go about it. The only logical means of getting one quickly into service was to affix iron plates onto a wooden hull, as had been done in France and England. That was already in the works with the USS *New Ironsides*, a standard screw and sail frigate with eighteen smoothbore and rifled cannons. The 4,000-ton ship was 238 feet long, clad in 4 inches of armor plate above the waterline. Ordered from a Philadelphia shipyard in August 1861, she wouldn't launch until May the following year, long after the Rebel ship was supposed to be completed. Something had to be done fast. In late April 1861, Welles began assembling the fourteen warships available for immediate service to blockade the Southern ports. He then created an ironclad board, consisting of himself and several naval officers, to review the more than one hundred ideas they received from inventors, shipwrights, and cranks. One was for a rubber-clad ship from which cannonballs would bounce off.

The most famous shipbuilder in the country was Donald McKay, whose fast and beautiful clipper ships like the *Flying Cloud* had captured the world's imagination. He wrote, "The time for line of battle ship is over. No ship constructed on the old system are capable of sustaining fifteen minutes' fight against one of the new iron monsters without being blown to pieces." Not surprisingly, McKay was one of the contenders to build the ironclad.

His proposal would cost over one million dollars.

A Connecticut businessman named Cornelius Bushnell proved to be the catalyst for what would become the Union's answer to the *Merrimac*. Bushnell hailed from the same family line as David Bushnell, the creator of the *Turtle*, the wooden Yankee submersible that attempted to sink a British warship in New York in 1776. Cornelius was not an inventor or even a shipbuilder, but he did own an iron foundry in New York. He also had rich and influential friends. He was aware of the panic sweeping the North over the proposed Confederate ironclad and suggested to Welles that the Swedish-born inventor John Ericsson might be the man to conceive and build a Union ironclad in time to stop the *Merrimac*.

As related previously, Ericsson had already had some trouble with the navy. He was owed a great deal of money for his design and construction of the ill-fated *Princeton*. The scandal created by Robert Stockton's finger-pointing blame on Ericsson was enough to keep the inventor from having anything to do with the United States Navy. But Bushnell went to New York and met with the arrogant, egotistical Ericsson. With flattery and praise, Bushnell coaxed the inventor into showing him a concept for an ironclad, which Ericsson had been working on for years.

Bushnell viewed a cardboard model of a small, smooth-hulled ship with a bump or protrusion on top. It was radical, but the businessman saw potential. He took the model and Ericsson's sketches to Washington and showed them to the Ironclad Board. An oft-repeated story tells that Lincoln saw the model and said, "Like the western girl who put her foot in the stocking, 'It strikes me that there is something in it.'" The board wanted to meet the inventor, and Ericsson was persuaded to present his design. It was a hard sell, but Ericsson eventually won them over. He and Bushnell, along with New York and Connecticut businessmen, would underwrite the $275,000 cost of building the ship in ninety days. But they would only be paid by the government in $50,000 increments as the work went along. The navy was not convinced, parallel to what was happening in Richmond, that the new ironclad would even float. Essentially the ship would be privately owned. The final payment would only be made if and when the ironclad fought and defeated the Rebel ship. No government contract before or since ever had such restrictions. But Ericsson and his backers were convinced they were right.

Just eight days after Bushnell first saw the cardboard model, the contract to build the ironclad was signed and work began.

The iron keel for the strange new craft was laid at the Greenpoint Shipyard along the East River in Brooklyn in full view of the ferries and shores of Manhattan.

Much of the iron was rolled at the Rensselaer Iron Works in Troy, New York.

Unlike the *Merrimac*, the Union ship wouldn't be clad in iron but built entirely in iron, from keel to turret. It was essentially two ships, the Upper Vessel and the Lower Vessel. The Upper Vessel was 172 feet in length and 44 feet in beam, and it rested like the lid on a shoebox over the Lower Vessel, the underwater portion. Plated in two layers of half-inch

Photo # NH 60660   "Transverse Section through Turret" of USS Monitor, published circa 1862

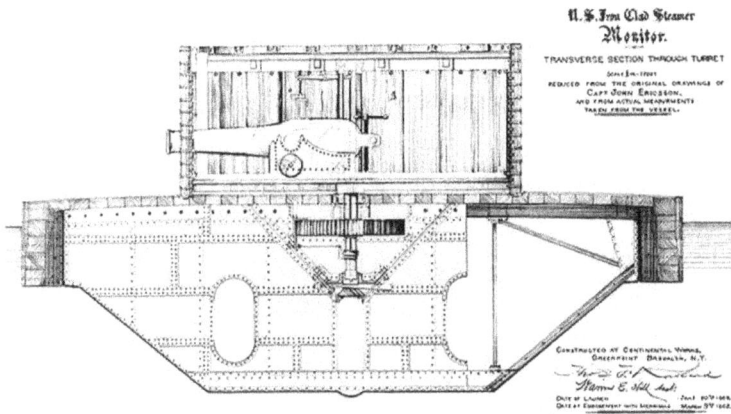

A transverse diagram of *Monitor's* hull through the turret pintle.

thick iron, the deck was made of 7 inches of pine set on 10-inch beams of oak. This was the only wood used in the main hull. The ends curved into points at either end. Ericsson wanted no compound curves in the entire ship, which made it simpler to construct in addition to being stronger. The only openings in the deck were the 20-foot circular opening for the turret, twin removable smokestacks, and several "deadlights," each eight inches in diameter with clear glass set in watertight gaskets. They provided natural light to the interior. Under the bow was a single hawsepipe for the anchor. Just aft of this was the pilothouse, a 4-foot square cube made of 9-inch iron plates stacked up with viewing slits on all four sides.

Below the deck was the Lower Vessel, which was 50 feet shorter than the overhanging decking. The hull was divided by a single heavy transverse bulkhead with access hatches on either side. This was the support for the 120-ton turret.

Plated in half-inch iron, the after hull contained the 320-horsepower engine, twin boilers, and coal bins. Ericsson had designed a unique blower system using belts to bring 7,000 cubic feet of air per hour into the engine room for the fireboxes and to ventilate the spaces.

A departure from tradition, the officers' quarters were forward of the beam. Each was personally designed by Ericsson to be comfortable, if somewhat cramped. Everyone had at least one of the deadlights in the overhead. They were paneled in black walnut and contained a bunk, porcelain sink, and small desk. The crew's quarters was a room 16 by 20 feet on the centerline between the port powder magazine and the starboard shell room. The crew hung their hammocks from hooks on the overhead. All the living spaces had wooden decking and walls. Aside from oil lamps, the deadlights in the overhead provided an eerie greenish illumination when water sloughed over the flat deck.

While cramped, the crew generally agreed that the accommodations were better than on most navy ships. The new ironclad had more than forty patentable inventions, in contrast to the *Merrimac's* single patent. Ericsson invented a toilet that used cutoffs and valves, a design still used on American submarines eighty years later.

The turret, whose eight curved layers of 1-inch iron plates were rolled at Novelty Iron Works in New York, had to be first drilled, riveted, and assembled at the foundry, then shipped by rail in pieces to the shipyard. It weighed 120 tons and was 20 feet in diameter. Nine feet high, the overhead was made of crisscrossing 2-inch and 6-inch iron bars to provide light and ventilation. The turret base rotated on a carefully machined bronze ring that Ericsson assured would be watertight by its sheer weight. The center pintle was 9 inches in diameter and geared for a small steam engine run by a single operator.

The turret deck was a grating with two openings for the passage of shell and powder. These had to be aligned with corresponding openings in the deck to allow ammunition to be brought up.

The only entry and egress from the ship were through the turret via ladders through the overhead grating.

The twin 11-inch Dahlgren smoothbore guns were set on rails with brass wheels and an Ericsson-designed recoil system. The rails and wheels were so carefully machined that a single man could roll the 5-ton gun with little effort. In order to give the long cannon more room within the turret, 18 inches were cut off the muzzles. The twin ports had swinging shutters to protect the crew when in the process of reloading. Small openings were allowed for the rammers and sponges to use when the shutters were closed. Block and tackle hoisted the shot up from the magazines. More cannonballs waited on a ring around the turret base. Each gun could fire a 168-pound shot over a mile using 15 pounds of powder.

Painted on the turret ring were markings to give the gun crew instant reference to where the guns were aimed. It was too dangerous to fire directly forward over the pilothouse. The guns could be fired individually or together by a single gun captain with a lanyard. Each gun needed a crew of eight men and one young "powder monkey" to bring the powder from the magazine.

The crew numbered eight officers and forty enlisted men. About ten percent of the crew was black, not unusual in the Union Navy. But there was no racial friction among the crew.

Exactly ninety-seven days after her keel was laid, the ironclad was launched on January 30, 1862. A large crowd watched the hull, not yet bearing the turret, slide into the waters of the East River. "Get a good look at her now," one man said to an onlooker, "because she won't be afloat once she hits the water."

But as Ericsson had often stated, the iron ship floated like a duck. The deck remained 10 inches above the surface of the water. The ironclad displaced 950 tons, and to the surprise of the navy officials, had a draft of exactly 11 feet, 5 inches, precisely as Ericsson had predicted.

The turret was fitted on February 17. It proved to rotate smoothly with only 25 pounds of steam pressure at a rate of one full revolution in 22.5 seconds.

The first test of the engine was not promising, but adjustments to the pistons and steam valves soon had the small vessel moving at a constant 6 knots, three less than Ericsson had planned. On February 26, the United States Navy commissioned the USS *Monitor* as its newest ship. Yet she was still not fully paid for. That would have to wait until she proved herself against the much-feared Rebel ironclad.

THE BATTLE THAT CHANGED HISTORY

On March 8, the *Merrimac* steamed down the Elizabeth River and rounded Sewall's Point to attack the Union blockading squadron. USS *Minnesota*, a steam and sail frigate, USS *Congress*, and USS *Cumberland*, both sail frigates, were anchored at Hampton Roads. They had been fore-warned about the Rebel ironclad but were confident in their own heavy guns and well-drilled crews. But as history has long since shown, their wooden hulls were no match for an iron ship. The *Merrimac* rammed and ultimately sank *Cumberland*, with the *Merrimac*'s ram still embedded in the frigate's hull. However, *Cumberland* managed to damage the ironclad with her heavy guns. The *Merrimac* battered *Congress* into surrender, and that frigate also sank, burning until her magazines exploded at midnight. Only *Minnesota* managed to escape destruction by slipping her anchor chain and backing away to shallow water. With more than four hundred men dead and two ships sunk, it was the worst defeat for the United States Navy until Pearl Harbor nearly eighty years later.

Merrimac, her crew tired but flushed with victory, moved back to Sewell's Point to make repairs and wait until morning.

The *Monitor*'s arrival that night after being towed through a storm changed history. At eight o'clock the following morning, the two iron-clads met in fateful battle. But even after three hours of furious fighting, neither could significantly damage the other. When the *Merrimac* with-drew on the ebb tide, the battle was over. *Minnesota* was still afloat, the *Monitor* remained close by, and the world had changed.

The *Merrimac* and the *Monitor* were highly innovative in their own ways. But neither was a truly seagoing vessel, being underpowered, hard to steer, and overweight. The *Merrimac* never steamed beyond Hampton Roads, while the *Monitor* nearly sank twice as she was towed the four hundred miles from New York to the Capes. Neither ironclad survived the year. The *Merrimac* was grounded and burned on the James River when the Union forces recaptured Norfolk. The *Monitor* sank in a storm off Cape Hatteras on December 31, 1862.

The consequences of the Battle of Hampton Roads were not yet apparent to many, except perhaps the few far-sighted naval tacticians. When the two ships, each of which was less than a week out of commis-sioning, began their short but momentous battle, the leaders of every other western navy held their breath. Iron and steam had proved, in a way no one could deny, their superiority over wood and sail. It would be at least thirty more years before the last sailing warships would be retired, but their long era was coming to an end.

The ironclads duel for the first and last time at Hampton Roads, March 9, 1862.

It was Admiral Sir John "Jacky" Fisher, First Sea Lord of the Admiralty, who, in 1904, realized the Royal Navy's superiority was largely based on numbers. In fact it was woefully out of date. He went over the ship list and struck out whole classes of cruisers, battleships, and sail frigates that were almost as old as he was. "Scrap the lot!" he roared with his characteristic pugnacity. The result was a ship that was as innovative as the two ironclads of the Civil War—the ten-gun HMS *Dreadnought*. An all-big-gun battleship, *Dreadnought* instantly made every other navy obsolete. Just as in March 1862, the world of naval combat had changed.

America entered the world stage in the last decade of the nineteenth century. The Spanish-American War, largely an invention of Assistant Secretary of the Navy Theodore Roosevelt, newspaper publisher William Randolph Hearst, and Massachusetts Senator Henry Cabot Lodge, was the new nation's "coming out party." "Remember the *Maine*! To hell with Spain!" were the slogans that inflamed a nation that had forgotten the bloodshed and sorrow of the Civil War. The excuse was to help the enslaved Cubans throw off the yoke of the Spanish oppressors. In reality, the Cubans were well on their way to independence from Spain, even without Yankee help.

America had a brand-new navy consisting of the biggest and most modern ships with powerful engines and guns. Roosevelt was eager for the chance to flex his navy's muscles. But one ship, the newest, was on the wrong side of the continent. The next essay describes the event that captivated the nation and proved a catalyst for the most ambitious civil engineering project in history.

THE RACE OF THE USS *OREGON*

Published in *Naval History*, June 2020

In the spring of 1898, a single United States battleship became the idol of the entire nation as she steamed from San Francisco to Florida to take part in one of the two major naval battles of the Spanish-American War. On the way she also proved the necessity of a canal between the Pacific and Atlantic Oceans. Known with affection and respect as the "Bulldog of the Navy," the USS *Oregon* had a long, varied career that ended half a century after being in the national spotlight.

Beginning in 1893, revolution and independence were rallying cries for the people of Cuba. Spain had ruled Cuba with an iron fist for nearly four hundred years. By 1898, six thousand Cubans under General Antonio Maseyo had been waging an increasingly successful guerilla war against 80,000 Spanish troops sent to hold the empire's most valuable Caribbean colony. Cubans living in the United States pressed for American support in driving the Spanish out. But more was at stake than Cuban rights and lives. In the era of robber barons and powerful trusts, many American businessmen were eager to profit from the Caribbean island's rich tobacco, sugar, and ore resources.

Spain had lost much of its empire in the New World and the Pacific. Only Cuba and Puerto Rico remained island bastions in the Caribbean, while the Philippines and Guam held the line in the Pacific. Spain had a large fleet to protect these last colonial possessions. But the ships were outmoded, worn out, and manned by ill-trained and poorly motivated men.

A decade before Great Britain launched the revolutionary battleship *Dreadnought* in 1906, the United States was still short of having a navy capable of challenging any European or Asian fleet. America's capital ships were not much more advanced than the *Monitor* of the Civil War. But by 1898, the U.S. Navy was at last coming into its own.

The spark that ignited the "splendid little war" happened on the night of February 15, 1898, when the protected cruiser USS *Maine,* sent to Havana to protect American interest, exploded and sank with a loss of 253 officers and men. Almost immediately, the yellow press, led by William Randolph Hearst, spread the word that Spanish mines had sunk the ship. Although there is strong evidence that *Maine* sank from the ignition of a powder magazine caused by a slow-burning fire in an adjacent coal bunker, no one was willing to believe this. The nation raged about Spanish treachery and demanded that President William McKinley declare war on Spain. One of the most outspoken promoters of war was the assistant secretary of the navy and the man who had ordered the *Maine* to Havana in the first place, Theodore Roosevelt.

Roosevelt was a close friend and confidant of sea power theorist Captain Alfred Thayer Mahan, who favored a massive naval building program. In 1895 Roosevelt wrote, "If only the people who are ignorant about our navy could see these great warships in all their majesty and beauty, and could realize how well-fitted they are to uphold the honor of America."

With his finger on the country's pulse and that of Wall Street, Roosevelt flexed the navy's muscles in the event of war with Spain. Even as he planned on leading a cavalry regiment into Cuba, he put his efforts into assembling as much seaborne firepower as possible. He had his bespectacled eyes on one ship in particular, the newest battleship in the navy, the USS *Oregon.* The third ship in the *Indiana* class, which included *Massachusetts, Oregon* was built at Union Iron Works in San Francisco, launched in 1893, and commissioned in 1896.

USS *Oregon* was a large ship for her time, displacing over 10,000 tons with a length of 350 feet and a beam of 67 feet. Two triple-expansion reciprocating engines could drive her through the water at a top speed of nearly 17 knots. With two turrets fitted with two 13-inch rifled cannons and four 8-inch guns, four 6-inch rapid-fire rifles, and twelve 3-inch rapid-fire rifles, *Oregon's* 470 officers and men wielded great firepower.

USS *Oregon* in 1898.

The only problem was that she was in Bremerton, Washington, in the wrong ocean.

Roosevelt was more preemptive than his often-absent superior, Navy Secretary John Long, and convinced McKinley to order the *Oregon* to join the North Atlantic squadron.

She would have to sail nearly 15,000 miles around South America. Time was of the essence. The Hearst press condemned McKinley daily for not having enough spine to challenge the decadent and tyrannical Spaniards.

Oregon received her orders on March 1 and weighed anchor on March 3. Reaching San Francisco three days later, her crew began loading nearly a thousand tons of coal and several hundred tons of shells and powder. Her commanding officer, Captain Alexander McCormick, fell ill and was replaced by Annapolis graduate Captain Charles Clark. His orders were to leave for their first port of call, Callao, Peru, on March 18.

The ship was painted in the peacetime scheme of white hull and buff superstructure and the *Oregon*'s guns were a gleaming black as she left the Golden Gate in her wake. Aboard was a young sea cadet, William Leahy, who would one day be an admiral and chief of staff to two presidents.

One of *Oregon's* assistant engineers, Joseph Mason Reeves, who would rise to the rank of admiral, wrote to his mother during the voyage around South America. He wrote, "Captain Clark is a good one. I think he isn't going to have the *Oregon* [become] a second *Maine* if he can prevent it." Racing at a sustained speed of 12 knots, *Oregon's* ram bow threw up a boiling "bone in her teeth." This would earn her the nickname "Bulldog of the Navy."

Chief Engineer R. J. Milligan knew that the fresh water used in the boilers and what was available for the crew was not sufficient for the entire voyage and suggested that the crew drink the water that had already gone through the boilers. This would extend her range. Surprisingly, the crew greeted this with equanimity and accepted the hardship, a measure of their motivation and patriotism.

This was the first transfer of a capital ship from one coast to another in a time of war and proved to be a boon for the navy's public image. Marconi's wireless telegraphy was still in its infancy in 1898, and all telegrams had to be sent by cable. *Oregon,* on her dash down the coast of the United States, Mexico, and Central and South America, was out of direct touch with shore. The only means of keeping track of her progress was from telegrams sent by U.S. consulates reporting her position. The Hearst and Pulitzer press published daily articles on the ship's progress. Americans followed the *Oregon's* race with increasing interest.

Captain Clark had one serious problem to deal with on the run south. A smoldering fire in one of the coal bunkers needed to be found and extinguished. These were common in coal-burning ships and not normally dangerous. But *Oregon* was a warship and carried a hundred tons of propellant powder for her guns. While he had no way of knowing *Maine's* destruction was likely due to the same source, his decision to find and extinguish the slow fire might very well have saved *Oregon* from the same terrible fate. Clark did not reduce speed as volunteers dug into the bunker and located the smoldering pyre. The hot mass of glowing coal was hauled up and thrown overboard.

The ship reached Callao on April 4 after a run of 4,112 miles in sixteen days. This was a record for such a large ship. But there was little rest for her crew as they again loaded coal from a barge for the run to the

Strait of Magellan. The ship's band played patriotic music and popular airs to keep the crew's spirits up in the increasingly humid equatorial climate. The men, stripped to the waist, were coated in black coal dust and sweat as the heavy canvas bags were hoisted up and shoveled into the half-empty bunkers below. It was dirty, hot, exhausting work. But other than a few dozen men fainting from the heat, they never faltered in their duty.

While at Callao, Clark received a cable from Washington that the Spanish torpedo boat *Temerario* had left the Uruguayan port of Montevideo and might be headed south to intercept and attack the *Oregon*. War had not yet been declared, but Clark told his lookouts and crew to be alert for any strange craft as the battleship pointed her prow to the southeast.

On April 11, President McKinley asked Congress for a declaration of war. Clark did not yet know this as *Oregon* steamed down the Chilean coast.

The battleship turned into the western end of the strait on the afternoon of April 15, too late to attempt navigating the stormy, confined waters before night fell. Then a violent storm struck the area, and huge waves rolled unbroken over the decks, burying all but her superstructure in foaming green water. Clark dropped two anchors in a bay on Tamar Island to wait out the storm. The following morning *Oregon* resumed her transit of the narrow strait and tied up at Punta Arenas on April 18. After provisioning and finishing some needed maintenance, she headed east and emerged into the Atlantic Ocean on April 21. USS *Oregon* was halfway to her goal. Now Clark's concerns were focused on the possible appearance of the *Temerario*.

Halfway around the world, in the western Pacific, events that would profoundly affect the crew of the USS *Oregon* were taking place. Commodore George Dewey, a scion of a navy legacy that went back to the War of 1812, commanded the Asiatic squadron, then based in Hong Kong. Aboard his flagship USS *Olympia,* he received orders to take his squadron to Manila and confront the Spanish fleet there.

The Spanish force in Manila consisted of eight heavy and light cruisers and three gunboats, while Dewey's fleet had five protected cruisers

Oregon rounding Cape Horn by Robert Hopkin. Actually, the ship went through the Strait of Magellan.

and two gunboats. The Spanish numerical superiority was more than compensated for by American firepower and excellent training. The Battle of Manila Bay on May 1 was a resounding victory for Dewey and the United States Navy. Dewey himself became a national hero.

The *Oregon* put into Rio de Janeiro on April 30, which, due to the International Date Line was the same day as the battle in Manila. While her crew labored to load seven hundred tons of coal into her bunkers, a Brazilian cruiser patrolled the harbor to protect the battleship from Spanish torpedo boats and sabotage. Word of the victory at Manila and the declaration of war sparked a wave of celebration and an increased rush to continue to Cuba.

In a letter posted from Rio, Assistant Engineer Reeves wrote, "There were loud shouts of 'Remember the *Maine!*' The navy's battle cry of this war and one that will most surely make a Yankee sailor's blood boil and make him more anxious to die than to ever strike our flag to any Spaniard man of war. Within two weeks I think the *Oregon*, single handed will sink or capture two of Spain's heaviest armored vessels."

With increased patriotic fervor firing the boilers as much as coal, *Oregon* left Rio on May 4. Cables from Washington reported four Spanish armored cruisers and three torpedo boats headed west from the Cape Verde Islands. Their course and orders were unknown. But *Oregon* now had company, the gunboat USS *Marietta*, and a recently purchased light cruiser, the *Nictheroy*. *Oregon* led them north as her crew prepared the ship for imminent battle. All her elegant woodwork, furnishings, and paneling—any fire hazard—was removed and thrown overboard. Her spotless white hull and upperworks were painted a flat gray.

On May 8, she steamed into Bahia, Brazil, announcing they would be there for several days. This was intended to fool any Spanish spies. In fact, they were on their way the next day. Clark had cabled Washington that "*Oregon* could steam fourteen knots for hours and in a running fight might beat off or even cripple the Spanish fleet. With present amount of coal on board will be in good fighting trim and could reach West Indies."

The battleship arrived in Barbados, whose population was decidedly anti-Spanish. But in order to confuse any Spanish sympathizers, Clark sailed that night with all the deck and cabin lights blazing as he headed west. Then all the lights were doused and the ship made a radical turn toward Florida.

On May 24, with her crew standing on deck in their tropical whites, *Oregon* entered Jupiter Inlet on the east coast of Florida sixty-six days after leaving San Francisco. She had steamed nearly 15,000 miles in just over two months, a remarkable feat for a pre-dreadnought warship driven by reciprocating engines. The press called it a "triumph of American technology and seamanship."

The Navy Department was heartened to learn that *Oregon* and her crew were ready for battle and that the ship had suffered no damage or mechanical failures during her long voyage. Moreover, the race of the *Oregon* proved that the United States could produce warships capable of protecting national interests on the world stage, exactly as Roosevelt and Mahan had insisted. But there was another unforeseen result of the voyage. If the United States were to become a global seafaring power, a canal had to be constructed between the Pacific and Atlantic. A two-month delay in moving ships from one ocean to another was completely unworkable. This was one major motivation for building the Panama Canal and another war Theodore Roosevelt would one day wage.

Oregon was at the naval base at Key West, awaiting orders from Rear Admiral William Samson, commander of the North Atlantic Squadron. Samson learned that Commodore Winfield Scott Schley, leading the detached "Flying Squadron," had found and blockaded the Spanish fleet in the port of Santiago de Cuba on the southern coast.

Admiral Pascual Cervera was in desperate straits. Governor General Ramon Blanco ordered him to move his fleet out to save them from American capture. He knew well the massed naval strength lurking outside the harbor entrance.

The American force consisted of five battleships, including *Oregon's* sister ships *Indiana* and *Massachusetts*, the new *Iowa*, the second-rate battleship *Texas*, the protected cruisers *New York* and *Brooklyn*, both of which were sisters to the *Maine*, the cruiser *New Orleans*, and a torpedo boat, the *Porter*. Divided into two squadrons, they patrolled east and west of the harbor entrance, waiting for the Spanish to emerge.

On the early morning of July 3, *New York*, *Massachusetts*, and three other ships sailed to Guantanamo Bay for coal while Samson conferred with the commander of the army forces, General Rufus Shafter. The western squadron was down to the *Brooklyn* and the armed yacht *Vixen* when Cervera, standing on the bridge of the magnificent cruiser *Infanta Maria Teresa*, led four large and light cruisers and two destroyers out to confront the enemy.

Cervera sent the cruisers *Cristóbal Colón* and *Almirante Oquendo* east with the destroyers while *Infanta Maria Teresa* and *Vizcaya* headed for the *Brooklyn*. This caused some confusion in the opening stages of the battle. The *Iowa* fired the first shot at 9:30 A.M. In moments, *Indiana*, *Texas*, and *Oregon* opened fire on the enemy ships. But then Cervera, realizing his ships were slower and far outgunned by the American battleships, turned his fleet southwest, followed by the *Vizcaya*, *Cristóbal Colón*, and *Almirante Oquendo*.

The only ship in the east squadron with enough speed to catch the fleeing Spanish was the *Oregon*. She charged west, passing and then being followed by the *Indiana* and *Brooklyn*.

Reeves wrote to his mother on July 7, "At last was the one chance we had been wishing for so long. Here was the *Oregon*'s chance to try her speed and her gunpower." *Oregon* and *Brooklyn* caught *Cristóbal Colón* sixty miles west at Cape Cruz. There *Oregon*'s 13-inch batteries fired at the Spanish ship.

Cristóbal Colón had left Spain in such haste that her main armament was not even fitted into the turrets. She could not fire back. Her captain and crew watched in horrified fascination as tall white waterspouts erupted from the blue sea as the huge Yankee shells exploded. With nowhere to go and no way to fight, *Cristóbal Colón* struck her colors at 1:13 P.M. and was scuttled just off the coast. Then *Oregon* turned to take on the last surviving enemy ships.

Knowing he had no chance in a battle, Cervera beached his flagship, followed by the *Almirante Oquendo* and *Vizcaya*, which had already been savaged by the *Oregon*'s 13-inch, 8-inch, and 6-inch guns.

"The *Almirante* and *Vizcaya* are simply torn and ripped to pieces," Reeves continued. "*Oregon* destroyed them almost alone and most mercilessly. She [*Vizcaya*] was afire in a dozen places and three of her magazines blew up."

The *Iowa*, joined by the *New York* and *Indiana*, chased down and severely damaged the torpedo boat *Furor*. The Battle of Santiago de Cuba lasted only four hours and left Spain without a fleet to support her army. Santiago surrendered on July 17.

Oregon, having fought in her first naval engagement, was considered the hero of the day. But this was not the end of her career.

After Emilio Aguinaldo ousted the Spanish from the Philippines and established the First Philippine Republic, *Oregon* was sent back to the Pacific to support the American troops fighting there. In 1900, she was sent to China to support land forces during the Boxer Rebellion. After remaining in the Far East for a year, *Oregon* returned to the states for an overhaul at Puget Sound Navy Yard. She was in San Francisco for the 1915 Panama-Pacific International Exposition.

The old battlewagon was still afloat when the Japanese attacked Pearl Harbor. Then considered an "unclassified" ship, *Oregon* was sold for scrap. Yet she still had a role to play. Stripped of her superstructure, *Oregon*'s hull served as a munitions barge during the Invasion of Guam in 1944.

She was finally scrapped in Japan in 1956, fifty-eight years after her historic race around South America. Ironically, the ship that had shown the urgent need for a passage between the Pacific and Atlantic never steamed through the Panama Canal.

Even though sail had long since given way to steam, the world's oceans were still home to many a tall ship with soaring masts carrying clouds of white sail. Relics of a bygone era, windjammers still evoked a sense of nostalgia in the first decades of the new century. And as astonishing as it may seem, one of those lofty ships was still capable of waging war on its enemies. In the Atlantic and Pacific, an old German windjammer was flying its nation's colors and attacking British and French steamships. The next essay tells the remarkable story of the last fighting sailing ship in the world.

SMS *SEEADLER*: THE LAST FIGHTING SAIL

Published in *Military History*, September 2018

The age of fighting sail lasted more than three hundred years, from 1540 during the reign of King Henry VIII until the advent of steam-powered ironclads in the American Civil War. The sight of a majestic windjammer under clouds of canvas was not uncommon during the years of the Great War. They were the last vestiges of the romantic age of sail. One of those ships was not what it appeared. Rather than a harmless sail-powered merchant ship crossing the seas, it was a deadly predator, a shark among the minnows. Her name was SMS *Seeadler*, the last page in the three-century saga of fighting sail.

By the autumn of 1916, the Great War had raged for more than two years. The Royal Navy blockaded Imperial Germany. Even as the Kaiser's armies drove hard to take Paris, the nation, heavily dependent on foreign wheat and fertilizer, was forced to live off its hump. The mighty High Seas Fleet was bottled up in Keil and Wilhelmshaven. The Battle of Jutland in May had not destroyed the German fleet, but the Kaiser was loathe to risk his navy by venturing out to the North Sea again. The only ray of hope came from the U-boat and the commerce raider. Submarines were already proving their worth against Allied ships. A few commerce raiders, armed liners, and merchant ships had slipped past the Royal Navy early in the war to prowl among vulnerable Allied shipping lanes.

In 1916, Captain Count Felix von Luckner, a tall, powerfully built Prussian aristocrat, and a few members of the German high command proposed to Kaiser Wilhelm II that a large sailing ship, properly armed and disguised, could slip past the British blockade and raid the shipping lanes. The scheme was unthinkable, even ludicrous. Yet it had some compelling advantages. Most raiders were subject to one serious limitation: coal. Germany had few colonies around the world, and consequently almost no coaling stations. German raiders had to either capture British colliers or have German ones meet them in isolated areas of the ocean. Therefore any vessel that could remain at sea for long periods without fueling had an advantage. Windjammers were the ultimate sailing ships. Far larger than the lovely sleek clippers that preceded them, the huge square-rigged barks had three, four, and even five masts to carry acres of white canvas. Often built of iron and steel rather than wood, they could sail under the most difficult weather conditions. They were the aegis of the age of sail. A large sailing ship would never be suspected of being a raider. As Luckner said to Kaiser Wilhelm, "Your Majesty, if our Admiralty says it's impossible and ridiculous, then I'm sure it can be done. The British Admiralty will think it impossible also."

Born in Dresden in 1881 and the son of a Prussian cavalry officer, Luckner left home in 1894 under the name Phelax Luedige to become a sailor. He sailed to the four corners of the world, amassing the skill of working with sails and spars. Years of sailing gave him unparalleled experience. He became fluent in English and Norwegian. He developed a love for the four-masted bark *Pinmore*, built in 1882. Still under the name Phelax Luedige, he returned to Germany and studied navigation, then joined the merchant marines as a petty officer aboard the small liner *Petropolis*. A year later, he joined the German Naval Reserve and gained a commission as a lieutenant. He went home, resplendent in gold braid. Luckner was promoted to captain on February

Captain Count Felix von Luckner.

3, 1912, while Germany and Great Britain built giant dreadnoughts of ever-increasing power and speed. His skill and bravery—he twice saved sailors from drowning—caught the attention of Kaiser Wilhelm II.

Luckner commanded light cruisers at the battles of Heligoland Bight in 1915 and Jutland the following year. Then he heard about the German Navy's idea to convert an old square rigger into an armed commerce raider and threw himself into the project. It was just the kind of daring adventure Luckner could make into a success. Not only would his prodigious experience in sailing ships be a major factor, but it appealed to his sense of the dramatic. He spoke perfect Norwegian, so the vessel would be disguised as a harmless, neutral Norwegian bark.

With that was born the SMS (Seiner Majestt, or His Majesty's Ship) *Seeadler*, or "Sea Eagle."

She was launched in Scotland in 1888 as the *Pass of Balmaha*. She was known to be fast and easy to handle. How the German Navy acquired her was a sea story in itself. While sailing to Arkhangel in Russia with a cargo of American cotton, she was stopped in the North Sea by a Royal Navy cruiser. Even though America was still neutral in 1916, the ship was seized and a British crew was put aboard to sail her to Scapa Flow. But then fate intervened in the form of a German U-boat. The tables were turned and the Germans took the *Pass of Balmaha* to the North Sea port of Bremerhaven. At 4,500 tons and a length of just over 250 feet, the ship was large enough for Luckner's purposes. She was extensively converted, beginning with a 950-horsepower auxiliary diesel engine and propeller shaft fitted just ahead of the rudder. This would provide propulsion even when the winds were slack. Her instruments and gear were well-used, weather-beaten, and Norwegian-made. Two 4.2-inch guns were concealed behind false stacks of lumber at the port and starboard bows. The gunners were trained to load, aim, and fire at specific targets on enemy ships.

But that was only the beginning of her extreme makeover. The intent was to make the bark seem like a harmless square rigger with a crew of slovenly, ill-disciplined sailors. But appearances were deceptive.

As Luckner put it, the *Pass of Balmaha* became "a mystery ship of trick panels and trick doors." In addition to quarters for her sixty-four officers and crew, she could carry up to four hundred prisoners—that is,

SMS *Seeadler* under full sail.

the crews from ships Luckner captured. The "cells" were cunningly hidden behind false panels in the hold that appeared to be stacks of crates and cargo. They were carefully constructed to be invisible to a British Navy boarding party.

As will be seen in the next essay, this was not an exclusively German subterfuge. The Royal Navy had already used disguised steamers to lure U-boats to the surface in order to sink them. In each case it was a matter of making a ship look harmless, even as it prowled the seas like a wolf in the fold.

Luckner was adamant that the prisoner accommodations have plenty of bunks, toilets, and even games and reading material. "I wanted them to feel as though they were my guests." This was more than his streak of gentlemanly chivalry. His "guests" would be more likely to behave and not sound the alarm when *Seeadler* approached another victim.

As for the crew, they were all German Navy volunteers chosen for their experience in sailing ships. Several spoke fluent Norwegian. One man, a slender and smooth-cheeked youth named Schmidt, was chosen to play the role of the captain's Norwegian wife, complete with wig, dress, and makeup. Every man had worked out his "identity" as a Norwegian sailor or officer, right down to fake family letters, keepsakes and photos, clothing, and personal idiosyncrasies. They chewed tobacco and learned the words to ribald Norwegian drinking songs. Luckner himself learned to chew tobacco, saying it helped, when asked an embarrassing question, to chew the plug, think for a long moment, then spit elegantly.

In early November 1916, the ship was ready, fully loaded, and manned. Now all she needed to pass through the blockade was a false identity. The bark *Maleta*, similar to *Seeadler*, was loading in Copenhagen. Luckner traveled to the port and signed on as a longshoreman using his former identity of Phelax Luedige. He crept aboard and stole the ship's logbook. The *Seeadler* would have a bona fide identity. But the German High Command delayed her sailing until after the real *Maleta* sailed, throwing off the timetable. Luckner changed the name on the log and all ship's papers to the *Hero*, a bark of dubious registry. But there was a catch. The erasures and alterations to the papers were too obvious. Luckner had a daring idea. He called the ship's carpenter and told him to use an axe to smash all the portholes, railings, furniture, and bunks and make sure to cover everything in seawater. When the job was done, it appeared the *Hero* had been through a violent gale. And of course, her papers, sodden and stained, were hard to read clearly. This was the Luckner touch: innovation and nerve.

Seeadler left Bremerhaven two days before Christmas, and her first mission was to get past a huge minefield. A storm came to Luckner's aid by forcing the bark to sail heeled far over on her beam-ends, which allowed her to ride safely over the submerged mines. Then a British cruiser, HMS *Avenger*, steamed close and ordered the bark to heave to for boarding and inspection. The Royal Navy officer saw a loaded lumber ship that had recently been battered by Baltic storms and a crew of smelly, undisciplined Norwegians who showed little respect for his rank or duty. The captain, a tall brute of a man named Knudsen with a plug of tobacco wedged in his cheek, showed him the ship's papers, which were water-stained and nearly unreadable. Knudsen, in his thick Norwegian accent, complimented the officer on his warm camel's hair duffel coat. He then introduced his wife, Josephine, lying on the damp cabin settee with a painful toothache. The Royal Navy officer saw no further reason to detain the obviously innocent Norwegian bark and returned to his ship. As HMS *Avenger* steamed away, the signal flags read "Bon Voyage."

Luckner and *Seeadler* had passed their first test. As they cleared the British Isles and headed out to sea, they shed the disguise. The lumber cargo was cast overboard to reveal the two guns. But some traces of the camouflage remained to lure unsuspecting prey into the Sea Eagle's claws. Thus prepared, Luckner sailed into the broad North Atlantic in search of prey. He would soon be known as the "Sea Devil."

His orders limited him to only attacking other sailing ships. The idea of an old bark capturing a steamship was ridiculous, but to Luckner, the challenge was too good to pass up. He had his first chance on January 9, 1917, when the masthead lookout saw smoke on the horizon. It was the 3,200-ton British steamer *Gladys Royale*, bound for Buenos Aries. After running up the Norwegian flag, Luckner used what would be his signature ploy, a request for a chronometer reading. This was common for sailing vessels, which needed accurate time for navigation. The *Gladys Royale* hove to under *Seeadler*'s port bow, then Luckner ordered the German Navy ensign raised and a shot fired across the steamer's bow. Three more shots forced the British captain to stop his engines and row over to the German ship. "You bloody well fooled me," he fumed at the grinning German captain.

The steamer's crew were brought on board the *Seeadler* and given quarters below while an explosive charge was placed in the steamer's hull. That night, Luckner's first victim went to the bottom. The next day, flushed with victory, *Seeadler* found another steamer; this time the prey was the 3,100-ton British steamer *Lundy Island*. But the British captain did not fall for the innocent request for a chronometer reading and attempted to run for it. Luckner raised the German flag and fired two shots into the ship's funnel and hull. Beaten, the steamer surrendered and the crew was taken aboard. In two days, Luckner had taken and sunk two British ships without a single life lost.

The British captains began a spirited checkers tournament while their crews enjoyed the run of the German ship, albeit under guard. But there were no problems due to Luckner's courtly treatment of his prisoners. Remarkably, the so-called prisoners were paid their regular wages while on board and participated in shipboard maintenance. Even more astonishingly, after Luckner stated that the first man to sight a ship would receive the equivalent of fifty marks and a bottle of champagne, almost every prisoner and even the two British captains lined the railings to spot the *Seeadler's* next target.

"Never," recalled Luckner, "had a ship such a lookout."

On January 21, the crew spotted the French bark *Charles Gounod* and approached with the same request for a chronometer reading. This ship was easily taken, and along with the crew, several cases of good French wine were brought on board. Over the next three weeks, two more windjammers from Canada and Italy fell to *Seeadler* without any resistance, and the hold was soon packed with over a hundred prisoners. Still no lives had been lost.

On February 3, 1917, the French square-rigger *Antonin*, a fast and well-handled ship, made a run for it. Luckner chose not to use his engine but engaged in a chase under full sail. At last he caught up and fired his machine guns at the French ship. They surrendered with the French captains swearing so loudly it could be heard over the span of water between the two ships.

In less than a month, *Seeadler* had sunk six ships. Still, the wily Sea Devil pressed on toward the South Atlantic. On February 19, Luckner was confronted with his past. The bark *Pinmore*, on which he had sailed as the young runaway Phelax Luedige, was captured. With a sense of nostalgia, Luckner rowed alone over to the old windjammer and walked the decks of his youth. He even found where he had carved his name, "Phelax Luedige," into the stern rail. Then pragmatism intervened. He chose to put some of his crew on board the *Pinmore* and sail to Rio de Janeiro to load some needed supplies. With his usual flair for innovation, Luckner got away with this daring venture and rendezvoused with the

Seeadler a few days later. But he then had to give the hardest order of his naval career. With a heavy heart, he ordered the *Pinmore* sunk. Staying below in his cabin, he tried not to listen to the dull rumble of the charges that sank a much-loved relic of his past.

But he had other things on his mind. While in Rio, he met a Royal Navy officer from HMS *Glasgow*, a light cruiser, who told him that his ship and HMS *Amethyst* were preparing to find and sink a German raider working off the Brazilian coast. With this timely warning, Luckner bent on full sail to head south toward Cape Horn at the tip of South America. Along the way he sank three more windjammers.

The 3,600-ton steamer *Horngarth* was spotted on March 11. The ship had not only a wireless but also a 5-inch deck gun. Luckner had to put the wireless out of action before the British could raise the alarm. When the standard request for a chronometer reading went unanswered, he started a small fire on the main deckhouse and raised a distress flag, something no ship could ignore. At last *Horngarth* came close. Then Luckner had his "wife," Josephine—in reality, "That rascal Schmidt"— parade demurely along the deck to distract the British sailors. Then he raised the German ensign and fired a shot directly into the wireless room. When *Horngarth*'s crew attempted to return fire, Luckner selected men with megaphones to yell out in English, "torpedoes are clear!" That made the British captain back down and surrender.

But Luckner's perfect record had been broken with the death of a British officer, who had died from wounds during the battle. He was buried with full military honors by the Germans and British. Now *Seeadler* had more than 275 prisoners. This prompted Luckner to use his next prize, the French bark *Cambronne*. Her captain was relieved to find that his ship wouldn't be sunk but was to take the *Seeadler* prisoners to Rio. The bark's topmasts were cut down to slow her. Luckner sailed north, still within sight of the French ship. After dark he turned south and headed for the Horn. But unlike the other ruses, this did not work. The Royal Navy soon realized *Seeadler* was headed for the Pacific and sent *Glasgow* and *Amethyst* to find and sink her.

By this time, the United States had declared war on Germany. From June 15 to July 5, 1917, Luckner captured and sank three small American schooners: the *A. B. Johnson,* the *R. C. Slade,* and the *Manila.* These were slim pickings compared to what he had found in the Atlantic, but he had other concerns. The British Navy was hunting for him and he was low on provisions. On the last day of July, the German raider anchored in the calm lagoon of Mopelia Atoll in the Society Islands. The crew and prisoners went ashore to feast on turtle soup, lobster, eggs, and fruit. But disaster struck when a strong current dragged *Seeadler's* anchor, and she was driven onto a submerged reef. Despite desperate efforts by the crew, her keel was broken in five places. Luckner knew it was the end of the voyage. He ordered everything salvageable taken off and the ship burned. As the Germans and Americans watched, the gallant windjammer burned to the waterline. A village of sorts was constructed of the ship's timbers and sailcloth on the beach.

But the audacious Luckner was not done. He selected five volunteers, outfitted a launch with sails, provisions, and weapons, and tried to capture the first island trading ship they came across. But after a 28-day journey to Fiji, they had no luck. In an island port, a British officer and armed soldiers confronted them. Knowing that resistance would only result in needless death, Luckner surrendered. His 224-day odyssey had ended. But in his wake were fourteen ships sunk, including three steamers, and more than $25 million in damages to the Allies. It was the last hurrah of fighting sail. For the rest of his life, Felix von Luckner was respected and revered for his daring, cunning, and chivalry toward his enemies. He may have been the Sea Devil, but he was truly the last of his kind.

Subterfuge was the key element in the short but amazing success of the *Seeadler.* But many more ships used stealth, guile, and even dirty tricks to lure enemy vessels close. The Royal Navy used these so-called Q-ships to bring the hidden killers of the sea—the U-boats—to the surface where they could be attacked and sunk. But it was a dangerous venture and resulted in more loss for the Q-ships than the submarines. The following essay tells the story of the Royal Navy's audacious attempts to counter the U-boat threat.

BRITAIN'S DEVIOUS U-BOAT KILLERS

The British Admiralty had a particular dislike and disdain for the emerging use of submarines in warfare. They considered the submarine "dastardly, unethical, and un-English, the weapon of cowards who refuse to fight like men on the surface." Yet there was a certain irony in this statement when the means of defeating the U-boats was equally devious. This essay relates a time and place when the tradition-bound Royal Navy realized unsportsmanlike trickery was acceptable to win the war at sea.

April 1917 was one of the most critical points in the naval war. In December of the previous year, Admiral Henning von Holtzendorff had written a memo to Kaiser Wilhelm II that if the U-boats were given free rein to conduct unrestricted warfare, they could sink 600,000 tons of ships per month. This would bring Great Britain to its knees. To the alarm of the Admiralty, Allied and neutral shipping losses climbed from 560,000 tons in February to 580,000 tons in March, then to a shocking high of 850,000 tons in April. The Western Approaches, the area of ocean between the Irish land's end and the Bay of Biscay, was becoming a graveyard of shipping.

At that time there were about 130 U-boats in service, but only half were operational at any moment. The best of them were 420 feet long, displaced 820 tons, and carried sixteen torpedoes and a well-trained crew of seventy men. They were true undersea predators, far deadlier than the earlier models that had prowled the North Sea in 1914.

The Royal Navy mined the North Sea, the Channel, and the German Bight off the coast, but there was virtually no defense in the open sea. Destroyers and patrol boats were helpless against hidden subs. As long as a U-boat remained submerged, it was invulnerable. A submerged U-boat with fully charged batteries could travel eighty miles. There was no way to track or follow a submerged U-boat. They could surface and attack anywhere, any time.

It remained for the Admiralty to find a means of defeating the U-boat menace. Prior to the sinking of *Lusitania*, Winston Churchill, in his role as First Lord of the Admiralty, made the first move in Britain's covert war on German submarines. In his zest for daring and even foolhardy schemes, he ordered that British trawlers tow submerged Royal Navy submarines and communicate by telephone cables. When a U-boat was sighted, the trawler sent an alert to the British sub, which then cut the tow and maneuvered to attack the U-boat. This unusual ploy worked in June and July 1915, sinking two U-boats. The captain of *U-40*, sunk by the *C-24* and rescued by the trawler *Taranaki*, loudly declared that his sub had been sunk by a "dirty trick."

The towed sub tactic was hardly the solution. What was needed were more ships. With the U-boats eating away at merchant shipping, the deficit between losses and new construction widened. Churchill ordered every ship that could carry cargo or troops to be found. Old sailing ships, worn-out tramp steamers, and even trawlers were collected from Britain, Scandinavia, Canada, and the United States. Old, worn-out steamers demanded exorbitant prices. Yet they failed to make up the losses.

The effort, along with increased ship construction, totaled about 1,152,000 tons of shipping into service. But this was only about a quarter of what had been lost to the Germans. The Admiralty canceled the construction of six cruisers and three battleships to boost merchant shipping tonnage.

When the war started in the summer of 1914, U-boats conducted their attacks under an article of the 1907 Hague Convention governing war at sea, generally known as "cruiser warfare." Upon stopping a ship, a submarine must board her to determine its nationality, destination, and cargo. Ships of any nation carrying war materiel for Great Britain could be sunk, but only after the crew and passengers were safely off in lifeboats. This changed after the sinking of the Cunard liner *Lusitania* in May 1915. Among the 1,261 persons who died after the *U-20* torpedoed the liner, 118 were American. The "deed for which a Hun would blush" inflamed American passions and pushed President Woodrow Wilson closer to the decision to declare war on Germany. In Berlin, Chancellor Theobald Bethman-Holweg, a moderate, was desperate to avoid a war with the huge nation across the Atlantic. He knew full well it would mean Germany's defeat, but Admiral Alfred von Tirpitz, Secretary for Naval Affairs, fiercely opposed him. Tirpitz and the naval high command were stubbornly certain that unrestricted submarine warfare on Allied and neutral shipping would cripple Britain in six months, then Germany could face America on nearly equal terms.

Kaiser Wilhelm vacillated until September 1915, when Admiral Hugo von Pohl, Commander-in-Chief of the High Seas Fleet, withdrew all U-boats from the sea, soothing simmering American emotions. But the pressure was still on. With the land war in an endless stalemate, the only certain means to bring the war to a close was to starve Great Britain by putting its merchant fleet on the bottom. In the first seven months of 1915, U-boats sank 790,000 tons of Allied and neutral shipping, of which about 570,000 tons had been British. This was nowhere near the total that would have to be sunk if U-boats were to bring Britain to the surrender table. They would have to sink at least 600,000 tons each month for a year—in other words, 7.2 million tons in all. This was impossible under the strict rules that governed restricted submarine warfare.

The SMS *U-20*, a typical German submarine of WWI. This is the sub that sank the *Lusitania* in May 1915. *Imperial War Museum*

Caught between the American rock and the hard place of winning the war, Kaiser Wilhelm chose a compromise in February 1916. All Allied ships in the War Zone were to be attacked without warning, as were all armed Allied ships on the open seas. Passenger ships were to be unmolested. Regarding neutral and unarmed ships outside the War Zone around the British Isles, Wilhelm insisted that the rules of cruiser warfare be observed. While this was about as civilized as a naval war could be, it put the U-boats at considerable risk. With no other choice, they went on patrol with this restriction.

But the winds of war were already turning against the U-boats. Early anti-submarine tactics and weapons were ineffectual. It became apparent that the only sure way to sink a U-boat was to bring it to the surface, where gunfire could penetrate the pressure hull and sink the sub. Submarines were deadly underwater but fragile on the surface. The trick was in enticing the sub to come up. A sub commander used his meager supply of expensive torpedoes sparingly for large merchantmen and warships. Small freighters of less than 5,000 tons displacement could be sunk by fire from the U-boat's deck gun or by placing scuttling charges in the hull. In either case, a U-boat had to be on the surface. This led to the genesis of the Q-ship.

In order to advance the use of disguised armed ships, First Sea Lord Admiral Sir John Jellicoe appointed Rear Admiral Alexander Duff as head of an official anti-submarine division in December 1916. Duff had been in command of the light cruiser *Birmingham* when it rammed the *U-15* on August 9, 1914, the first German sub to be sunk in the war. Duff began by establishing specific routes for merchant ships that changed on a regular basis to confuse U-boats, and most significantly, arming the next generation of Q-ships.

He collected scores of small, nondescript freighters of less than 6,000 tons of displacement. They looked like the tramp steamers found in every port in the world—rusty, old, and of basic construction—although their engines and boilers were upgraded to give them more speed. Deckhouses were cut down to conceal gun mounts hidden behind collapsible walls.

Duff originally called them "special service ships" or "mystery ships." The term "Q-ship" may have come from Queenstown in Ireland, where many of the ships were based. They were manned by trained reserve navy crews and not averse to flying the flags of neutral Brazil, Argentina, Norway, Finland, Iceland, or the United States.

Even in the ultratraditional Royal Navy, Q-ships had much leeway to do and try any subterfuge, any deviousness that would persuade a wary U-boat captain to surface. Image was everything. Q-ships always assumed they were under scrutiny through a U-boat's periscope. In order to make the crack Royal Navy Reserve crew appear as harmless, slovenly foreign sailors and passengers, they grew long hair and beards and wore nondescript civilian clothing. Every aspect of "spit and polish" was buried in favor of sloppy, lazy, and even insubordinate behavior. They assiduously avoided acting like trained sailors, going so far as having fistfights on deck, refusing to salute, and adopting forbidden habits like smoking pipes and chewing tobacco.

The more unkempt the ship appeared, the more likely it was to entice a U-boat to surface for a gun attack.

When a periscope was sighted, the Q-ship's captain watched the sub's movements through concealed holes in the superstructure. A common ruse was for a specially trained "panic party" to throw itself into a lifeboat and frantically row away to escape the attack. In order for this ploy to work, Q-ships often carried double the normal number needed for a small freighter.

So was that plodding old rust bucket in the War Zone exactly what it appeared, or was it in fact a predator, a wolf in sheep's clothing? One of those innocent-looking tramp steamers was commanded by a man who would go down in history as the most successful U-boat killer of the First World War.

Well before the creation of an official Q-ship program, there had been engagements between disguised ships and U-boats. Croydon-born Lieutenant Commander Gordon Campbell was clever, daring, and audacious to a fault. He also possessed the one quality that Q-ship captains needed in abundance: patience. Campbell was thirty years old when he took his first decoy ship to sea in 1915. Campbell and HMS *Farnborough*'s crew had to wait nine months for their first chance at a German U-boat. In the meantime, exercising a latent skill as a theater director, Campbell refined the deception. Almost as if he had read the same book as *Seeadler*'s Felix

A view of a "panic party" lowering from *Tamarisk*,
1917.

Luckner, he disguised one crewman as his wife, complete with a simu-
lated baby, to sit in a lounge chair and read a book. He ceaselessly drilled
the crew on the two 6-pounder and five 12-pounder guns.

His chance finally came on March 26, 1916, off the southern coast
of Ireland. A crewmember spotted a torpedo coming at them. It missed,
passing harmlessly behind the ship. Campbell told his men to show no
reaction. It took great courage and presence of mind to maintain the
deception even under torpedo attack.

While a hit might kill some of the crew, the ship probably would not
sink. Decoy ships often had their holds stuffed with cork, empty barrels,
balsa wood, and other "unsinkable" materials. The gunners were ready
when the *U-68* surfaced directly astern and passed alongside the *Farnborough*. "Let go!" Campbell bellowed. The white Royal Navy ensign was

Captain Gordon Campbell, VC, the scourge of German U-boats.

raised and the guns opened fire. In minutes, the U-boat sank with its hull riddled with shell holes. This was only the first of three victories for Gordon Campbell.

Almost a year passed before Gordon Campbell again faced a U-boat. The date was February 17, 1917, while the German subs were sinking almost 600,000 tons per month. Now under the aegis of Admiral Duff's new division, *Farnborough* was hit by a torpedo a hundred miles southwest of Queenstown. While any competent naval officer would consider this a catastrophe, Campbell's standing orders were for the deck officer to alter the ship's course and speed to ensure a hit. Immediately the "panic party" went into action, making their headlong dash into the lifeboats as haphazard as possible. But as the two boats hit the water and rowed away, the sub still had not surfaced.

By this time the Kriegsmarine was aware of the new threat. Now every merchantman sailing alone was suspect, and the U-boats became extremely wary when approaching a ship. The captains carefully studied the rusty old ships, searching for any sign of false bulwarks or depth charge racks. The Q-ships were being called *Unterseeboot Falle*, or "U-boat trap." One of the safest tactics was to surface two or three miles from the ship and shell it with the sub's 4.1-inch deck gun.

This was the most nerve-racking time for the Q-ship crew. It was harrowing having to remain concealed beside their own guns while enemy shells exploded among them. All they could do was hope the U-boat commander chose to come closer. Then it would be their turn. Some U-boat captains used a torpedo to ensure a kill without the risk.

The *U-83*, under *Kapitanleutnant* Bruno Hoppe, was not taking any chances. He continued to study the ship, noting that it did not seem to be sinking, even though most of its crew had fled in panic. Hoppe's periscope came so close to one of the lifeboats that the crew spoke in whispers so as not to be heard by the prowling German. Then, *U-83* moved close enough to the *Farnborough* that Campbell saw the gray hull under the surface. Then Hoppe decided to come up, breaking the surface only a hundred yards away, a perfect target for Campbell's skilled gunners.

Campbell was well-acquainted with submarines, having spent some time with a Royal Navy sub flotilla the previous year. He knew that once a sub surfaced, it would take several minutes to submerge again. The first 12-pounder shell decapitated Hoppe as he climbed from the conning tower hatch. His gun crew was caught unawares as their skipper's headless corpse fell back into the conning tower. Confusion and panic ensued as the British guns fired again. With forty-five holes torn in the hull, *U-83* sank, leaving only two survivors. Thirty-five Germans died.

Campbell was awarded the Victoria Cross. Fifteen members of his crew also received decorations. The details of Campbell's VC were never released, prompting the name "The Mystery VC."

In June 1917, Campbell commanded the heavily armed HMS *Pargust*, a 2,800-ton Devonport-converted collier. She carried two 4.1-inch guns, four 12-pounders, and two 14-inch underwater torpedo tubes. But the latter were not as formidable as they might seem. It was virtually impossible to accurately aim and fire the torpedoes, as the ship could not maneuver like a submarine could.

Off the south coast of Ireland, *Pargust* was hit by a torpedo from the mine-carrying submarine *UC-29*. Campbell added to the "panic party" appearance with further touches, including a bowler-hat-wearing "captain" complete with a stuffed parrot in a cage. Every aspect of his crew's reaction was intended to make the U-boat captain come closer to *Pargust*'s guns or torpedoes.

After half an hour, the *UC-29* surfaced fifty yards away. Campbell ordered the gun crews to open fire. A torpedo was launched but missed the submarine. Several shells hit the sub, which then exploded, most likely from one of its own mines.

By the summer of 1917, the Q-ship versus U-boat war reached a climax. Six Q-ships had been sunk, while at least twelve U-boats died from Q-ship action. It was now virtually impossible to entice U-boats to the surface. The most legendary battle between a Q-ship and U-boat took place in the Bay of Biscay on August 8. HMS *Dunraven* was a new twist to the Q-ship concept. Instead of looking like an old tramp steamer, *Dunraven* portrayed a 3,000-ton armed merchant steamer. She had a single 4.1-inch gun visible on her stern but was also armed with torpedo tubes, and two stern-depth charge racks, and four more guns concealed behind false bulwarks. Having the ship appear as an armed merchantman was intended to goad a U-boat captain, unaware of *Dunraven*'s great firepower, into making a surfaced attack. In command was the Q-ship ace, Gordon Campbell. But this was one battle he would lose.

At midday, the *U-61*, cruising on the surface, approached *Dunraven* and submerged. Campbell made sure his ship gave the appearance of running in panic from the sub, even reducing speed to allow the submerged sub to catch up. His tactic worked and *U-61* surfaced and opened fire with its deck gun from two miles away. It was the opening of a battle unlike any ever fought at sea.

One shell came close and a great cloud of steam rose from the ship. It was another ruse, a special system that blasted steam as if from a ruptured boiler. Then the stern gun fired back, but under Campbell's orders, none came close. He sent distress calls on an open frequency sure to be heard by the U-boat. When the *U-61* was half a mile away, Campbell sent off the panic party. It was a masterful performance, even leaving one boat dangling in the davits. The gunfire continued, and one German shell hit *Dunraven's* stern among the ready ammunition. An explosion sent a fireball into the air. This was no ruse. *Dunraven* was badly hit. A fire started and a depth charge went off. The concealed gun crews remained at their stations as the sub came closer. With the black smoke obscuring their aim, Campbell had to wait. Two more depth charges cooked off in what Campbell described as a "terrific explosion." This destroyed one of the concealed 4.1-inch guns, but the crew was unhurt. The fire spread quickly.

Blazing wood and hot shrapnel made the deck a deadly hell. The magnitude and number of explosions alerted the *U-61* that they were dealing with a Q-ship and they submerged. Even though the fire was certain to reach the magazines, Campbell continued to watch and wait. At 1:23, *Dunraven* took a torpedo hit and Campbell ordered, "Abandon ship!" A second panic party entered the boats, but the remaining gunners stayed aboard with their captain.

The battle of wits and courage continued as more ammunition exploded. *U-61* surfaced off *Dunraven's* stern and poured shells into the hull, safe from any return fire. At 2:53, the *U-61* submerged and passed *Dunraven's* port side, whereupon Campbell, watching the periscope, launched a torpedo, which missed. The sub apparently did not notice it. Another was launched but failed to detonate upon striking. Having had enough, the *U-61* moved off and returned to Germany. Now Campbell truly abandoned his ship, which sank later that evening, white ensign flying. Gordon Campbell was awarded a bar to his Victoria Cross, making him the most decorated naval officer of the Great War.

Campbell served thirty years in the Royal Navy and retired as a Rear Admiral in 1929.

Altogether there were more than two hundred Q-ships, of which twenty-seven were sunk, having defeated between twelve and fourteen submarines. The ratio was certainly no victory for the Royal Navy. They played only a minor role in the U-boat war, but their very existence was a factor in the Kaiser's decision to unleash unrestricted submarine warfare in February 1917. This was the spark that ignited the United States' declaration of war in April. From that point on, the convoy system and great numbers of destroyers at last eliminated the U-boat threat.

The concept of sending surface ships out to raid enemy merchants went back to the corsairs of the Barbary Coast of Africa in the Middle Ages. For nearly four centuries the concept continued and expanded until raiders and privateers were an accepted element of naval warfare. However fast and powerful surface ships were by the beginning of the Second World War, they were limited by how much fuel they could carry and their vulnerability to being spotted from the air. During the Great War, surface raiders held the winning hand. The SMS *Emden*, part of Admiral Maximilian von Spee's East Asia Squadron, had roamed the Pacific and Indian Oceans in 1915, doing great damage to British merchant ships and commerce.

During the eighteen years between the Great War and the German invasion of Poland, much had changed in naval weapons and tactics. The birth of the aircraft carrier meant that a fleet could send air patrols out to find an enemy far beyond the visible horizon. Wireless radios and the early development of radar were advances that only time would reveal.

The next essay relates how one senior German officer used the might of the Third Reich to build and deploy new and modern surface warships to find and destroy enemy convoys.

HUNTING THE *GRAF SPEE*

The African Lion deserves its undisputed title as "King of the Beasts," but even with its great strength, sharp claws, and blinding speed, a pack of smaller jackals working in cooperation can defeat it. In the last three months of 1939, one of Nazi Germany's deadliest lions was the German cruiser *Admiral Graff Spee*, a fast and heavily armed commerce raider with nine kills to its credit. In her brief but stunning career, *Graf Spee* was one of the only successful German surface raiders of the Second World War. But it only took three Royal Navy jackals to kill the lion.

In the cool predawn of August 21, 1939, the hulking dark shape of a warship slipped out of the German naval port of Wilhelmshaven on the North Sea coast and headed north into the cold waters between England and Norway. Forty-eight hours later the ship was well out into the broad Atlantic Ocean, safe from prying British eyes. This was the opening move in a naval campaign that would become legend. The ship was the *Admiral Graf Spee*, a compact and powerful cruiser with six 11-inch guns. Painted a light gray to blend in with the misty horizon that often covered the Atlantic, *Graf Spee* was one of the first of Grossadmiral Erich Raeder's surface raiders.

In his supreme role as the senior officer in Hitler's Kriegsmarine, Raeder was at last implementing his long-anticipated Plan Z, unleashing a fleet of fast, powerfully armed, deadly surface raiders on a daring campaign to destroy Britain's sea commerce. At the war's outset, Britain possessed about two thousand merchant ships and another thousand coastal vessels of less than 2,000 tons each, totaling around 4 million tons of cargo capacity. Another three million tons came from countries conquered by

Panzerschiff *Graf Spee* in 1936. *Imperial War Museum*

Germany, while another million tons were being launched each year. Britain required about fifty-five million tons of imports of food, oil, cotton, wool, and other industrial products annually. Raeder aimed to sink more tonnage than Britain could endure and force the capitulation. In essence, his raiders had to sink ships faster than Britain could replace them.

Grossadmiral Erich Raeder was a strong advocate of fast surface commerce raiders. But he was more a tactician than a strategist, a remnant of his time with the battle cruisers under Hipper. He never developed a broad strategy, instead using his meager force in hit-and-run raids and attacks. This old maritime practice went back to Sir Francis Drake in Elizabethan times. Issuing a letter of marque to a ship and captain to raid and capture merchant ships flying an enemy flag was common during the Napoleonic era, American Revolution, Civil War, and Great War. The only difference in Raeder's plan was that the raiders were exclusively German Navy warships.

Originally, Plan Z was to have the use of several dozen fast and powerful battleships, heavy cruisers, and aircraft carriers. In reality, the Kriegsmarine never deployed an aircraft carrier. With no ports out of the range of enemy planes and having little access to the Atlantic, the lone German carrier, *Graf Zeppelin,* was never completed.

Hitler, who had assured Raeder that the war wouldn't start until at least 1943, preempted this grand building program by planning the invasion of Poland in the fall of 1939. Raeder had to work with what he had. His only advantage was that the Royal Navy was largely equipped with vessels launched during or shortly after the Great War. After signing the naval treaties of 1922 and 1931, the Admiralty scrapped most of the expensive capital ships, leaving a nucleus of aircraft carriers, battleships, cruisers, and a leavening of light cruisers and destroyers.

Raeder's ships were all new, having been launched since 1931 and fitted with the latest naval technology and engines. They were, for the most part, fast, heavily armed, and armored and were the equal of their larger British counterparts. But there were too few of them.

Among them were the *Deutschland* class of euphemistically named "pocket battleships," a limited breed that was more of a cruiser than a true battleship. In fact, the "pocket battleship" title was hung on the class by the British media. Official German papers used the term *Panzerschiffen,* or armored ships.

Yet they represented major advantages in warship design and construction. *Graf Spee,* named for the commander of the Imperial German Navy's East Asia squadron in 1914, Admiral Maximillian von Spee, was the second of three ships of the class. *Graf Spee* was built at the Reichsmarinewerft shipyards in Wilhelmshaven between 1932 and 1934. She was commissioned into the Nazi Kriegsmarine in June 1936. Even before the fall of the Weimar Republic, Germany was already violating the stringent terms of the 1919 Treaty of Versailles that limited the tonnage of battleships. Registered at 10,000 gross tons displacement, the *Deutschland* class actually tipped the scales at 15,000 tons. A number of new innovations were included in their construction, such as the unprecedented use of electric arc welding to join plates instead of rivets. This saved several hundred tons and resulted in a cleaner underwater profile.

Rather than the standard steam turbines, *Graf Spee* and her sisters were powered by eight MAN diesels in quadruple sets, totaling over 54,000 shaft horsepower. For a ship of 15,000 tons, that was a lot of power. Compare this to the American *Iowa*-class battleships, which, at 45,000 tons, three times as much as *Graf Spee,* had only twice her horsepower.

Her twin bronze propellers drove the 610-foot hull through the sea at a speed of 28.6 knots for 16,000 nautical miles. A battleship's main reason for being was the main armament. Each of the six 11-inch guns could fire an armor-piercing or high-explosive shell weighing nearly 700 pounds over a distance of twenty-two nautical miles. Eight 5.9-inch rifles in twin turrets, a caliber that had served Germany well since the Great War, packed a strong punch for shorter ranges. *Graf Spee*'s crew complement was large for a ship of her size, with thirty-five officers and nearly nine hundred enlisted men. Atop the teak deck was the citadel of the superstructure, from where her commander, navigation, and gunnery officers fought the ship in battle.

An Arado 196 floatplane was mounted on a catapult. *Graf Spee* carried twin quadruple-tube torpedo launchers. This made for a powerful and dangerous raider thrust into the vulnerable Allied sea lanes.

For the *Graf Spee*, the gods of war were most generous. Her raiding career lasted less than four months but has long since entered naval legend. Part of this was due to her commander, *Kapitän zur See* Hans Langsdorff, a forty-five-year-old native of Bergen in Mecklenburg. He came from a family with a religious and legal heritage. In 1898, the family moved to Düsseldorf, where the young Hans met Graf Maximillian von Spee, who inspired the boy to join the German Navy in 1912. As a junior officer on minesweepers, Langsdorff earned the Iron Cross during the Battle of Jutland in 1916.

Even during the interwar years, while depression-ridden Germany languished under the burden of international ostracism, Langsdorff rose in the ranks of the Kriegsmarine. By 1936, Lieutenant Commander Langsdorff was serving aboard the *Graf Spee* in support of the fascist regime in the Spanish Civil War. He gained recognition for his excellent administrative and operational skills and was promoted to *Kapitän zur See* of the *Graf Spee* the following year. He recognized the honor of commanding the ship named for his childhood hero, who had died aboard his flagship, the armored cruiser SMS *Scharnhorst*, during the Battle of the Falklands in December 1914.

Langsdorff was known for being both an officer and a gentleman, a true distinction among the often brutish military officers of the Third

Reich. He looked after his men and acted honorably and with great civility in his duties. In time, even his enemies labeled him the "gentleman raider."

On the way to the South Atlantic in late August, Langsdorff waited for his inevitable orders to seek out, intercept, and destroy all Allied shipping. This was the core of Raeder's Z Plan, and warships like the *Graf Spee* were well suited for the job. But there were limitations. The lack of friendly bases where he could make repairs was a matter of concern. The 20,000-ton tanker *Altmark* rendezvoused with *Graf Spee* south of the Canary Islands on the day Hitler invaded Poland. With war now raging, Langsdorff knew the Royal Navy and its allies would be hunting him.

In his role as a commerce raider, Langsdorff was ordered to avoid contact and battle with enemy naval forces. On September 11, while refueling from the *Altmark*, the Arado floatplane pilot reported a large warship approaching. This was the cruiser HMS *Cumberland*, which was part of Force G, a four-ship squadron patrolling the South Atlantic. Langsdorff broke off the refueling, and the two ships sailed in different directions. Luck was with the Germans that day.

It was not until September 26 that orders came from Raeder to "begin attacks on British shipping under the rules of Cruiser Warfare." The 1907 Hague Convention, of which Germany was a signatory, required that all merchant ships be stopped and searched to determine if they carried war materiel before being sunk. The safety of passengers and crew must be assured before the ship could be sunk. Langsdorff had his marching orders and began hunting. The sea was a "target-rich environment," with busy shipping lanes from South America and Africa running up to the Mediterranean and Europe. Ships carried oil from the Soviet Union, iron ore from Portuguese Timor and Java, and rubber from Malaya and the Dutch East Indies. A thousand other vital goods needed by Great Britain were carried on unarmed and unescorted ships.

Graf Spee's Arado floatplanes scoured the sea for likely victims, flying low to avoid being seen by the often lazy lookouts of merchant vessels. Radioing Langsdorff upon a sighting, the plane remained airborne to keep watch for any sign of enemy warships. Langsdorff, having carefully trained his crew, raced to intercept the ship. He relied on speed and shock to overwhelm his prize. *Graf Spee*'s radiomen listened for calls on the international distress frequencies, and at the first sign that his prey was calling for help, Langsdorff directed his best gunners to fire the precise 4.1-inch guns to knock out the merchant ship's radio equipment. This required pinpoint accuracy, but his gunners never failed Langsdorff. He intended to prevent any distress calls and avoid bloodshed.

After signaling by blinker light that he was sending over an armed party, Langsdorff never had any trouble seizing the ship. His first victim was the Booth Line Steamship *Clement* off the coast of Brazil on the last day of September. After taking the captain and chief engineer prisoner, the crew was permitted to go into the lifeboats. For the first time, *Graf Spee*'s main guns fired shots in anger, sinking the vessel after thirty shots and two torpedoes. This was not as good shooting as Langsdorff had intended, and he continued to drill his gunners to be more effective with their shots. As he departed the area, Langsdorff ordered his radioman to send a distress call to the British naval base in Brazil to alert them of the stranded merchant crew. This was soon to be Langsdorff's hallmark. He did his best not to kill, injure, or even endanger the defenseless seamen.

On October 5, the *Graf Spee* captured the steamer *Newton Beach*, which was boarded by a prize crew of junior officers and about a dozen enlisted men. Two days later, the freighter *Ashlea* was stopped, boarded, searched, and sunk. Her crew and passengers were initially put on the *Newton Beach*, but her slow speed meant she couldn't keep up with the fast German warship. Langsdorff reluctantly took the merchant sailors onto his own ship, having set up livable, if not comfortable, quarters deep under the waterline where they could be guarded. *Newton Beach* was sent to the bottom with scuttling charges on October 8.

In early October, an improvised Anglo-French effort assembled a small fleet of carriers, including the *Ark Royal* (soon to be famous for launching the Swordfish torpedo planes at the *Bismarck*), *Hermes*, *Eagle*, and the French *Béarn*. In addition to several light cruisers and destroyers were the battle cruiser *Renown* and two French battleships, *Dunkerque* and *Strasbourg*. Divided into eight separate groups, they patrolled the vast expanse of the South Atlantic for the German raider. The next time the Admiralty assembled such might to find a single ship was in May 1941 to sink the *Bismarck*. But as things turned out, only one of those battle groups would find the *Graf Spee*. This was Force G, commanded by Commodore Henry Harwood. Force G consisted of the cruisers *Cumberland* and *Exeter* and was supplemented by the light cruisers *Ajax* and *Achilles*. Based on the east coast of South America, Harwood's force was strung out from Rio de Janeiro to Montevideo, Buenos Aires, and the Falkland Islands, the latter being the site of Admiral von Spee's defeat twenty-five years earlier.

Henry Harwood was typical of the new breed of Royal Navy commanders. Born in London in 1888, he joined the navy in 1904 and served on dreadnoughts until 1929, when he was given command of a destroyer, HMS *Warwick*, and was second in command of the division. He was known for his expertise in surface-launched torpedoes. While he had served on capital ships, Harwood was most at home on the fast and nimble cruisers and destroyers. This gave him an edge when pitted against a more powerful single foe. Even though he was already fifty-one years of age, Harwood was aggressive, eager, and decisive. He would have been well-suited to serve under Admiral Horatio Nelson.

On October 10, Langsdorff captured the merchant ship *Huntsman*. But by now *Graf Spee* was overcrowded. Sending a coded message to the *Altmark*, Langsdorff put a prize crew aboard the *Huntsman* and told them to meet *Graf Spee* and *Altmark* at a specified rendezvous. After refueling, Langsdorff transferred his prisoners to the German tanker and sank the *Huntsman*.

Langsdorff was careful never to remain near a recent attack. Five days elapsed before the Arado plane spotted the steamer *Trevanion*. By now the German gunners and crew were good at their duties, and *Trevanion* was captured, again without the loss of a single life.

After this successful run, Langsdorff decided to change his hunting area. As October turned into November, he slipped around the Cape of Good Hope and into the southern Indian Ocean, staying well off the coast to avoid being seen by Allied vessels in Cape Town. By doing this, he hoped he would confuse the Royal Navy as to his location. Langsdorff was actually following in the maritime footsteps of the late seventeenth-century pirates, including Captain William Kidd. He knew time was inevitably running out. So far his ship had steamed more than 30,000 miles, and the ship's diesels were badly in need of overhaul. But his orders and mission were paramount. In mid-November, *Graf Spee* sank the tanker *Africa Shell* and stopped but did not sink a Dutch freighter, which was not carrying war materiel.

The Indian Ocean proved to have fewer targets for his guns, and Langsdorff, hoping the British had been decoyed, turned south and shaped a course back to the Atlantic and his tanker. On November 26, his tanks were refilled and temporary repairs were made. To further confuse the enemy, Langsdorff had his crew construct a dummy gun turret on the bridge level of her superstructure and add a false second funnel aft of the aircraft catapult. These modifications substantially altered *Graf Spee*'s silhouette. With half the Royal Navy hunting him, Langsdorff hoped to make his ship unrecognizable at a distance.

In early December the Arado spotted the steamer *Doric Star*. This ship not only did not stop when an 11-inch shell was fired across her bow, but her radioman also managed to send off the Morse signal "RRR," meaning a surface raider was attacking them. The German gunners destroyed the radio shack. After hastily transferring the crew to the warship, Langsdorff sank the steamer with his heavy guns.

But this time Harwood, who had been monitoring all radio traffic, had a good fix on *Graf Spee*'s location. After studying the charts, he made a shrewd guess that Langsdorff might be headed for the mouth of the River Plate at Montevideo in Uruguay.

On December 5, the steamer *Tairoa* fell victim to Langsdorff. The vessel's radioman kept up a steady stream of distress calls until a 4.1-inch shell hit the radio aerial. The German captain was again doing his best to avoid killing any merchant sailors. In this respect Langsdorff was taking dangerous chances. Had he been more merciless, his last two victims might not have gotten off distress calls. He again rendezvoused with the *Altmark*. His 143 prisoners were transferred to the tanker as he refueled. But there was no time to make repairs to his diesels, which periodically made dark smoke, increasing the risk of being seen by an enemy warship.

On December 7, *Graf Spee* stopped and boarded the steamer *Streon-shal*. In her safe, the boarding party found documents and charts which revealed that four British cargo ships were scheduled to depart Montevideo on December 10.

Harwood, having called *Exeter* and *Achilles* from the Falklands and Rio, was waiting for him. He was faced with a challenge that could either advance his naval career or end it, not to mention lead to his death. His three ships possessed less firepower than their single opponent. Together their main armament could fire a total of 3,100 pounds of shell, while *Graf Spee* could unleash 4,700 pounds in a single salvo. *Graf Spee*'s hull armor was immune to the 6-inch armor-piercing shells of the *Ajax* and *Achilles*. Only *Exeter*'s heavier 8-inch projectiles could damage the German ship's vitals. In naval combat, the larger gun usually wins.

The situation Harwood was facing was not unique. Another Royal Navy admiral had once been confronted with a life-or-death decision concerning several lightly armed British cruisers facing a powerful German battle cruiser. In this case, it ended his career. It had been just over twenty-five years earlier in the Mediterranean Sea. While the specific circumstances of the two battles were different, they bear some consideration, as they affected Harwood's decisions in December 1939.

On the eve of the Great War in August 1914, General Joseph Joffre, commander of all French ground forces, assembled the 19th Army Corps in French Algeria. It was vital to bring the army to the port of Marseilles in southern France. The French Navy's weak Mediterranean fleet was hard-pressed to protect the vulnerable troop convoy from the huge German battle cruiser SMS *Goeben*, a titan with ten 11-inch guns. She was accompanied by the light cruiser *Breslau*.

The only force capable of protecting the troopships was the Royal Navy's Mediterranean fleet, under the command of Vice Admiral Sir Archibald Berkeley Milne. He had three fast and powerful battle cruisers: *Indomitable*, *Inflexible*, and his flagship *Indefatigable*. In addition, the British force had four older armored cruisers: *Warrior, Black Prince, Duke of Edinburgh*, and the flagship of Rear Admiral Sir Ernest Troubridge,

Defence. Four light cruisers and sixteen fast destroyers leavened the force. Starting on July 30, Milne received the first of a series of confusing wireless orders. They came not from the First Sea Lord of the Admiralty, Prince Louis of Battenberg, an experienced naval officer, but from the self-aggrandizing sage of the Royal Navy, First Lord of the Admiralty Winston Churchill. With the same zeal and impetuousness that would become his hallmark, Churchill bombarded Milne with orders that made it clear that he was to protect the French transports at all costs. Milne knew that the Admiralty was most concerned about *Goeben*. He called Rear Admiral Troubridge to his base on Malta and showed him the Admiralty's orders. His prime task was to protect the troopships, but he was warned not to "engage superior forces."

On August 4, the day Great Britain declared war on Germany, *Goeben* and *Breslau* were almost done coaling at Sicily. Rear Admiral Wilhelm Souchon, in command of the *Goeben*, was not about to risk his ships against the might of three bigger battle cruisers. Germany and Turkey had formed a defensive alliance in their war against Russia. Since there was scant chance of attacking the French troopships and absolutely no chance of breaking out into the Atlantic, he planned to head east to the Aegean Sea and Turkey.

Milne sent Troubridge and his four armored cruisers to watch the north and south approaches to the Strait of Messina for the emergence of the German warships. He again cautioned Troubridge not to engage a superior force.

Souchon turned southeast around the toe of Italy. Troubridge was hot on his trail. But now his ships were the weaker antagonist. *Warrior, Defence, Duke of Edinburgh,* and *Black Prince* displaced an average of 14,000 tons and, despite their designation, had thinner armor than any battle cruiser. Moreover, he knew well that *Goeben*'s 11-inch guns could fire shells weighing a ton at him from 16,000 yards away, while his 9.2-inch guns could only reach half that distance. His smaller shells wouldn't have much effect on the thick German armor. In a stern chase, he would be within *Goeben*'s range for over an hour before his ships could fire back. In broad daylight, that meant certain destruction for his force.

Troubridge, the great-grandson of one of Nelson's "Band of Brothers" at the Battles of the Nile and Trafalgar (See Chapter 2), faced a momentous challenge. Not only was British control of the Mediterranean at stake, but his family name also had to be upheld. A favorite at the Admiralty and a personal friend of King George V, this wouldn't protect him if he failed in his duty.

He was determined to follow and, if possible, stop *Goeben* from reaching her goal. He followed the German ships through the night of August 6. Troubridge planned to move in and attack at dawn, which would give him an advantage. *Goeben* and *Breslau* would be silhouetted by the rising sun, while his own ships would be indistinguishable in the western gloom. This was the only way he could negate the great reach of *Goeben*'s 11-inch guns.

Yet after conferring with *Defence*'s flag captain, Troubridge accepted that his four ships could never get within the range of their 9.2-inch guns before *Goeben* would blow them out of the water. When Troubridge informed Milne that he would not attack, his superior chastised him. This put more pressure on Troubridge, whose pride and reputation were paramount. But he also realized that a major naval defeat at the start of the war would be disastrous to British morale.

He followed *Goeben* as the Germans continued east toward Cape Matapan on the southernmost tip of the Peloponnesian Peninsula. In the end, *Goeben* and *Breslau* reached the safety of the Aegean Sea and soon entered the Sea of Marmara at the entrance to the Black Sea. There she was commissioned into the Turkish Navy and proved to be a serious threat to the Russian fleet at Sevastopol. The loss of *Goeben* infuriated the Admiralty, particularly the normally soft-spoken First Sea Lord, Prince Louis of Battenberg. He charged that Troubridge's "amazing misconduct had failed in the task assigned to him. The escape of *Goeben* must forever remain a shameful episode in this war. The flag officer responsible cannot be trusted further with command afloat. Any continued service in this command constitutes a danger to the navy."

Troubridge returned to England to face a court-martial. He couldn't be charged with cowardice, since his reputation for bravery was well known, but the charge of negligence and failure to carry out orders was harder to dismiss. Troubridge defended himself with the statement that he had been told by the Admiralty and Milne "not to engage a superior enemy force," of which *Goeben* certainly qualified. He had made it plain to Milne on August 2 that he had no intention of engaging the superior force in open waters in daylight unless supported by battle cruisers. Milne, who was present at the proceedings, was hostile to his former subordinate. He testified that it would have been difficult, if not impossible, for *Goeben* to concentrate her fire on four ships at once effectively, and Troubridge could have materially damaged or hampered the German battle cruiser.

The court finally acquitted Troubridge, agreeing that he had "acted properly in not hazarding his force against a superior foe."

But the general opinion in the navy was against Troubridge, and he never again received a command at sea.

Troubridge was vindicated in a ghastly way when, in the November 1914 Battle of Coronel, two British armored cruisers, *Monmouth* and *Good Hope*, were destroyed without getting close to Admiral Maximillian von Spee's two heavier and better-armed armored cruisers *Scharnhorst* and *Gneisenau*. Every man on the two ships died. Worse, *Defence, Warrior*, and *Black Prince* were all blown up by German shells at the Battle of Jutland less than two years later. None of the three armored cruisers could inflict any significant damage on the bigger German battle cruisers or dreadnoughts. In retrospect, this is what would have happened to Troubridge's armored cruisers had he closed with *Goeben*. *Goeben* and *Breslau* never again emerged from the Black Sea. The beleaguered Troubridge had achieved one of his many conflicting orders.

Now, twenty-five years later, Commodore Henry Harwood was faced with nearly the same tactical situation. He was about to confront what was still called a "superior force." Harwood, unlike Troubridge, had no conflicting orders from the Admiralty. He was to find, approach, and sink the *Graf Spee*. While he enjoyed a three-to-one advantage in ships, his cruisers were hardly a match for *Graf Spee*'s firepower. Only the 8,400-ton *York*-class *Exeter*'s six 8-inch guns could significantly damage the German warship. But *Exeter*'s gun range was far short of the *Graf Spee*'s 11-inch shells. As with Troubridge's armored cruisers, Harwood's ships would be under German fire for the entire time it took them to reach their own range. As for the *Leander*-class light cruisers, *Ajax* and

Achilles, each of which displaced just over 7,000 tons, their eight 6-inch guns were little threat to *Graf Spee*'s heavy armor. They could damage the superstructure but do little harm to her turrets, engines, or hull. Harwood's only advantage was in numbers. He planned to give *Graf Spee* too many jackals for the lion to fight off.

Harwood called for *Cumberland* to join him, but the other cruiser would need at least two days' steaming time to reach the River Plate. He would divide his ships into two divisions. *Ajax* and *Achilles* were to remain separate from *Exeter*. This would permit the ships to call out "flank marking," the practice of spotting and identifying the fall of shot from each ship. The three British cruisers could coordinate their fire. It also prevented *Graf Spee* from concentrating all her big guns on a single ship.

But Hans Langsdorff was at another disadvantage. On December 12, her single Arado floatplane suffered a serious mechanical failure and was out of action. This deprived Langsdorff of his ability to scout the sea beyond the visible horizon. He knew British warships were searching for him. *Altmark* was as vulnerable as any merchant ship, and there were no friendly ports in the South Atlantic he could reach in time. His main gun

HMS *Achilles*, one of the ships to hunt *Graf Spee* in 1939. *Imperial War Museum*

armament was partially depleted, and his engines were badly in need of overhaul. Germany was seven thousand miles away. Langsdorff was no coward. He had seen battle and tasted blood. He knew he could depend on his ship and the skill of his gunners and crew. But he was under orders from Raeder to avoid combat unless there was no choice. All Langsdorff could do was head for the River Plate, attack and sink the four British ships, then make a speed run to Germany, where he stood a fair chance of sneaking into a German port.

As dawn rose on the clear morning of December 13, 1939, *Graf Spee* was cruising northwest at 24 knots when the ship's lookouts spotted two masts on the horizon off the starboard bow. It was about 0535 hours. Langsdorff waited, trying to determine if the masts belonged to the escort ships for the convoy he was hunting. Soon the ships, now three of them, about fourteen miles away, were determined to be the cruiser *Exeter* and two smaller vessels. Langsdorff first thought them destroyers but soon identified them as *Leander* class. He decided to fight. His guns should reduce the smaller cruisers to scrap before their lighter guns could reach his ship. Increasing his speed to 28 knots, he called his crew to battle stations. Then he and his officers climbed into the tall, narrow pyramidal tower and took their stations. This area was not armored.

Because the light gray paint scheme used by the Kriegsmarine blended into the pale gray morning, it was just after 0600 when Harwood's lookouts spotted the oncoming German cruiser. One Admiralty report says that the *Graf Spee* was first detected from its plume of dark diesel smoke, but this would have been seen far earlier. Harwood called his crews to battle stations and put his plan into effect. *Ajax* and *Achilles* pulled away from *Exeter* and began an enveloping maneuver.

Langsdorff saw this and chose to divide his firepower. As the range decreased, *Graf Spee*'s two heavy main turrets swiveled to meet the *Exeter*, while the smaller 5.9-inch turrets aimed at Harwood's flagship and the *Achilles*. His smaller guns had nearly the same range and size as those on the *Leander* cruisers. All three British ships were in range, and at 0617, the six guns blossomed massive orange fireballs as the heavy 11-inch shells screamed toward *Exeter*. Tall waterspouts of white foam burst from the gray-green surface of the sea as the shells detonated. Another salvo erupted from the main turrets. *Exeter*, racing at her maximum speed, was straddled by the second salvo but never faltered. Then her own forward guns fired at 0620 hours, followed by *Ajax* one minute later. *Achilles*, still out of range, finally answered with her own guns at 0624 hours.

Graf Spee's heavy shells began scoring on *Exeter*, putting her forward turrets out of action a few minutes later. Her aircraft catapult and bridge were severely wrecked. The damage control parties were busy putting out fires. But the ship continued to move closer.

Harwood ordered his two cruisers to spread out and maintain a withering fire on the German ship. Their smaller shells did not affect the hull or turret armor, but the thin plating of the superstructure was being ripped open. Steel splinters twice wounded Langsdorff, and more than sixty of his men had already been killed or wounded. *Exeter* turned away. Harwood drove in, all guns blazing, until a 5.9-inch shell hit *Ajax's* rear turret.

Langsdorff knew that the two cruisers were moving in for a torpedo attack. Although there is no evidence that he knew who his opponent was, it would have been a likely move for Harwood to do just that. Langsdorff turned west and increased speed to outmaneuver the British ships. He ordered a smoke screen, and in moments, a steady plume of dark gray smoke fell like a death shroud over the German ship. This partially obscured her from the British gunners.

Then, at 0700 hours, *Exeter* rejoined the battle, firing with her single remaining aft turret. *Graf Spee's* aft turret roared out, and the British cruiser was hit again. Now listing to port, she broke off for the final time. Sixty of her crew lay dead and twenty-seven were wounded. But the tough *Exeter* had hit *Graf Spee*, inflicting damage to her hull and superstructure. In fact, the German ship had been hit by at least three 8-inch and seventeen 6-inch armor-piercing shells. The machinery needed to purify the diesel fuel and lubricating oil was destroyed, along with the water purification plant. A large hole had been torn in the bows where the armor belt was thinnest. Remarkably, not one of the British prisoners from the steamer *Streonshal* was injured. It was time for Langsdorff to break off and leave. It was 0724 hours, just two hours since his lookouts had spotted the British cruisers. At this point the British and Germans launched torpedoes at the extreme range of 9,000 yards, but none struck home.

The mouth of the River Plate beckoned, and the *Graf Spee* slipped into the safe, quiet waters of the estuary. Harwood regrouped his battered ships and followed but did not attempt to engage. He had the German raider just where he wanted her. The three cruisers took up blocking stations outside the three-mile territorial limit.

Langsdorff radioed Berlin with his status and requested that he remain in the neutral port for fifteen days while he made emergency repairs. Raeder, after consulting a furious Hitler, granted the request. In an attempt to prod Langsdorff to remain in port, the British Admiralty began transmitting messages on frequencies known to be monitored by German Intelligence. These messages were sent to several powerful British squadrons and capital ships to set course to Uruguayan waters. The Royal Navy was hoping that the Uruguayan government would grant the German captain seventy-two hours, giving the carrier *Ark Royal* and the battle cruiser *Renown* time to join Harwood.

Langsdorff quickly arranged for his fifty-nine wounded and the sixty-two prisoners to be ferried ashore. The wounded were taken to hospitals under the supervision of the German consul. His dead were buried with full military honors in a public cemetery in the city.

Under the international rules of neutrality, if *Graf Spee* remained in Uruguayan waters for more than seventy-two hours, Langsdorff risked having his ship and crew interned for the duration of the war. "Under no circumstances are you to allow your ship to be interned in Uruguayan waters," Raeder messaged him. There was a good reason for choosing internment in Buenos Aires over Montevideo. The Uruguayan government, while neutral, had a good relationship with Great Britain. If *Graf Spee* was interned in Uruguay, there was every chance the government would allow the Royal Navy to inspect the ship with all its classified equipment, engines, and weapons. This couldn't be permitted.

Langsdorff briefly considered making a dash for Buenos Aires under the more congenial Argentine government. But this was almost certainly doomed to fail. Buenos Aires was more than three hundred miles away.

At least four British ships were waiting, now including the undamaged *Cumberland*. Having expended most of its main and secondary armament, it was obvious that the *Graf Spee* couldn't fight off a determined attack by several British ships.

Langsdorff sent Raeder a message on December 16, listing his options. Hitler first insisted that Langsdorff fight to the death, but Raeder persuaded the Führer to permit him to scuttle the ship. At least the crew would survive and there was a chance of having them returned to Germany.

Langsdorff made the fatal decision. On the morning of December 18, under careful supervision, his crew dismantled and destroyed as much of the ship's classified equipment as possible. This included the radio, coding machinery, radar, and fire control equipment. But in the rush to finish before the seventy-two-hour deadline, some vital gear, such as the radar rangefinder, was missed. Langsdorff sent the bulk of his crew ashore while he and forty volunteers remained aboard to take the ship beyond the three-mile limit. There they set several high-explosive charges among the engines and against the hull. By now a huge crowd of spectators had gathered on shore in anticipation of a naval battle. Instead, they saw a strange submarine surface and move close to the German cruiser. A launch carried Langsdorff and his crew to the sub. With the Royal Navy and Uruguayans watching expectantly, the sub slipped away and submerged. Twenty minutes later, the charges went off. Huge yellow flashes erupted from *Graf Spee*'s superstructure and hatches in the ship's decks. A massive black column of smoke rose into the air as *Admiral Graf Spee* settled thirty-six feet into the mud of the estuary.

The submarine had been sent from Argentina to take the Germans to Buenos Aires, where they were safe from the Royal Navy. The remainder of *Graf Spee*'s crew were interned in Uruguay. The wreck burned for two days. Most of the superstructure remained above the surface, while the six 11-inch guns protruded menacingly from the water lapping around them.

The pro-German Argentine government welcomed Langsdorff and his crew. There, Langsdorff, residing in a hotel, sent telegrams to Berlin explaining what he had done. But he had one more duty to perform.

After writing letters to his wife, he made out his will and committed suicide with a single gunshot to his head. He was lying upon *Graf Spee*'s naval ensign. His letter to his superiors read, in part, "I alone bear the responsibility for scuttling the panzerschiff *Admiral Graf Spee*. I am happy to pay with my life for any possible reflection on the honor of the flag. I shall face my fate with firm faith in the cause and the future of the nation and of my Führer."

Kapitän zur See Hans Langsdorff was buried in the German section of the La Chacarita Cemetery in Buenos Aires with full military honors. Eventually the crew interned in Uruguay were taken to Argentina to join their comrades, where they remained until the end of the war. While they were treated well, they were anxious to return to Germany. But being in Argentina probably saved their lives. If they had gone back to Germany, they would almost certainly have been inducted into the U-boat service. Nearly 30,000 U-boat sailors died in the war.

In 1942, a dummy Montevideo salvage corporation set up by the British examined the wreck. There they salvaged the intact radar range-finder. The Royal Navy used it to develop countermeasures that would foil the Kriegsmarine, exactly as Langsdorff had feared. The wreck of the *Graf Spee* remained visible for years until it was cut up and removed as a hazard to navigation in 2004.

In all, the *Admiral Graf Spee* sank nine merchant ships totaling just over 50,000 gross registered tons, or four times her own displacement. Even though it ended in an ignominious defeat, *Graf Spee*'s brief but wildly successful campaign was solid proof, in Raeder's opinion, that his Plan Z could indeed become a significant threat to the Allied war effort. In the end, he, too, was proven wrong.

Coincidentally, Admiral Maximillian von Spee had died aboard his flagship SMS *Scharnhorst* only 1,100 miles from where his namesake would be scuttled almost exactly twenty-five years later.

After the battle, First Sea Lord Admiral Sir Dudley Pound wrote to Harwood, "Even if you had lost all your ships you would have done the right thing. Your action has reversed the findings of the Troubridge court-martial and proved how wrong they were." Pound, who had been an officer in the Royal Navy since before the Great War, was convinced Troubridge had thrown away his chance of a victory in 1914. He believed Harwood had proved his point.

But a sharp reader will notice that Pound did *not* say, ". . . lost all your ships *and* sank *Graf Spee*, you would have done the right thing." We will never know.

With Great Britain fully engaged in a war, her subjects faced a grim reality and an even more horrific possibility. Hitler seemed to have every intention of invading England. The brave fighter pilots and determined men and women of RAF Fighter Command fought to stop a Nazi occupation of the British Isles. While no Briton truly believed the Germans could win, they took prudent steps to protect their children from the horrors of an invasion. In 1940, even as the RAF valiantly scoured the skies of Luftwaffe bombers, an organization was formed to carry hundreds of children to safe haven in Canada. Selected liners would carry them under adult protection until the danger was past. But under the cold waters of the North Atlantic lurked another danger. The U-boat. The next essay tells the story of one such ship and many innocent, brave children who found themselves fighting to survive against impossible odds.

THE LOST CHILDREN OF 1940 – SINKING OF SS *CITY OF BENARES*

Published in *World War II History*, February 2016
Second publishing, *Titanic International Society Quarterly* #112, Summer 2020

In the summer of 1940, the world watched with rapt attention as the citizens, airmen, sailors, and soldiers of Great Britain steeled themselves for imminent invasion by the ever-victorious German Army. From July 31 to September 15, the daily air raids by the Luftwaffe's huge armadas rained death and destruction on airfields and cities. Only the determined efforts of RAF Fighter Command denied the Luftwaffe what they most needed: air superiority.

And in the end, the German air raids became a matter of vengeful reprisals on an implacable British spirit that refused to die.

Many more than the lives of hundreds of young and brave airmen had been lost while Britain fought on, and not all were adults who understood the risks they faced. Some were innocent children doomed to die a cold and terrifying death far out to sea on what they thought was a great adventure.

On June 17, three weeks after the evacuation of Dunkirk, Undersecretary of State for Dominion Affairs Geoffrey Shakespeare formed the Children's Overseas Reception Board (CORB), which developed a means to evacuate children from the British Isles to relatives overseas. CORB, sanctioned by Prime Minister Winston Churchill and his cabinet, was intended to save as many children as possible from starvation, death, and imprisonment. The government would cover most of the cost. Applications were arranged through schools and churches.

In two months, more than 211,000 children were registered. They would be accompanied by one teacher and a nurse for every fifteen children. Traveling without passports, they were issued CORB-numbered luggage tags and ID tags. It was meant as a temporary measure, and the evacuees would be returned home after the end of the war. By August, 24,000 children, with 1,000 adult volunteers, were prepared to cross the sea. Canada would receive the largest percentage, followed by Australia, New Zealand, and South Africa. Others were bound for the United States. Ocean liners provided by several shipping companies would join organized convoys in Liverpool and sail west.

The parents, understandably concerned for the safety of their children, were assured by CORB representatives that Royal Navy warships would escort the transport ships. That was true, but only up to a point. The Royal Navy had to stretch its assets as far as possible. With dozens of convoys on the open seas, a thousand miles of coastline to patrol, and few experienced crews, priority went to the protection of the Home Islands.

Another fear was the German surface raiders. The heavy cruisers *Scharnhorst* and *Gneisenau*, along with the so-called pocket battleships *Admiral Hipper* and *Lutzow*, were already causing great damage to Allied shipping. The big battleships *Bismarck* and *Tirpitz* would soon be turned loose in the shipping lanes. The Royal Navy had much to concern it.

But in the summer of 1940, the threat of German submarines was still deemed slight. This assumption was already out of date. Prior to the fall of France, German U-boats had sailed from Kiel and Wilhelmshaven on the Baltic coast of Germany and couldn't range far out into the north Atlantic for long periods. However, the Kriegsmarine quickly established U-boat flotillas in western France at St. Nazaire, Lorient, Brest, and La Rochelle, adding greatly to the U-boat range. By August, the undersea predators could not only stay on patrol in the north Atlantic for several days, but they could also easily reach the East Coast of the United States.

With the German policy of unrestricted submarine warfare in place, no vessels, even passenger liners, were safe.

Bess Walder was a fifteen-year-old London schoolgirl. She and her younger brother, Louis, had been among the first children to be registered for the CORB program. Bernard and Rosina Walder had followed the events on the continent as far back as the Spanish Civil War. Stories

Bess Walder, one of the few CORB survivors of the *City of Benares*.

of terrible atrocities and barbarism from Poland, Belgium, Denmark, the Low Countries, and France left little doubt about what lay in store for innocent civilians if the Nazis came.

Bernard Walder, an air raid warden, had watched the red glow of flames in the night sky over London as he helped herd people into shelters. Every night he watched the fire brigades fight the fires, faces black with soot and agony. It was time to get his son and daughter to safety. Finally, the letter from the CORB arrived. When the children were told they would be taking a ship to Canada, they were ecstatic. "Wonderful! When can we go?" exclaimed nine-year-old Louis, who thought it would be a great adventure and imagined he might see real cowboys and Indians.

On the morning of September 9, Bess and Louis, each carrying their single small suitcases, were taken to Euston Station for an unknown port. Rosina hugged her daughter and said, "Now grow up to be a good girl." Then she wept while her husband told Bess, "Look out for your brother." Bess, not understanding the pain her parents were feeling, said she would.

Only later did Bess realize that her parents feared they would never see their children again.

Once the train rolled out, the bewildering climate of fear dissipated, and the children, excited at an ocean voyage, began to play and chat. After several train delays from bombings, they arrived in the port city of Liverpool on September 11 and were directed to a large hall with hundreds of straw mattresses on the floor.

A girl of Bess's age, Beth Cummings, was a Liverpudlian whose widowed mother was determined to get her daughter to Canada. The two girls became friends. Colin Richardson, an eleven-year-old from North London, wore a thick red jacket made by his mother. It was stuffed with Kapok to make it into a lifejacket. "Never take this off," she told him as they said their goodbyes.

The next morning, after a quick breakfast, they were herded down the streets to the docks, where the ships of Convoy OB-213 were preparing to depart.

Bess, Louis, and Beth stared wide-eyed at the huge vessel towering over the dock, the Ellerman City Line's SS *City of Benares,* queen of the England-to-India run. She was an 11,080-ton, 480-foot liner launched in 1935. She was known for her speed, her best defense against submarines, and painted a dusky brown for camouflage. Some of her stewards were dressed in turbans, blue sashes, and pointed slippers to amuse the children for their first sea voyage. Bess Walder remembered the stewards called them "Little Madams" and "Little Sirs."

The liner was still fitted out for the comfort of her passengers. Among them were Mary Cornish, a concert pianist and CORB escort.

The Ellerman City Line's SS *City of Benares* in 1939.

On Friday, September 13, the *City of Benares*, as one of twenty ships of Convoy OB-213, left Liverpool for Quebec and Montreal. On board were 191 passengers, 90 of which were children, along with 216 officers and crew.

Convoy OB-213 was commanded by Rear Admiral E. J. G. Mackinnon, who chose the *City of Benares* as his flagship. Captain Landles Nicoll maintained the lead position in the center line of the westbound convoy.

The children were given tours of the ship and shown their cabins. Each one was told where their lifeboat station was and how to put on the bulky lifebelts. Yet even with the dark reality of the danger that awaited them, few children felt any fear. Bess Walder shared a cabin with two other girls. Comfortable bunks, wardrobes, and clean bathrooms were provided. The boys, who included Louis Walder, Fred Steels, and Paul Shearing, all not yet twelve years of age, occupied the port cabins while the girls were on the starboard side. Bess knew her brother was in good hands, and she could just have fun with Beth and the other girls, being treated like young ladies. The stewards and escorts were always there to give them whatever they wanted, including ice cream, chocolate, ham, beef, vegetables, fresh fruit, and bread, fast becoming luxuries in England. The youngest children had a special playroom with a huge rocking horse that could carry three of them. There was an attempt to hold classes, but the level of excitement was too high for much boring study.

The destroyer HMS *Winchelsea*, two corvettes, HMS *Gloxinia* and HMS *Gladiolus*, and two armed sloops comprised OB-213's escort.

After the convoy rounded the northwest tip of Ireland, a large four-engine aircraft was seen to the south. It was a Focke-Wulf Condor reconnaissance plane on patrol, looking for convoys. Mackinnon and Nicoll knew their chances of avoiding any German subs were slim. The passengers and children were given more lifeboat drills and told to sleep in their lifebelts.

On the morning of September 17, OB-213 reached 17 degrees longitude, where the escorts were ordered to join an eastbound convoy. From that point on, the ships of OB-213 were undefended. But the news that the RAF had claimed 180 German planes two days before bolstered the spirits of the passengers and crews of the remaining ships.

At 8 P.M., forty-one-year-old escort Mary Cornish put down the fifteen girls in her care and went to meet her friends for coffee in the lounge. After a couple of hours they decided to walk out on deck.

At 10:02 P.M. Greenwich Mean Time, 250 miles off Rockall, Ireland, the German Type VIIB submarine *U-48* found convoy OB-213.

The Type VII was the most successful of the Kriegsmarine's U-boats. More than seven hundred Type VII U-boats were built at ten yards in Germany from 1936 until the end of the war. Propelled by twin six-cylinder, four-stroke diesel engines and two electric motors, the subs could reach speeds of 17 knots surfaced and 9 knots submerged. Their cruising range of nearly eight thousand miles made them ideal for prowling the waters of the Atlantic. Günther Prien, the "Bull of Scapa Flow," commanded *U-47*, a Type VII boat. Another was *U-99*'s Otto Kretschmer, who sank thirty-five Allied ships.

Constructed at Kiel's Germaniawerst and launched in March 1939, the *U-48* was small for Atlantic duty, displacing little more than 850 tons submerged. At 248 feet long, she was almost as large as the newest *Salmon*-class submarines entering service with the United States Navy. She carried fourteen G7A torpedoes for her four bow and one stern tubes. Most of her crew of four officers and forty-six men had been together since being commissioned in the summer of 1939. The boat was assigned to the Seventh Flotilla in Lorient, France.

On her fifth patrol in April 1940, *U-48* joined a wolfpack off Cape Finisterre on the French coast. Their intended target was a troop convoy carrying 25,000 Australian and New Zealand troops to England aboard the converted liners *Queen Mary* and *Mauritania*. The ships were the most-prized targets for the U-boat fleet. But previous sinkings in the area had alerted the liners and they changed course.

Now on her seventh war patrol, *U-48* was under the command of her third captain, *Kapitanleutnant* Heinrich Bleichrodt. She was nine days out of Lorient, looking for Allied convoys. Most of the time she ran on the surface in order to pick up sighting reports from the prowling Condors. Already, *U-48* had sunk five others ships in convoy SC-3. She still carried six torpedoes.

A storm had been building all day, and by 11 GMT on the night of September 17, the rain was slicing across the convoys, driven by a bitter wind. A Force Ten gale was building. The ships, trying to maintain their place in the columns, were more concerned with the storm than looking for U-boats. The ocean's crenelated gray surface made it impossible to see a periscope, but an attack was unlikely during a storm. But Bleichrodt, who would soon become known for his aggressiveness, chose the largest ship in the center line, the *City of Benares*.

With the weather steadily growing worse, the *U-48* was able to approach undetected.

At 11:45 P.M. GMT, he fired two torpedoes from his bow tubes. Both missed the ship, and the lookouts failed to see them in the turbulent waves.

But *U-48* was not done. At one minute after midnight, Bleichrodt fired again. This torpedo struck the *City of Benares* on her port side, just under the children's sleeping quarters.

The ship was mortally wounded. The G7A torpedo's 617-pound warhead destroyed a large area under the main deck. The blast ruptured steam and water lines and damaged the generators. The cold Atlantic rushed in.

Mary Cornish was just stepping off the stairs down to the main deck when she heard a loud THUMP! and felt the entire ship shudder. Suddenly the stairway and corridor below were cluttered with fallen debris and water. She realized her girls were in danger and pushed along the dark corridor to reach them.

Young Bess Walder was asleep when the torpedo hit. Instantly she was awake, knowing what had happened. Around her, the three-berth room was heaving from the ship's increasing list. The wardrobe door fell open, dumping things on the deck. She tried to get the girl in the lower bunk to awaken, but she refused, not recognizing the danger.

Eleven-year-old Fred Steels fell from his bunk in one of the boys' cabins, trapped under the fallen wardrobe cabinet. He heard alarms sounding and managed to force his way free. Water sprayed from burst pipes at the sink, and Steels knew they'd been torpedoed. He yelled to the other boys, "We've been hit!" But like Bess's roommate, they were slow to respond. Finally, Paul Shearing on the lower bunk rose, and they put on their lifebelts. With another boy, they made their way out to the corridor. It was already crowded with running and screaming passengers and crew.

They had to get to the lifeboats, but every step was like climbing up a mountain in an earthquake. When they reached the upper deck, Fred Steels saw a huge smoking hole in the deck. A dirty seaman picked him and Shearing up and threw them into a lifeboat.

Colin Richardson was reading a penny novel in his bunk when he heard the torpedo explode underneath his cabin. At first he thought the ship had collided with another, but the familiar scent of explosives told him it was a torpedo. He'd been through German raids before being sent to Surrey to live with his grandparents.

Fourteen-year-old Beth Cummings thought she'd had a bad dream, but when she awoke to alarms and loud crashing sounds, she tried to turn on the light. It didn't work. That was when she realized the deck was slanted. They were sinking. She got into her lifebelt and reached the corridor, finding Bess already there. "We have to get to the boats," she said, trying to be heard over the din of alarms and shouting.

The two girls helped a third girl named Joan, who was very seasick. Bess had lost her little brother, Louis. She had to find him, but in all the chaos, she didn't know where to look. They were trying to do what they'd been told about reaching the lifeboats, but the drill had been done in daylight, in calm seas and without panic.

The boat deck was totally different from what they'd seen a few days before. The lurching ship's motion caused the hanging boats to swing wildly in their davits while the crew tried to fill and launch them. Some adults were hysterical, while others remained calm and helped the children.

On the port side, the boats swung far out away from the side of the ship, while those on the high starboard side were almost impossible to lower as they caught and bumped on the ship's rivets.

In the melee was Mary Cornish, who'd managed to corral some of her girls up to her assigned boat. She put them in and went down for the last girl but could not find her.

Boat Number 2, carrying Colin Richardson, wearing the red jacket his mother had given him, was lowered into the water. But as soon as it touched the waves, it was swamped and stayed afloat only because of its buoyancy cells. Colin was sitting in freezing water up to his neck.

The wind was rising, whipping icy spray from the waves.

On the port side, the overloaded boat Number 8 swung back and forth at the end of the falls and smashed into the unyielding side of the ship. Nearly every person in the boat was thrown into the heaving waves. One of them was young Louis Walder. He struggled to stay afloat until an older boy named George Crawford managed to pull him back aboard. But when George tried to pull another child out, he fell overboard and was lost.

Fifteen minutes after the torpedo hit, the *City of Benares* was almost gone. The lifeboats were being tossed in the storm like corks. In the water-filled Boat Number 8, four crewmen worked feverishly to bail but succumbed to cold and died. Young Colin helped to lift them from the boat and over the side. Removing the bodies helped to keep the boat afloat. An elderly nurse next to Colin sank into despair and listlessness. Colin tried to comfort her and keep her awake. He realized to fall asleep meant death. The water was only a few degrees above freezing.

Beth and Bess had managed to stay together. The crew was herding them into Boat Number 5 on the starboard side. One of the last boats to be lowered, it was grossly overloaded. When it hit the water, it was almost immediately swamped. Then a heavy wave flipped it over, and everybody in it was dumped into the sea. Bess and Beth, choking on seawater forced into their mouths and nostrils by the wind, fought to stay afloat. Bess was a good swimmer and struggled to find the boat. She saw it in the dim light, managing to reach it and cling to the keel with numbed hands. And then she saw her friend Beth also holding desperately to the clinker planking. She saw a dozen other pairs of hands hanging onto the wet planks. The howl of the wind and roar of the waves drowned out their cries for help.

By the time Cornish reached the boat deck, her boat was gone. An officer ordered her to go to Boat Number 12, already filled with men and boys. She resolved to take care of them. Boat Number 12 was the last one launched. It reached the water as the doomed *City of Benares* heeled far over and seemed to descend like a huge steel cliff. The men began to pump the steel Flemings cranks that drove the propeller and move them to the relative safety of open water.

Among the boys were Fred Steels and Paul Shearing. The children no longer felt the joy of an exciting ocean voyage. All they saw now was a vast, tossing gray and black ocean with towering seas crashing over them. Fred Steels, freezing in the wind and spray, saw what the men were doing and bent to add his tiny weight to the task. At least it would keep him warm.

Mary Cornish comforted and held a young boy who shivered violently from cold and fear. As she rubbed his shoulders, she saw men and women in the water, some waving for help while others floated limply in their lifebelts. Already many of the ship's passengers and crew had died from the explosion, drowning, or exposure to the near-freezing water. Cornish, feeling deep despair but trying not to show it, held the boy and said in a soothing voice, "Don't worry, it's only a torpedo."

Just then, the glare of a searchlight cut through the dark night, spreading pools of light on the stormy seas. The *U-48* had moved into the area to see the results of the attack. At 12:30 A.M., as Bleichrodt watched, the *City of Benares* sank, taking with her Rear Admiral Mackinnon, Captain Nicoll, and almost 258 others.

The *U-48* moved away, searching for more targets. Bleichrodt had no way of knowing he'd sunk a ship carrying nearly a hundred children.

Back in Liverpool, the Royal Navy's Office of Western Approaches copied a message that a ship in Convoy OB-213 had been torpedoed. They contacted the eastbound destroyer HMS *Hurricane*. "Proceed with utmost dispatch to position 56.43 North, 21.15 West, where survivors are reported in boats." Lieutenant Commander Crofton Simms immediately ordered a 180-degree turn to the west and headed for the site of the attack, 300 miles away.

The weather was against them and the survivors. Even as the first storm abated, giving the weakened swimmers and people in the boats a glimmer of hope, a new, stronger storm came in. It was even more violent, scattering the boats and causing the swimmers to swallow seawater as their strength ebbed.

Bess, Beth, and the other ten survivors tried to climb higher on their overturned boat, but their fingers were too numb to do more than hang on. One by one, the other pairs of hands lost their grip and fell away until only Bess, Beth, and two Indian crewmen were left. There was no food, no drinking water, and no rescue in sight. Bess would not give up. Beth thought of her mother, now alone. She, too, was determined to live.

Hurricane's knife-like bow sliced into the mountainous seas, rising up covered in green water, only to crash down again. Simms pushed his ship hard, desperate to reach the site of the sinking in time. All through the night, the survivors clung to life. Some succeeded; most fell insensible and slid into the waiting water, never to be seen again.

Hurricane reached the area by mid-afternoon. The crew readied the longboats and skiffs, gathered blankets and slings to lift survivors. Lookouts clad in heavy foul-weather gear were posted on the bow and mast. Simms heard calls of "Boat in the water!" The storm was still strong but seemed to be slacking off. They stopped alongside the first boat. Inside were only corpses. Each tiny body was carried in the arms of Royal Navy sailors, weeping in sorrow.

With deepening fear, *Hurricane* moved on to the next boat, Number 11, with twenty drenched survivors. Only two of the fifteen CORB children were still alive. One of them was Louis Walder. Strong but gentle hands lifted them into slings and up ladders into the ship. Sailors threw woolen blankets over them and dispensed hot tea as they led them into warm, dry rooms where a surgeon lieutenant tended to them. The children were given the officers' quarters to sleep in.

Boat Number 9, which had carried thirty-three people, only had eight still alive. Colin Richardson was carried aboard. He was totally numb below the waist and wore only his pajamas and the red jacket that had saved his life.

The searchers finally reached the overturned boat with Bess and Beth hanging on to the keel. A Navy coxswain named Albert Gorman reached out to Bess. "Come on, darling, let go." But the girls' hands were so stiff they had to be carefully pried loose. Then the two girls were gently lifted into the boat and taken to the ship.

Hurricane rescued 117 survivors.

Simms stayed in the area for several more hours but finally turned east to Scotland.

Bess became despondent despite her rescue. She lost her brother, Louis, and would never know what had happened to him. "I promised my parents I'd take care of him!"

The next day, the door to her room opened, and in stepped Captain Simms. "Sit up, miss. I've got a present for you."

Behind him was Louis, safe and sound. He hadn't known Bess was on board, either. While receiving a tour of the ship from Simms, he recognized Bess's dressing gown. Simms realized they had both Walder children.

When Bess saw her brother, she said, in both relief and anger, "Where have you been?" Then they embraced.

As *Hurricane* sped away, the sea appeared empty but for scattered bits of floating wreckage, deck chairs, lifebelts, and broken planking.

But there was still one more lifeboat out there. Boat Number 12, carrying Mary Cornish, five boys, and forty adults, had not been seen. The storm had scattered the boats far and wide, and the broad gray-green swells hid the tiny craft from view. Steels, trying to remain brave, saw bodies in the water—some of them children, just like him.

For the next seven days, the lone boat drifted aimlessly. The only officer, Ronnie Cooper, rationed out the small supply of water and tinned biscuits. The days dragged by. The pitiful human cargo grew weaker and weaker. On the eighth day, just after noon, a lone RAF Sunderland flying boat flew over them. Low on fuel, it couldn't land, but Cooper knew it had seen them. Fifteen minutes later, another plane flew low and dropped supplies and a note saying help was on the way.

Then on Thursday, September 26, a destroyer, HMS *Anthony*, found them. The forty-six survivors in Boat Number 12 were the last to be rescued, almost ten days after the sinking.

Bess and Louis Walder were the only brother and sister to be rescued. Some families had lost two, three, and four children. The Grumman family lost all five of their children when the *City of Benares* sank. The final death toll of the ninety CORB children on the *City of Benares* was seventy-seven, ranging from six to fifteen years old.

By the beginning of 1941, it was obvious that Hitler had no immediate plans to invade England. The need to send children overseas became less urgent. The German invasion of the Soviet Union was the turning point of the European war. Hitler would never again have the supremacy he had enjoyed in the summer of 1940. Soon many children returned home. When the United States entered the war upon Germany's declaration of war on December 11, 1941, the convoy system grew larger with better escorts. The inclusion of the B-24s finally closed the curtain on the U-boat threat.

Kapitanleutnant Heinrich Bleichrodt sank twenty-four ships by the end of the war, totaling more than 124,000 gross tons. He was charged with war crimes at Nuremberg, including the sinking of *City of Benares*. Bleichrodt maintained the ship was a legitimate target and that his actions were appropriate. Some of his crew expressed shock at the loss of the children.

An ongoing debate centers on two factors: If the *City of Benares* had been openly declared carrying women and children on a humanitarian mission, the German government and Admiral Doenitz would have declared her off-limits to submarine attack. The Third Reich was still willing, as late as the fall of 1940, to avoid inflaming world opinion with an attack on a ship full of children. But she was running at the head of the convoy, was the largest ship in OB-213, and the flagship of Admiral Mackinnon. On the other hand, there is no evidence that Bleichrodt would have left her unmolested even had he known.

There was a happy ending for two of the CORB children. Bess Walder became a teacher and headmistress and later married Jeff Cummings, Beth's brother.

Without a doubt, the most famous battleship of the Second World War was the German ship *Bismarck*. The subject of a 1960 motion picture and a popular Johnny Horton song, *Bismarck* had a short but violent career. For all her power, *Bismarck* achieved only one success, the sinking of HMS *Hood* on May 24, 1941. The next essay takes a look at the *Bismarck* legend, particularly the myth that she was the most powerful battleship in the world. This is one time when the bark was far worse than the bite.

SINKING THE *BISMARCK* MYTH

Published in *World War II History*, October 2016

In 1960, Twentieth Century Fox released *Sink the Bismarck!*, based on C. S. Forrester's bestselling *The Last Nine Days of the Bismarck*. The documentary-style film tells a gripping and reasonably factual account of history's most famous sea chase.

In an early scene, the German Fleet Admiral Günther Lütjens addresses the battleship's crew as they head out to the Atlantic.

With the typically bellicose posturing usually portrayed in war films, Lütjens proclaims, "Officers and men of the *Bismarck*! This is the Fleet Commander. I can now tell you that we are going out into the North Atlantic to attack the British convoys. We are going to sink their ships until they no longer dare to let them sail! It is true we are only two ships. But the world has never *seen* such ships! We are sailing in the largest, the most powerful battleship afloat, superior to anything in the British Navy! We are faster, we are unsinkable!"

From that point on, the viewer is left with little doubt of the German warship's invincibility and power. Yet this isn't true.

Bear in mind that the movie was made in 1959, eighteen years after the *Bismarck* sunk. This has become the *Bismarck* legend. But most legends have no more validity than what one accepts at face value.

Like many other historical icons, *Bismarck*'s power has been greatly magnified and distorted. William Stevenson writes about the *Bismarck* chase in Chapter 28 of his landmark 1976 book, *A Man Called Intrepid*. Stevenson, who headed up British Security Coordination in New York from 1940 to 1945, oversaw British and American intelligence operations. But Stevenson, who was in a position to know better, wrote that *Bismarck* was "the most powerful battleship in the world."

In fact, rather than being the most powerful battleship, she was actually among the ranks of less heavily armed capital warships in 1941. True, her design, fire control, engines, and gunnery were superb. But those factors alone don't warrant top billing. The development of heavy warships since 1906, when HMS *Dreadnought*, the first all-big-gun ship, was launched, was steadily climbing in size and power. But it was most often a constant duel between size, weight of armor, speed, and gun caliber.

During the First World War, the old tactic of battleships steaming in parallel lines, battering away at one another, ended at Jutland on May 31, 1916, when two huge fleets met off Danish Jutland in the North Sea. When it was over, three British battle cruisers had blown up. But the main force of the German High Seas Fleet and the British Grand Fleet had suffered little crippling damage. Even when the biggest guns were employed, armor protection mattered most. Unfortunately, some naval design experts had yet to learn this fact.

All Jutland proved was that the old way of ending wars with battleships was over.

When the Third Reich dawned in 1934, Germany had already begun a shipbuilding program. Destroyers, cruisers, and, most effectively, U-boats were constructed in great numbers. Grossadmiral Erich Raeder, commander of the Kriegsmarine, commissioned several fast surface raiders of various sizes and armaments. A certain hazy sense of purpose surrounds these ships. They were referred to, at various times, as battle cruisers, heavy cruisers, and even battleships. Since the battle cruisers were traditionally meant to act as fast scouts rather than capital ships, this betrays an uncertainty in the Kriegsmarine as to what their role was meant to be.

Not so for *Bismarck*, laid down in 1936 and launched at the Blohm & Voss Shipyard near Hamburg on St. Valentine's Day, 1939. Attending the ceremony was Adolf Hitler himself. The new battleship was to be armed with eight 15-inch guns in four turrets and twelve 5.9-inch rifles in six turrets. At nearly 50,000 tons and protected by 13 inches of armor, *Bismarck* was the biggest warship ever built in Germany. With both radar and advanced fire control systems to aim her guns, she was

The new German battleship *Bismarck*, the "most powerful ship afloat," in 1940. *Imperial War Museum*

capable of doing great damage to other warships and totally destroying any unarmored merchant ship with ease.

The Royal Navy watched her progress with trepidation. When war broke out, the primary target of Germany's warships were the Atlantic convoys that provided Britain with vital supplies of food and raw materials. They carried munitions, planes, tanks, food, supplies, and troops to Great Britain's armies. If the vulnerable transports and tankers could be sunk, it was only a matter of time before England would fall. The worry over what *Bismarck* could do to convoys gave the Royal Navy all the reason they needed to stop her.

In the spring of 1941, *Bismarck* was undergoing sea trials in the Baltic Sea. When she and her consort, the *Prinz Eugen*, finally left Norwegian waters to head out to the Atlantic in May, sixteen British convoys were headed for the Mediterranean or the British Isles. Even with Royal Navy destroyers, cruisers, and battleships providing escort, they were all vulnerable to *Bismarck's* huge guns. The fate of Great Britain was uncertain. *Scharnhorst* and *Gneisenau* had sunk twenty-two ships totaling 115,000 tons. And they had nowhere near *Bismarck's* firepower. *Bismarck* was the all-consuming obsession of the British Admiralty.

For six days, through good and bad weather, good luck and tragedy, two fleets and nearly three dozen warships tried to find *Bismarck*. On May 24, the pride of the Royal Navy, the huge battle cruiser HMS *Hood*, met up with *Bismarck* in the Denmark Strait. When *Hood* and the terror of the seas met for the first and last time, it came down to the two biggest kids on the block slugging it out to see who was toughest. One was an old fighter with a heavier punch but a shorter reach, while the other was a young boxer who could hit faster. Less than ten minutes after they opened fire on each other, the "Mighty *Hood*" received a hit near her main ammunition magazines and exploded in a massive detonation that killed all but three of her 1,400 crewmen. What really mattered wasn't the size of the guns. It was range, armor protection, and accuracy. *Hood* and *Bismarck* carried almost identical main armaments.

Hood's loss was a deep blow to Great Britain and only steeled their resolve. To the rest of the world watching the sea drama unfolding, it seemed to prove that the *Bismarck* was invincible. Sinking the *Hood* was a propaganda bonanza for the Third Reich. Avenging the *Hood* was a rallying cry for England. Neither side could back down.

The Royal Navy scraped together every ship they could, and in the end, by the sheerest luck and steadfast determination, two British battleships finally turned *Bismarck* into a flaming wreck.

For more than seventy years, *Bismarck*'s superiority has been taken for granted. The 1960 Fox movie added to the legend, and in time, it became fact. But how did it start? Who was the first to make that statement? After careful research of German and British archives from the Imperial War Museum and the Naval Historical Center, the author could not find a single public pre-1941 proclamation of *Bismarck* as "the most powerful and/or biggest battleship in the world." Not even the German War Ministry or the Propaganda Ministry seem to have made such a claim. Josef Goebbels, Minister of Propaganda, certainly the master of deceit and spin control, would have been the logical one to say it, but he was too smart. Any naval expert would have challenged a boast of *Bismarck*'s strength, and the Third Reich would have lost face. The closest to such a claim was during her launching at Kiel. Adolf Hitler proudly stated *Bismarck* and her sister, *Tirpitz*, were the "most powerful warships ever built in Germany." That, too, isn't fully accurate. Back in 1916, during the height of the Great War, SMS *Bayern* was launched. She was the first of the Kaiser's new superdreadnoughts. She carried no less than eight 15-inch guns, the same as *Bismarck* would carry twenty-three years later. Hitler seems to have forgotten this minor point.

The most the Germans could honestly say, if the German Propaganda Ministry would ever recognize such a word, is that *Bismarck* was the newest and most advanced warship in the world.

After carefully studying the major warships of the time, it appears the mighty *Bismarck*'s bark was worse than its bite. Naval guns, by the spring of 1941, were as good as they would ever get. Their size and range increased from the early 12-inch cannons used on the pioneering HMS *Dreadnought* in 1906, growing by leaps and bounds by the beginning of the Great War. Soon, even 13.5-inch guns were overtaken by the massive 15-inch guns of the colossal *Queen Elizabeth*-class superdreadnoughts. They set the standard in the Royal Navy that held sway for the next twenty years. But there were exceptions.

For the sister ships HMS *Nelson* and HMS *Rodney*, launched in 1920 and 1922, respectively, nine 16-inch guns were fitted. With three triple-gun turrets, they were later matched by the American *South Dakota*, *North Carolina*, and *Iowa*-class battleships. They were the heaviest guns ever mounted on a British warship. The pendulum between more guns and bigger guns swung back and forth, partially due to cost and the configuration of the proposed vessel. By the years before World War II, the newest battleship in the Royal Navy was the *King George V*, with ten 14-inch guns in three turrets. The forward and aft guns were set in two ponderous four-gun turrets, while the last two were set in a high-mounted twin turret. This illustrates the capricious nature of battleship design in the interwar period. For the United States Navy after the Great War, the 14-inch gun was the standard, appearing on nearly every battleship from the USS *Nevada* until the launching of the three wartime battleship classes in 1941. *Nevada* carried ten 14-inch guns, while the later USS *Arizona* boasted twelve guns in four turrets.

Let's not forget France and Italy. France's largest battleships, *Jean Bart* and *Richelieu*, carried eight 15-inch guns. Italy's capital battleship *Vittorio Veneto* had nine guns of the same caliber and rated at 40,000 tons and 780 feet long.

Of course any examination of World War II battleships must include the Japanese superbattleships. HIJMS (His Imperial Japanese Majesty's Ship) *Yamato* had been launched by the time of the *Bismarck* chase but wouldn't be commissioned until December. At nearly 70,000 tons, *Yamato* carried nine immense 18.1-inch guns, the largest ever mounted on a ship. She was the apogee of battleship design, but this did not protect her and her later sister, *Musashi*, from being sunk. Not by naval guns but by carrier-based aircraft.

In order to clearly illustrate how *Bismarck*'s armament was less than equal to many, if not most, of the world's major warships, it will be necessary to look at certain criteria. Here we focus on the main armaments: caliber, weight of shell, and range. Certainly these are the most important elements for a battleship, indeed its very reason for existence. Using a simple formula of the number of guns multiplied by the size provides Total Gun Caliber (TGC). This is only meant as a means of ranking a ship's gun size. Another formula, Total Weight of Broadside (TWB), is also used as a means of ranking. Of course many other factors need to be considered, such as range, rate of fire, fire control, and accuracy. As a new, highly advanced warship with state-of-the-art German engineering, *Bismarck* was arguably technologically superior to anything in the Royal Navy in 1941. The chart below uses TGC and TWB to rank the major warships of Germany, Great Britain, the United States, Italy, France, and Japan as of 1941.

World Battleships Ranking, 1941

Ship	Length/ Tons	Guns/ Caliber	TGC	Shell Weight/ Range	TWB	TGC/ TWB Rank
Bismarck	798/ 42,000	8/15-inch	120	1,800/ 35,000m	14,400 lbs/ 6.857 tons	8/8
Hood	860/ 46,000	8/15-inch	120	1,900/ 29,000m	15,200 lbs/ 7.238 tons	7/7
King George V	745/ 42,200	10/14-inch	140	1,590/ 36,000m	15,900 lbs/ 7.571 tons	6/6
Nelson	710/ 33,730	9/16-inch	144	2,480/ 35,000m	18,432 lbs/ 8.777 tons	4/3
Nevada	538/ 27,500	10/14-inch	140	1,500/ 36,000m	15,000 lbs/ 7.142 tons	5/7
Arizona	608/ 29,158	12/14-inch	168	1,500/ 36,800m	18,000 lbs/ 8.571 tons	3/6
Tennessee	624/ 33,190	12/14-inch	168	1,500/ 36,800m	18,000 lbs/ 8.571 tons	3/6
Vitorrio Veneto	780/ 37,000	9/15-inch	135	1,950/ 42,000m	17,550 lbs/ 8.397 tons	7/6
Richelieu	813/ 47,500	8/15-inch	120	1,950/ 41,700m	15,600 lbs/ 7.428 tons	5/6
Nagato	760/ 39,200	12/16-inch	198	2,200/ 30,200m	26,400 lbs/ 12.5 tons	1/2
Yamato	839/ 64,000	9/18-inch	168	3,500/ 42,000m**	31,500 lbs/ 15 tons	2/1

** Approximate estimated weight of 18-inch AP shell
Source:
Jane's Fighting Ships, 1922
Jane's Fighting Ships, 1924
Jane's Fighting Ships, 1941
Jane's Fighting Ships, 1943–44

After a look at the TGC and TWB ratings, some surprising results emerge. It is obvious which ship ranks highest. Japan's massive *Yamato*, with a TGC of 168, ranks second behind *Nagato* at 198. Yet as TWB is rated, the numbers are reversed. *Nagato* could fire a heavier broadside than her newer, bigger descendant. Interestingly, the U.S. Navy's *Arizona* and *Tennessee* had the same 168 TGC as *Yamato*, although their gun range and weight of broadside were inferior since they were older. Overall, Japan's battlewagons rank highest, while the United States and Great

Britain hover above France and Italy. Yet the mighty *Bismarck*, "the Terror of the Seas," as Johnny Horton's 1959 novelty song proclaimed, is dead last. As shown above, *Hood* and *Bismarck* were evenly matched. Both had a TGC of 120 and a nearly identical TWB of 7.238 tons and 6.857 tons, respectively. In fact, *Hood*'s shells weighed 1,900 pounds compared to her opponent's 1,800-pound projectiles. Yet even with heavier shells, *Hood*'s 29,000-meter range was 6,000 meters less than *Bismarck*'s. Only *Bismarck*'s range and gunnery were superior. In the end, it was armor, or in the case of *Hood*, the lack of it, that mattered. In fact, during the Battle of the Denmark Strait, it was not *Bismarck*'s fire-control radar that led to *Hood*'s destruction. *Bismarck* had fired on the shadowing British light cruisers *Suffolk* and *Norfolk* the day before, knocking out her radar. The heavy cruiser *Prinz Eugen* was leading her bigger sister and using her own radar when *Bismarck* fired the fatal salvo.

So how did the world come to accept the boast? Just as *Titanic* was never called unsinkable until after she was at the bottom, *Bismarck* was only the most powerful long after she had been sunk. It was part of the legend. And the Royal Navy, having lost the vaunted *Hood* and then destroyed the German behemoth, looked better if *Bismarck* had been the superior vessel.

The truth is, for just nine short days, *Bismarck* was the newest and most advanced battleship in the world. But sooner or later, she would have met her match, as all boastful bullies eventually do.

Bismarck's very existence and potential menace were more destructive than her guns. The Royal Navy committed eight battleships, two carriers, several cruisers and destroyers, several land-based squadrons, and legions of radio-direction stations to find and destroy her. Eleven convoys were diverted, burning more fuel and delaying their arrivals. This in itself was almost enough to justify building the *Bismarck*. Other than the sinking of *Hood*, she never lived up to Raeder's promises.

Bismarck's one victim was the mighty *Hood*, the pride of the Royal Navy. Actually a battle cruiser, *Hood* was the victim of short-sighted naval standards written during the Great War. Considered more than adequate at the time, they doomed the great ship to sink in the icy waters of the Denmark Strait. The following essay details the construction, career, and destruction of the most beloved ship in the Royal Navy.

HMS *HOOD*: DEATH OF THE BATTLE CRUISER

Published in *World War II History*, October 2019

The era of the battleship reached its apogee at Tsushima Strait in May 1905 when Admiral Heihachiro Togo's powerful Japanese battleships annihilated the Russian fleet in the Russo-Japanese War. After Tsushima, no single major naval engagement between capital ships would have more than a trifling effect on the outcome of any war. But the long-cherished belief that battleships could decide the fate of nations refused to die, even more than thirty years later. That was the case on a tragic day in May 1941, when two British warships, the new battleship HMS *Prince of Wales* and, the pride of the Royal Navy, the huge battle cruiser HMS *Hood*, emerged from the dawn to face the German battleship *Bismarck*.

Bismarck, the newest and largest warship ever built in Germany, was accompanied by the smaller but equally dangerous heavy cruiser *Prinz Eugen* as they raced southwest through the Denmark Strait toward the open Atlantic. *Prince of Wales* and *Hood* were there to stop the Germans at all costs.

The pivotal moment in a duel that lasted only minutes began at 5:51 A.M. on May 24, when the two Royal Navy warships turned to close with the two German ships on the western horizon. The range was 28,000 yards (15.8 miles). *Hood* had to move closer to give her shorter-ranging guns a better chance of hitting *Bismarck*. The guns on all four combatants began firing. Then another salvo from *Bismarck*'s huge 15-inch shells screamed in an unearthly howl from the skies. *Hood* was straddled by towering columns of water. A portentous moment in time seemed to freeze, then the massive warship erupted into a fireball that left only floating debris. In those horrifying seconds, the lives of 1,415 British officers and seamen were snuffed out as if they had never existed.

The mighty *Hood* had blown up. It was the worst single disaster for the Royal Navy in its four centuries of history. *Hood* was a favorite in Britain, and her loss was a terrible blow to British pride.

It was also *Bismarck*'s only victory. Three days later, she, too, lay on the bottom of the Atlantic, a victim of German hubris and British vengeance. Ironically, *Bismarck* sank on the thirty-sixth anniversary of Togo's victory at Tsushima, marking the zenith of the battleship and its final decline.

How could it have happened that the largest warship in the Royal Navy be snuffed out in an instant?

The reasons go back to April 13, 1907, when a new warship slid into the waters from the Armstrong-Whitworth Shipyard along the River Tyne. The new battle cruiser, HMS *Invincible*, was the first in a line of potent warships that would dominate Admiralty doctrine for the next ten years. Her 560-foot-long hull, displacing more than 17,000 tons, was the height of warship design. When fitted out, *Invincible* had thirty Yarrow water-tubed boilers conveying high-pressure steam to four modern Parsons Turbine engines that drove four screws to move her sleek hull through the seas at 28 knots. Her main decks carried four heavy turrets, each mounting two massive 12-inch rifles capable of firing shells weighing half a ton over a distance of twelve miles. Without a doubt, *Invincible* was the most radical concept in capital warship design. But hidden under her bristling guns and gray war paint, *Invincible* was at serious risk.

The battle cruiser concept was first set down by the father of the modern Royal Navy, First Sea Lord Admiral Sir John Arbuthnot "Jacky" Fisher. After ramrodding the innovative all-big-gun battleship HMS *Dreadnought* into being in 1906, Fisher developed the idea of fast, heavily armed but lightly armored battle cruisers. Fisher had decreed that in battle cruisers, "weight in armor should be sacrificed to weight invested in larger guns and heavy propulsion machinery to generate higher speeds." This became the rule by which all subsequent British battle cruisers were designed and launched. While there were marked differences in gun caliber, speed, and tonnage, they generally had only half the armor thickness around their turret barbettes, hull, and decks than a comparable dreadnought in the Grand Fleet. Most dreadnoughts, having more armor, were often 10 knots slower than the big battle cruisers. In a fast and furious naval engagement over a wide area, as at the Falklands in December 1914, Dogger Bank in January 1915, and Jutland in May 1916, big guns mounted on fast ships could mean the difference between victory and defeat, between survival and annihilation. Always a proponent of speed and big guns, Fisher knowingly and willingly sacrificed the safety afforded by heavy armor. Although battle cruisers could sweep far ahead of the main fleet and move in fast to engage capital ships at extreme range, they were as vulnerable as any light cruiser only half as big. Yet this did not seem to deter or even occur to the Admiralty in 1907.

Fisher's position and status at the Admiralty were such that no senior naval officer and few government officials could safely challenge him. He wielded immense power and brokered no opposition. Those who challenged Jacky Fisher were buried in his characteristic tsunami of tirades, threats, memos, and intimidation. Even so, few men disagreed with his daring dream of the "super cruiser" or "fast dreadnought." England led the race to build the fastest big-gun dreadnoughts in the years before and during the Great War. In all, thirteen such ships of increasing size and main gun caliber were constructed after *Invincible*, eventually culminating with HMS *Hood* in 1920. Soon Germany, Japan, Russia, France, and the United States followed suit, laying down the keels to their own battle cruisers.

But not all the other navies blindly agreed with the Fisher dogma. Admiral Alfred von Tirpitz, who, as secretary for naval affairs, held the same status in the Kaiser's Navy as Fisher in the Admiralty, felt that a warship's primary job was to remain afloat to fight and therefore chose to accept lower speed and smaller gun caliber in favor of thicker armor.

The fast battle cruisers were meant to scout far ahead of the main battle fleet, providing information on the enemy's strength, formation, course, and speed. The slower but more heavily armored dreadnoughts were the real power of a navy during the Great War, holding a status that could only be compared to the huge hydrogen bombs of the Cold War two generations later. While battle cruisers were never intended to engage enemy battleships, their big guns were too tempting for aggressive fleet commanders to discount in a clash of warships. In addition to thinner armor, they had one fatal flaw. During the battle of Dogger Bank on January 24, 1915, the SMS _Seydlitz_, flagship of the German battle cruiser force, received a penetrating hit on one of her aft gun turrets. The flash from the explosion went down the barbette to the shell room and powder magazines below the waterline. _Seydlitz_ was in imminent danger of exploding, but prompt action by an officer flooded the magazine and saved the ship. It should be explained that the term "barbette" usually means the entire rotating assembly of turret housing, guns, and the vertical trunk extending down into the hull.

The German Navy recognized the danger and began installing double sets of anti-flash doors in the barbettes of every capital ship. Both doors couldn't be open at the same time, so an explosion in the turret was stopped before it reached the powder magazines. The Royal Navy remained blissfully unaware of this same fatal flaw in their capital ships. Fisher left the Admiralty in 1915, still convinced of the value of his dream. In one respect, he had been right: Big guns and speed were essential factors in victory at sea. At the climactic battle of Jutland a year later, three of Admiral Sir David Beatty's battle cruisers exploded from exactly the same type of catastrophic hit on a turret. After watching the HMS _Indefatigable_, HMS _Queen Mary_, and HMS _Invincible_ blow up, Beatty said laconically, "There seems to be something wrong with our bloody ships today." Fisher's decree reaped a deadly harvest. More than three thousand officers and men died in the three ships.

Jutland also saw an hour-long duel between the heavy dreadnoughts of the German High Seas Fleet and the British Grand Fleet, none of which were lost or seriously damaged. This was undoubtedly due to their thicker armor preventing armor-piercing shells from penetrating the turrets. In any event, Jutland patently displayed the design fault in the turrets, and changes were made throughout the fleet. Yet Fisher did not recognize nor admit that his thin-skinned darlings were literally sitting ducks in a major engagement. After the battle, Fisher, never one to admit culpability, blamed the losses on the Royal Navy commanders and their lack of aggressiveness. "I have worked thirty years to build this fleet and they failed me."

In only one case did battle cruisers ever make any noteworthy contribution to the war. At the Battle of the Falklands in December 1914, HMS *Invincible* and HMS *Inflexible* were sent to the South Atlantic to intercept Admiral Maximillian von Spee's East Asia Squadron, which consisted of two armored cruisers, SMS *Scharnhorst* and SMS *Gneisenau*, and three light cruisers. Only the big guns of the British battle cruisers, carried by their great speed, assured victory.

The battle cruisers were forever doomed to be seagoing bastards, neither fish nor fowl. They carried big guns but did not dare engage equally armed ships. This was to have tragic consequences for a ship that had yet to be launched when Jutland dominated the headlines. Earlier that year, the Admiralty had learned of the proposed German *Mackensen*-class battle cruisers, rumored to be bigger and better armed than the new *Renown*-class. They hurriedly laid plans for a new super battle cruiser, the *Admiral*-class. The losses at Jutland forced the incorporation of thicker armor and anti-flash doors in the turret barbettes. All four keels of the new class were laid down, but only one would be completed. The collapse of the High Seas Fleet and the imminent end of the war convinced the Admiralty that the money for the other three ships could be better spent rebuilding Britain's merchant fleet, which U-boats had decimated. Only one of the mighty *Admiral*-class was launched and commissioned. The contract for the new warship was awarded to the John Brown Shipyards in Clydebank, Scotland, in April 1916. Her keel was laid down in September and her massive hull slid into the River Clyde on August 22, 1918, less than three months before the Armistice.

HMS *Hood*, named for the eighteenth-century Admiral Samuel Hood, was the first capital ship to be commissioned after the war ended. Her hull was constructed on the same slipways where the liners *Queen Mary* and *Queen Elizabeth* would be built in the 1930s.

Hood's motto was *Ventis Secundis*, Latin for "With Favorable Winds." From the start, *Hood* became a national favorite. The largest and most powerful warship in the fleet, she carried four main gun turrets, each mounting twin 15-inch Mark I rifles, capable of firing 1,900-pound armor-piercing shells to a maximum range of 30,000 yards. The four turrets, two forward and two aft, were designated "A," "B," "X," and "Y."

HMS *Hood* in 1924 during speed trials. *Imperial War Museum*

The magazines for each turret held 240 powder charges and shells. Her 860-foot hull was 104 feet wide at the widest point.

Drawing more than thirty feet, her side, deck, and barbette armor were heavier and thicker than any previous battle cruiser. She was more than a hundred feet longer, twenty feet wider, and 13,000 tons heavier than the largest battle cruisers in the Royal Navy. Initially, *Hood* displaced 42,300 tons, but the later installation of more armor increased her displacement to 45,000 tons. This made *Hood* ride four feet deeper in the water. In moderately heavy seas, the waves rode over her bows and across the deck, earning her the dubious reputation as "the largest submarine in the British Navy."

In 1939 and 1940, her original 5.5-inch secondary armament was replaced with more-efficient Mark 16 twin-mount dual-purpose 4.1-inch guns, each of which had its own magazine holding two hundred shells. *Hood* had four fixed 21-inch tubes for twenty-eight torpedoes fitted above the waterline aft of the rear funnel.

Twenty-four Yarrow boilers fed steam to the four huge Brown-Curtiss geared turbines, with a total of 144,000 shaft horsepower. This drove the *Hood* through the water at an impressive 31 knots, better than any of Fisher's vaunted wartime battle cruisers.

Hood's armor along the hull and the turret barbettes was adequate to protect against armor-piercing shells from a low trajectory, but she

remained vulnerable to plunging shells and bombs on her decks and turret roofs. This aspect of *Hood*'s vulnerability was never fully addressed.
In fact, her popularity and stature in the Royal Navy were a detriment
to any modernization or improvements that would have added to her
survivability. In 1941, *Hood* had no more armor protection than she had
been given in 1918.

Her armor was adequate for what the German Navy might have unleashed on her in the Great War but was too light for the later generation
of high-trajectory, high-velocity, armor-piercing rounds coming into use
by the end of the 1930s.

With that in mind, the Admiralty decreed that *Hood* was not to be
part of the main fleet but to operate in the classic battle cruiser role of
fast scout. This was her primary duty in the years before World War II.

In the early 1930s, in shipyards across the North Sea, Germany had
been violating the terms of the Treaty of Versailles by constructing a series of ever-larger surface warships. Curiously, there was no battle cruiser
among them, from the heavy cruisers to the so-called "Pocket Battleships"
to the titanic dreadnoughts launched in 1939 and 1940. While they dif-
fered greatly in size, gun caliber, and configuration, the Third Reich's big
warships were fast, powerful, and clad in heavy protective armor. Their
biggest and most modern were the sister battleships, *Bismarck* and *Tirpitz*.
Bismarck was launched in Hamburg on St. Valentine's Day in 1939, with
Adolf Hitler himself watching. While she was erroneously touted in the
Nazi press as the most powerful warship afloat, *Bismarck* was definitely
the largest and most advanced warship ever constructed in Germany.

The British Admiralty watched with trepidation as the new battleship finished her sea trials in the Baltic in 1941. By then most of the surface raiders had been sunk, damaged, or forced into port. The *Bismarck*
was a dangerous threat to the many vital Allied convoys in the Atlantic.
She would have to be stopped at all costs. But *Bismarck* was faster than
any battleship in the Royal Navy. So the Admiralty sent the only two
capital ships capable of catching and stopping *Bismarck*—*Hood* and
Prince of Wales.

But while the two largest combatants were almost equally armed
with eight 15-inch guns in four turrets, the scale was vastly tipped in the
German warship's favor.

Displacing over 50,000 tons fully loaded and with a hull 798 feet long, *Bismarck* had a beam of 118 feet. This made her heavier and wider than *Hood* and reflected the differing views of the German Navy's philosophy about armor. Her twelve Wagner high-pressure boilers drove the three-geared turbine's 148,000-horsepower shaft. Although *Bismarck* displaced five thousand tons more than her British opponent, she still nearly matched *Hood*'s 30-knot speed.

Bismarck's armor protection was even more impressive. A belt over twelve inches in thickness girded her hull while fourteen inches clad the four main gun turrets and barbettes. German armor was far superior in tensile strength than what was used in Britain. *Bismarck*'s armor constituted more than forty percent of her total displacement, as opposed to the thirty percent on *Hood*.

From a purely aesthetic standpoint, *Bismarck*'s design reflected the modern Bauhaus style of the 1930s. From her raked Atlantic clipper bow to the smooth curves of the hull to the curving cruiser stern, the German ship was undoubtedly more pleasing to the eye than the angular silhouette of most British warships.

But *Bismarck*'s real advantage rested in radar and fire control. Being a generation newer than *Hood*, *Bismarck* was equipped with three FUMO-23 search radar units. With direct input to the main fire control stations, these sets allowed *Bismarck* to fix the range of an enemy vessel quickly. *Hood* was also fitted with fire control radar, but her maneuvers in the fateful battle would negate their effective use.

Hood's only advantage was in the weight of her armor-piercing projectiles, which weighed 1,900 pounds as compared to her opponent's 1,800-pound shells. Yet even with heavier shells, *Hood*'s 29,000-yard effective range was 6,000 yards less than *Bismarck*'s.

We must examine the actual circumstances of the events of that morning in order to determine how *Hood* died. The Denmark Strait, a wide northeast-to-southwest channel that separates Greenland from Iceland, was where *Bismarck* and her smaller consort, the heavy cruiser *Prinz Eugen* were making their break for the open Atlantic. The Royal Navy had two light cruisers, HMS *Suffolk* and HMS *Norfolk*, patrolling in the strait to shadow the two German warships until the venerable

Hood and her brand-new companion, the battleship HMS *Prince of Wales*, could arrive. There was little doubt that *Hood*, the most powerful warship in the fleet, could easily take care of *Bismarck*.

During the night, *Bismarck*, which had been in the lead, fired on *Suffolk* and *Norfolk* in an attempt to sink or disable them. Five salvos of 15-inch shells rained down on the smaller, rapidly twisting ships without hitting them. But *Bismarck*'s FUMO-23 fire control radar was damaged by the concussion, and Admiral Günther Lütjens ordered the cruiser *Prinz Eugen* to take station in the lead with her own functioning radar. Thus it was Prinz Eugen in the lead when dawn approached on May 24. When the British and German squadrons first sighted each other at 5:30 A.M., the distance was 28,000 yards (15.8 miles), which put them on each other's horizon. Initially southeast of *Bismarck*, *Hood* was silhouetted against the rising dawn while the Germans were still lost in the gloom. This gave the Germans the initial advantage. Commanded by Vice Admiral Lancelot Holland, *Hood* and *Prince of Wales* opened fire at extreme range. The slightly smaller *Prinz Eugen* had nearly the same silhouette as *Bismarck* and was in the lead. This made Holland concentrate *Hood*'s fire on the cruiser. Both German ships aimed at the distinctive shape of the *Hood*, which was ahead of the *Prince of Wales*. Instead of relying on radar, the German fire control was initially directed by the excellent rangefinders high on *Bismarck*'s superstructure.

Hood's first salvo, fired at a range of 25,000 yards (14.2 miles) at 5:52 A.M., fell short. Holland, realizing they needed to be closer, ordered a twenty-degree starboard turn to the southwest to bring the two Royal Navy warships closer to *Bismarck* and *Prinz Eugen*. Well aware of his flagship's vulnerability to plunging fire, Holland apparently wanted to force the Germans to lower their guns so their fire would be on a flatter trajectory. The shells would hit *Hood*'s thicker side armor.

But the turn toward the Germans masked the three aft turrets of the *Prince of Wales* and *Hood*, depriving them of nearly half their firepower in the opening stage of the battle.

At exactly 5:55 A.M., Admiral Lütjens ordered Captain Ernst Lindemann to open fire on *Hood*. Holland saw the bright flashes of *Bismarck*'s eight heavy guns. A few seconds later, there was a roar like a speeding freight train as the huge shells screamed overhead. Tall white waterspouts towered as high as *Hood's* foretop. A sudden sharp shudder shook the 45,000-ton warship. *Hood* had been hit. *Prinz Eugen* added her eight smaller guns to the deadly duel but did little damage. Still, the old battle cruiser bored in, her guns reaching out to her distant enemy. Again the flashes, and again, the roar of heavy shells tore over *Hood*.

With their advanced fire control systems, the two German ships loosed four broadsides at the British. Being fresh out of the builder's yard, HMS *Prince of Wales* could not get all her guns going. *Hood* could only use her fore turrets. The range had closed to 16,500 yards (9.3 miles) when Holland ordered a turn twenty degrees to port, unmasking "X" and "Y" turrets. It was 5:56 A.M. Then a shell from *Bismarck's* fifth salvo struck close to the battle cruiser's mainmast on the aft boat deck. That was the killing blow.

A thunderous eruption of flame, steam, smoke, and flying debris instantly smothered the place where the mighty *Hood* had been. The sound of *Hood's* destruction roared over the cold waters of the Denmark Strait and echoed off the distant icy cliffs of Greenland.

Three minutes later. *Hood* was gone, her torn remains settling into the icy black waters 9,000 feet below. Three survivors out of her crew of more than 1,400 were picked out of the freezing water.

The first public announcement from the Admiralty on May 24 laconically reported that ". . . HMS *Hood* received an unlucky hit in a magazine and blew up."

In two best-selling books by C. S. Forester and William Shirer, the descriptions of how *Hood* died have become the stuff of seafaring folklore. According to both books, *Hood* had what was euphemistically called a "chink" in her deck armor on the Boat Deck between the two funnels. A 15-inch armor-piercing shell struck exactly at this spot at 5:56 A.M. and penetrated six decks and six bulkheads to explode in the main powder magazine, igniting 300 tons of high explosive cordite. Several jets of flame and smoke burst from her superstructure, and a huge sheet of fire rose between the funnels to a height of a thousand feet. A massive gray cloud cleared and revealed the bow and stern of *Hood* jutting out of the water like "two sharks until they sank."

The general public has long accepted these accounts, but they fall short in two major areas: There was no so-called "chink" in *Hood*'s deck armor, and there was no main gun magazine in that area to destroy *Hood*. The two forward and two aft gun barbettes were separated by nearly 400 feet. The twenty-four Yarrow boilers and their uptakes took up the intervening space under the funnels.

So the question remains, how could it happen?

Besides *Bismarck*'s shells, the only logical culprit had to be *Hood*'s lack of sufficient armor protection. When *Hood* was first designed in 1916, she was to be larger, faster, and more heavily armed than the biggest battle cruiser ever built up to that time. But Fisher's old refrain of a fast, heavily armed, lightly armored ship still held sway, and *Hood*'s armor was significantly thinner than a battleship of comparable size, even after her 1939 and 1940 refits. The numbers leave little doubt. In 1941, *Hood*'s main protection was along her hull to prevent penetration from heavy shells and torpedoes. The belt ranged from 6 inches thick at the bow and stern and increased to 12 inches along the most sensitive areas, such as the magazines and boilers. The barbettes, the main structure of the turret assembly, were sheathed in 12 inches of steel. The turret housings, the part which actually enclosed the guns, had 15 inches of armor on the front, which was intended to face the enemy warships, and 11 inches on the sides and rear. Yet despite the hard lessons of Jutland, *Hood*'s turret roof armor was only 5 inches thick, an inch less than the thickest deck armor plate.

While this would seem adequate, a battleship of the same era usually had hull and deck plating that ran between 12 and 15 inches in thickness. This would stop or deflect the heaviest armor-piercing shells then in use.

There is no evidence that *Bismarck*'s shells penetrated *Hood*'s barbettes in those three minutes of battle. Rather, it is well-established that the fatal blow struck somewhere amidships in a manner that managed to convey the detonation to one of the battle cruiser's aft powder magazines, located six decks down in the vessel's bowels. Considering her size, this bears closer examination.

In the Great War, a dreadnought's fire was directed visually from rangefinders in the foretop high over the superstructure, and most naval battles were fought at ranges of less than 15,000 yards (9 miles). But the advent of radar for fire control made it possible to fight naval engagements at ranges of more than 25,000 to 30,000 yards (14.2 to 17 miles), far beyond visual range. Main gun turrets could elevate the guns as high as 30 degrees, imparting a high-arc trajectory to the shell, then plunged downward into the decks of enemy ships. But *Hood*'s deck armor was only 2 inches thick at the bow and stern and increased to just over 6 inches on both the main and boat decks.

Accounts from witnesses on the light cruisers *Suffolk* and *Norfolk* and survivors from *Bismarck* described the cataclysm. To the majority of witnesses, the explosion was amidships near the funnels. *Hood*'s aft portion seemed to break away from the main hull and sank first. Apparently one or more of the magazines had exploded in the aft portion of the hull.

With the exception of *Prince of Wales*, all other ships viewed *Hood* from either port or starboard. The new battleship, being aft of *Hood*, had a view that revealed what really happened. Captain John C. Leach on *Prince of Wales*'s bridge later described the column of flame shooting up from the vicinity of *Hood*'s mainmast, which was on the aft portion of the boat deck and just forward of the "X" turret. He said the blast obscured and then obliterated the entire aft portion of *Hood*. While there were no main guns on the amidships superstructure, it did contain the twelve twin-mount 4.1-inch guns, each of which had its own magazine with two hundred shells.

The official board of inquiry report, released on June 2, 1941, stated that ". . . the probable cause of the loss of HMS *Hood* was direct penetration of the protection by one or more 15-inch shells at a range of 16,500 yards, resulting in the explosion of one or more of the aft magazines."

While the findings were straightforward, they almost immediately came under criticism. The circumstances of the battle and its aftermath meant there were no immediate verbatim statements taken of any of the witnesses, neither British nor German. Then other theories emerged, including one in which *Hood* had been destroyed by the internal detonation of her own torpedoes in the hull aft of the rear funnel. *Hood* did carry twenty-eight torpedoes, theoretically more than enough to destroy her. But from the start, there was good reason to discount this theory, and it was never given much credence.

A second inquiry, held in September, taking into evidence the testimony of over a hundred witnesses, was more thorough but came to much the same conclusion. *Hood* died from an explosion in either her 4.1-inch or 15-inch aft magazines. The most likely probability was that the 4.1-inch magazines, located closer to the mainmast, exploded first, starting an instantaneous chain of explosions in the larger magazine. This seems to fit the eyewitness accounts. If a shell had penetrated at this point, it could have started an intense fire in the engine room, which tore through the ventilators into the aft powder magazines. Another element that supports this is the multiple eruptions of smoke and fire witnessed by Captain Leach and surviving Germans that seemed to shoot up from the engine room vents. The engine rooms were located aft of the boilers on either side of the barbettes and magazines. If an explosion in the aft 4.1-inch magazines or the boiler rooms occurred, the blast would almost certainly have destroyed the bulkheads, which were only 4 inches thick.

The original long-accepted view of a "chink" in the deck armor allowing a shell to explode the magazines must be addressed. When *Hood* exploded, the combatants were about 16,000 yards apart, which meant that *Bismarck* would have had her guns elevated to about 14 degrees. This made the shells' trajectory nearly flat. Any shell coming in from an angle of 14 degrees couldn't have reached *Hood*'s aft magazines without first penetrating the 12-inch hull armor belt. While a so-called weak spot might have allowed a shell to enter the superstructure, it wouldn't have gone downward. At most, it would have torn across the width of the superstructure. Of course, this is where the 4.1-inch barbettes were located, with their corresponding magazines just below.

One theory involved a report from *Prince of Wales* that "unusual discharges" were coming from one of *Hood*'s forward guns. This testimony was taken at the second inquiry, suggesting she was about to suffer a Jutland-type of explosion. But the fact that the battle cruiser's aft portion was the center of the large explosion seems to refute this theory. Also, *Hood*'s bow would have been extremely difficult for anyone on the following battleship to see clearly.

The 2001 discovery and exploration of *Hood*'s grave revealed how violent the explosion had been. She lies in 9,200 feet of water with her remains scattered across three distinct debris fields. The large midsection is overturned, while the stern is several hundred feet away. The bow and superstructure are likewise separate from the main section. The wide gap between the main hull and stern proves conclusively that the magazines for either "X" or "Y" turrets did explode. The hull broke apart on the surface. The rudder is still set at port, exactly where Holland had ordered it just before the fatal blow. Curiously, *Hood's* bow is gone just forward of "A" turret. One possibility concerns a hit on *Prince of Wales*, which was taken under fire by *Bismarck* after the destruction of *Hood*. A 15-inch shell fell short, slid into the water eighty feet off her side, and penetrated the hull 30 feet below the waterline beneath the armor belt. It tore into the warren of compartments and bulkheads but failed to explode. This could conceivably have happened to *Hood*. One shell might have struck the water off her starboard quarter and exploded in the aft powder magazine. The wreck reveals that nearly the entire starboard hull in the region of the fuel oil tanks was torn open from an internal explosion. If a shell did penetrate and explode under the waterline, it could have ignited the fuel from stern to bow and possibly been responsible for blowing off *Hood's* bow and possibly igniting the aft magazines.

Obviously there are many theories and explanations for the sinking of *Hood*. But using Occam's razor, the most likely cause was a hit in or near one of the 4.1-inch magazines, which then, either directly or via the engine room, reached the 150 tons of cordite in the handling room of the aft turrets. At that point, the blast erupted upward through the ventilators and hatches that dotted the boat deck and superstructure, creating the "sheet of flame and smoke" described by so many witnesses. That blast obscured what was happening as the entire aft portion of the hull tore open and fell away. In any event, the explosion that killed *Hood* and over 1,400 men was almost certainly a result of the same type of blast that sank three British battle cruisers at Jutland almost exactly twenty-five years earlier. There lies the Mighty *Hood*, 150 fathoms down in a black, icy grave, the last monument to Jacky Fisher's flawed dream of the fast battle cruiser.

Despite the Battle of the Denmark Strait and the sinking of *Bismarck* being one of the most famous naval engagements in history, it played only a side role in the Battle of the Atlantic and the outcome of the war. The primacy of the battleship had reached its apogee at Tsushima. Never again would the big-gun warship play a significant role in the fate of wars and nations.

This was dramatically proven in late 1941 when HMS *Prince of Wales* and the battle cruiser HMS *Repulse* were sent to the Pacific to protect British interests in Singapore. On December 10, both warships sank with absurd ease by Japanese land-based aircraft using bombs and torpedoes. Even *Prince of Wales*'s heavier armor was not enough to protect her from Japanese air attack.

But a new concept, unheard of in 1907 when *Invincible* slid into the water, was appearing on the seas in the late 1920s. Due to the limitations of the 1922 Washington Naval Treaty, three of Britain's smaller battle cruisers, HMS *Courageous,* HMS *Furious*, and HMS *Glorious*, were converted into aircraft carriers. The United States followed this lead by converting its last two battle cruiser hulls on the way into the aircraft carriers USS *Lexington* and USS *Saratoga*. Ironically, the speed of the battle cruiser, as envisioned by Fisher, was the key to making them effective aircraft carriers. The big-gun warship had reached and passed its apogee and soon became a supporting element to the carrier.

The next two essays concern a single day in December 1941 when the United States Navy found itself at war with Imperial Japan. The first American shot of the Second World War was fired from Gun Number 3 on board the destroyer USS *Ward*. The story of the *Ward*'s fight with a Japanese midget submarine is well known, but there are some interesting aspects of the fight and its aftermath. The story of the *Ward* has a curious end three years after it entered history at Pearl Harbor.

USS *WARD*: PEARL HARBOR AND BEYOND

Many ships throughout history have been remembered for one specific event, but the subsequent years are totally forgotten. How many people recall that the *Carpathia*, six years after racing fifty miles to save the survivors of the sinking *Titanic*, was herself sunk by torpedoes from the German submarine *U-55*? Or that the German heavy cruiser *Prinz Eugen*, best remembered for her role as *Bismarck*'s escort during the May 1941 Battle of the Denmark Strait, survived the war to be made into a target ship during the Bikini Atoll atomic bomb tests in 1946?

Scores of ships had long and interesting careers after the events for which they are remembered. Such is the case with the American destroyer USS *Ward*.

Ward was already a remarkable ship before she arrived at Pearl Harbor in January 1941. As one of the 111 *Wickes*-class fast destroyers, she was built and launched in the chaotic last year of the Great War. A desperate need for fast escorts for Atlantic convoys and anti-submarine patrols led to the construction of the class at ten shipyards around the country. Mare Island Shipyard in Vallejo, California, laid down the keel on May 15, 1918, and launched her two weeks later on June 1. She was commissioned as USS *Ward* (DD-139) on July 24. Even for a crash wartime shipbuilding program, no other ship of the class was put into commission in less time. She was built in the standard *Wickes* design, a 1,200-ton flush deck with four squat funnels, known as the "four pipers." At 314 feet long, she was only two feet longer than the World War II *Balao*-class submarines. Twin steam turbine engines pushed her at a respectable 35 knots. Four deck-mounted 4-inch guns, twelve torpedo tubes, and twin

USS *Ward* circa 1941. *Official U.S. Navy Photo*

racks of depth charges gave the *Ward* plenty of punch for her dozen officers and two hundred enlisted men.

Named for Commander James Harmon Ward, the first officer in the Union Navy to be killed in action in the American Civil War, *Ward* was sent to the Atlantic to serve as one of the pocket ships to support the navy's three Curtiss NC flying boats during their 1919 flight from Newfoundland to the Azores. Returning to the Pacific, *Ward* was decommissioned in 1921. Twenty years later, as the war raged in Europe, *Ward* was again recommissioned and sent west to Pearl Harbor.

On December 5, 1941, Lieutenant Commander William W. Outerbridge took command of the old destroyer, then attached to Division 80. Raised in Ohio, the thirty-five-year-old Outerbridge was considered an excellent officer, having graduated from Annapolis in 1927. *Ward* was his first sea command, and he was eager to prove himself.

Even though she was already twenty-three years old, *Ward* was still a fast, nimble, and sturdily built warship.

In the cool predawn of December 7, 1941, the last night of peace, the moon was breaking through the clouds over the calm waters off southern Oahu. A restricted sea area off the coast was marked by sea buoys and constantly patrolled by minesweepers and patrol craft. Overhead, a PBY Catalina flying boat flew in lazy ovals.

At 0345 hours, the small coastal minesweeper USS *Condor* made its way across the restricted area. Her seventeen-man crew was tired and waiting for dawn and breakfast. The quartermaster of the watch on *Condor's* bridge spotted a small dark object in the water far in their wake. It was moving at 9 knots and appeared to be following them. At 0357 hours, *Condor* alerted the *Ward*, then on its second inshore patrol.

Outerbridge ordered the ship to battle stations. All eyes strained in the dark as *Ward* approached the location of the sighting, but after almost an hour, they found nothing. *Condor*, whose crew had lost sight of the object, resumed moving toward the red and black markers that denoted the entrance to the channel. The heavy anti-submarine nets had been left open in anticipation of her entry. What the crew of *Condor* did not know was that the object they saw was already sneaking up the channel into Pearl Harbor.

Seaman 1/C Ray Chavez, who died in 2019 at the age of 106, had told the author that he and the rest of the crew had been "working all night sweeping the eastern area. We were ready to head back to Pearl for chow. But the sighting of a possible sub sent everyone on deck. It was too dark and the moon kept disappearing behind clouds. I never saw a thing. But when we heard later that a Jap midget sub had made it into Pearl and was sunk by the *Monaghan*, we were sure it was the one following us."

At 0600 hours, the navy tug *Keosanqua* was heading out to meet the supply ship *Antares*, which had passed Barbers Point on the southwest tip of Oahu. *Antares* was towing a 500-ton barge (often mistakenly identified as a target sled), waiting for the tug to take the barge into the harbor. A pilot was on the tug to guide *Antares* through the channel. As the sun crested the eastern horizon, heralding another perfect Hawaiian Sunday morning, *Antares's* captain, Commander Lawrence Grannis, subsequently spotted a black object that appeared to be a small submarine. The ship's log states: "Sighted strange object bearing 226 degrees true, distance about 1,500 yards on starboard quarter." It was on a converging course between the barge and the ship and, according to Grannis, "appeared to be having some difficulty maintaining depth control."

Several officers and crew spotted it, and at 0630 hours, the sighting report was sent to the *Ward*, cruising a mile to the southwest. This time there was plenty of sunlight. With the *Ward* turning to parallel the *Antares's* starboard side, the small object was clearly defined with the sun behind it.

There was no doubt, even though no one on *Antares* and *Ward* had ever seen anything like it before. It was certainly a submarine, painted dark green and coated with sea growth. The oval-shaped conning tower was only about two feet high and had tiny glass ports. The sub was moving at 9 knots, clearly headed for the *Antares*.

Overhead, Ensign William Tanner of Patrol Squadron 14 out of Kaneohe Bay Naval Air Station also spotted the sub. But he assumed it was an American sub in distress. Circling low, his crew dropped two smoke markers to assist the *Ward* in finding it.

On *Ward's* bridge, the helmsman was the first to see the small conning tower. He and the quartermaster of the watch agreed it was some kind of submarine. The quartermaster called Lieutenant (jg) O. W. Gepner, *Ward's* executive officer. After seeing for himself, he called out, "Captain, come to the bridge!"

Outerbridge, catching some sleep on the chart room cot after the earlier alert, pulled a robe over his undershirt and boxers and came through the door to the wheelhouse. Gepner pointed to the sub and handed him the binoculars.

The time was 0637 hours. Despite his lack of command experience, Outerbridge knew they were seeing a sub in the restricted area—a clear violation. No subs were to enter the area without escort and approval from the commandant of the Fourteenth Naval District.

He made his decision quickly. "Call the crew to battle stations and go to full speed." It was 0640 hours. The water around *Ward's* stern boiled as she changed heading toward the sub. Immediately her crew emerged from hatches and doors to run for the gun mounts and depth charge racks. One man was already on Number 3 mount and had pulled a 4-inch shell from the holder. In less than a minute, *Ward* was ready for combat. From his lofty vantage point of more than a thousand feet, Tanner saw the three wakes as they neared their confrontation. The *Antares* was turning north to pass between the outer buoys that marked the channel entrance. The sub left a tiny wake that was also turning north but angling to intercept the larger ship's course.

The *Ward* was charging ahead at 25 knots to get between the two ships.

As she came abreast of the barge, Outerbridge ordered a turn to port, which pointed the bow into the area between the sub and the *Antares's* wake. All the guns were ready and he ordered them swung to starboard. Every man on watch on the bridge, in the guns, or on deck saw the small dark object as the *Ward* moved in.

Outerbridge, still in skivvies and robe, ordered the ship slowed as they came close to the sub. It was only about a hundred yards off the starboard bow.

At exactly 0645 hours, Outerbridge said, "Commence firing!" The phone talker on the bridge repeated the order.

Number 1 gun fired first. The gunner couldn't use his regular sights since the sub was too close. He aimed by peering right down the barrel "like a squirrel gun." The heavy Mark 9 gun boomed, clearly heard across the quiet waters off southern Oahu. It was the first American shot of the Second World War.

But it missed, hitting the water a hundred yards past the sub and raising a tall waterspout. The sub did not show any reaction. Then Number 3 gun atop the galley deckhouse boomed at a range of 50 yards, and this time it was a direct hit, punching a large hole where the conning tower met the hull. The sub rocked to starboard, then wallowed and slowed as *Ward* moved closer. Outerbridge ordered, "Cease fire!"

The sub sank and came under *Ward's* stern. "Roll four depth charges!" Overbridge ordered.

With four blasts on the ship's whistle, the crews on the stern rolled four Mark 3 420-pound depth charges into the roiling water behind the ship. The chief torpedoman said he clearly saw the sub directly over the first charge. Four successive rumbles sounded as huge boiling masses of white seawater blasted up from *Ward's* wake.

Then Ensign Tanner, recognizing this was probably a hostile sub, came in and dropped two Mark 3 depth charges where he had last seen the sub. Then he reported his actions to Kaneohe Bay.

There was no sign of the sub. *Ward* circled the site and only saw an iridescent slick of oil on the surface. The water was 1,200 feet deep.

At 0651, Outerbridge sent a coded message to the watch officer of the Fourteenth Naval District in Pearl Harbor. "We have dropped depth charges on submarine operating in defensive sea area." But almost immediately, he considered this message too ambiguous, as many false sub sightings had been reported in the last few months.

At 0653, he again sent a coded message: "We have attacked, fired upon, and dropped depth charges upon submarine operating in defensive sea area." This second message was intended to alert the navy that *Ward* had actually seen and fired on a sub, not merely dropped charges on a suspected sonar contact. The message was received by the Bishop Point's radio station and relayed to the Fourteenth Naval District.

For the next thirty minutes, nothing came of it.

Far to the north at Opana Point, the SCR-270B mobile radar station crew reported a large formation of planes coming in from the north. Their report was also ignored. But Privates George Elliott and Joe Lockard had also detected the incoming Japanese attack.

Exactly one hour and two minutes after Outerbridge sent his report, Commander Mitsuo Fuchida ordered the torpedo planes to attack the battleships at Ford Island. However, first blood between the Japanese and the Americans had been drawn by the USS *Ward*.

The *Ward* remained on station even while the Japanese bombs and torpedoes wreaked havoc, death, panic, and horrendous damage on Oahu. When the Day of Infamy was over, she moved past the beached USS *Nevada* near Hospital Point and toward her berth west of Ford Island. The island's naval air station had been heavily bombed, while several cruisers had been put out of action by bombs and torpedoes. To the east of Ford, huge columns of black smoke rose into the blue Hawaiian sky over the remains of America's proud battle fleet. December 7 was a day none of her crew would ever forget. But it was only the beginning of the war for the USS *Ward*.

As to the submarine, it was one of five 78-foot Type A two-man midget submarines—known as *Ko Hyoteki*, meaning Scaly Dragon—launched off the southern coast between 1215 and 0333 hours. One

Type A two-man midget submarines, known as *Ko Hyoteki* meaning Scaly Dragon.
Official U.S. Navy Photo

of the submarines, *I-24*, carried an officer whose name would be well known to the United States Navy in late 1945. Lieutenant Commander Mochitsura Hashimoto would command the *I-58*, which would torpedo the cruiser USS *Indianapolis*.

The *I-20* launched the submarine piloted by Ensign Ikira Hiroho and Petty Officer Yoshio Kariyama. They were the closest to the restricted area. In 2002, it was found exactly where *Ward* reported the sinking. Underwater surveys found it fully loaded with two Type 97 torpedoes and a large hole in the conning tower.

Outerbridge only held his command for a few months, having been transferred to the Office of the Chief of Naval Transportation in the Pentagon. He was awarded the Navy Cross for his actions on December 7, 1941. In the spring of 1944, as a full commander, he was given a new destroyer, USS *O'Brien* (DD-725). The *Sumner*-class destroyer, built at Maine's Bath Iron Works, was launched in December 1943, had a thousand tons more displacement than *Ward*, and was 60 feet longer and 10 feet wider in beam. Her twin turbines drove her hull at 34 knots. *O'Brien* was ordered to the Atlantic for the D-Day landings at Normandy. Her close-inshore supporting gunfire was so accurate that the heavy German coastal guns shifted fire from the battleship USS *Texas* and concentrated on the destroyer. *O'Brien* was badly damaged by direct fire, but after repairs in England, she escorted a convoy back to Boston.

Back in the Pacific by late 1944, she joined the Third Fleet and, later, the Seventh Fleet during the Philippines Campaign. It was there that she and her skipper, Commander William W. Outerbridge, reached a crossroads in history.

In late 1942, *Ward* had been ordered to the West Coast for conversion to a high-speed transport. The navy wisely chose to use the outmoded "four-pipers" for a special role as fast delivery transports. By removing two boilers and the two forward funnels, the ship lost 10 knots of speed but was still capable of a healthy 25 knots. Seventeen of the *Wickes*-class destroyers were converted in this manner. The *Ward* was refitted to hold as many as two hundred troops, several tons of cargo, or even aviation fuel. In her new role as APD-16 in February 1943, *Ward* was sent to the central and western Pacific to carry out whatever assignments the area commander needed.

Her first assignment in April took her to the Solomon Islands, where she transported troops and other vital supplies, ran dispatches and orders, transported wounded, and carried out anti-submarine patrols. Her new guns, which included fast-firing 3-inch 40mm and 20mm anti-aircraft guns, helped to break up an air raid on Tulagi. For the rest of the year, she operated in the Solomons area. In 1944, *Ward* escorted troop transports and convoys on more than a dozen amphibious operations in the Marshalls, Carolines, and Marianas Islands. On October 17, *Ward* carried troops to Dinagat Island for the opening phase of the invasion of Leyte in the Philippines. The next assault was at Ormoc Bay in early December, where *Ward* carried infantry troops to the beach. During her patrols along the coast, a flight of kamikaze planes approached.

Ward was already at battle stations and began filling the air with hot shrapnel. But one of the A6M7 Zero fighters, carrying a 250-kilogram bomb, dived in and crashed into *Ward* amidships, tearing open fuel tanks and setting off ready ammunition at the Number 2 and 3 gun mounts. The fire quickly spread out of control. The destroyer division commander ordered assistance for *Ward* from another destroyer. But even with the added manpower and firefighting assistance, *Ward* was clearly beyond salvage. Her crew was ordered to abandon ship. They climbed into rafts and boats as the old ship wallowed and burned. *Ward* was to be sunk by naval gunfire. In the cold equation of war, she was now a hazard to navigation. After recovering *Ward*'s crew, the destroyer's gunners went to their battle stations. The guns were loaded and trained on the helpless derelict. Some of the gunners, officers, and deck crew may have felt a subliminal sadness at being forced to sink one of their own. The guns barked out as 5-inch shells streaked over the water and hammered the stout old ship. Waterspouts erupted at the waterline as foam and spray vomited from the holes torn in the old steel hull.

After a dozen hits, all firing ceased. The destroyer's officers and crew watched with muted sadness as the USS *Ward* rolled on her side and began to sink. Soon only a spreading cape of bubbles and floating debris was left to mark the grave. There were no memorials or monuments, no epitaphs that remembered her role in the first day of the war. Few of the men watching realized what ship they had just sunk. But one man certainly did.

The duty to sink a derelict ship and remove a hazard to navigation was nothing new. It had been done scores of times during the war. But few men were called upon to sink a ship that had particular personal significance. The man who gave the orders to fire on the USS *Ward* had once stood on her bridge, binoculars in hand, looking at the tiny black conning tower of a Japanese midget submarine. His order to fire had been the first American salvo of the Second World War. From the bridge of the USS *O'Brien*, Commander William W. Outerbridge sank his first command. The date was December 7, 1944, exactly three years to the day after *Ward* entered history.

The wreck of the *Ward* was discovered by the *R/V Petrel* in December 2017, almost exactly seventy-six years after her role in the Day of

Infamy. But there remains one artifact of significance. During the 1942 conversion, *Ward's* Mark 9 guns were removed. Today, the Number 3 gun that fired the shot that sank the midget sub and drew first blood in the Second World War is on display in the Minnesota State Capitol in St. Paul. Many of *Ward's* 1941 crew were members of the Minnesota Naval Reserve. So today, there is a much-deserved monument to the USS *Ward*.

Battleship Row alongside Ford Island in Pearl Harbor is probably one of Hawaii's most popular tourist attractions. Every year, millions of visitors take the excursion boats out to the USS *Arizona* Memorial at anchorage F7 to see the remains of the sunken and shattered battleship that exploded and sank on that fateful day in 1941.

It is a melancholy and compelling place. In a way, *Arizona* is one of only three ships from the Japanese attack that still exists. USS *Utah* is still overturned on the far side of the island. USS *Oklahoma* lies on the sea floor 150 miles northeast of Oahu, where she sank in a storm while being towed to the coast. The line of proud warships anchored at Ford Island that morning was the pride of the U.S. Pacific Fleet. When the attack was over, the battleships *Nevada, West Virginia, California,* and *Oklahoma* were on the bottom of the harbor. Others, like the *Pennsylvania, Maryland,* and *Tennessee,* were damaged. The men who served on those ships would never forget the harrowing hours of the attack and the aftermath. The next essay tells the stories of five men who survived the attack on Battleship Row.

On a personal note, all the men quoted in the next essay were friends. Nearly all are gone now, Stuart Hedley having passed in August 2021.

I will miss them, and the nation has lost some incredible men.

VISIONS OF BATTLESHIP ROW

Published in *World War II History*, December 2016

One of the defining images of the twentieth century is the horrifying moment when the battleship USS *Arizona* exploded in a cataclysmic fire-ball at 0810 on the morning of Sunday, December 7, 1941. The Japanese attack on Pearl Harbor catapulted the nation into the most destructive war in human history. Nearly every American then could remember where they were and what they were doing on the Day of Infamy.

But there were thousands of young men whose lives and destinies were forever changed in those hours as the Japanese planes tore into the heart of the U.S. Pacific Fleet.

Today, they are the dwindling number of men who served on the ships moored alongside Ford Island's famous Battleship Row. Old men now, they are white-haired with slow movements and shuffling feet, but their minds, filled with vivid visions of an apocalypse they never imagined, are as sharp as ever.

Here they all remember the first moments when a quiet Sunday morning turned into a roaring chaos of war.

On that peaceful Sunday morning, nearly the entire fleet was in port. The battleship *California* was moored far ahead of the paired *Maryland* and *Oklahoma*, *Tennessee* and *West Virginia*, *Arizona* and *Vestal*, and the lone *Nevada*. *Pennsylvania* was in dry dock at the Navy Yard near the destroyers *Cassin* and *Downes* and the minelayer *Oglala*. More destroyers and submarines were tied to piers past the Navy Yard. The anti-aircraft training and target ship *Utah* and cruisers *Helena*, *Honolulu*, *Detroit*, and *Raleigh* were on the west side of Ford Island. All in all, more than ninety vessels were in Pearl Harbor that morning.

Author's computer-generated image of Battleship Row on December 7, 1941. *Author's Collection*

At 0755, the roar of aircraft engines shattered the early morning air. The first attack by 183 bombers and fighters was carefully planned to close in from all directions in a deadly inescapable web of destruction.

Akagi's First VT Squadron's twelve Nakajima B5N "Kate" torpedo bombers, led by Lieutenant Commander Shigeharu Murata, swept in a turn from the southeast to line up on the oblivious ships of Battleship Row. Behind them were twelve more from *Kaga*. Sixteen Kates from *Hiryu* and *Soryu* came in from the southwest toward the west side of Ford Island. Each carried a 1,870-pound Type 91 torpedo, specially modified to run in the shallow waters of the harbor. They were also fitted with two warheads to defeat the battleships' armor belt.

Far overhead, thirty Kate level bombers from the *Akagi* and *Kaga* put their crosshairs on the scrubbed teak decks of America's vaunted battle fleet. Under the fuselage of the Kates were 1,700-pound Type 99 armor-piercing bombs modified from 16-inch naval shells. Lieutenant

Commander Kakuichi Takahashi's twenty-seven Aichi D3A1 dive bombers from *Shokaku* attacked the Ford Island Naval Air Station and Hickam
Army Airfield with 550-pound Type 98 general-purpose bombs.

Another twenty-seven dive bombers from *Zuikaku* went after Wheeler Air Field and Schofield Barracks. Forty-four Mitsubishi A6M Zeros
provided an air umbrella for the attacking bombers.

None of the American sailors, Marines, soldiers, or airmen knew
they were about to go to war. The repair ship USS *Vestal* (AR-4) was tied
up on *Arizona*'s port side. "We were there to do some work on her," said
Radioman John Murphy of Oxnard, California. "I was coming off my
watch but wanted something to do. The Officer of the Deck suggested I
go 'next door' to the *Arizona* and make a mail run. I had to wait for the
OOD to sign the weather report before I could go over. The sky was clear
and quiet. Nothing was happening."

The USS *Nevada* (BB-36) was tied up aft of the *Arizona*. Her band
was just finishing "Morning Colors" when the Kates bored in and released their torpedoes.

USS *Oklahoma* (BB-37) was outboard of USS *Maryland*. "I was going to go ashore on liberty and was in the shower," said Yeoman 1/c Ray
Richmond. "Suddenly it felt as if someone had picked up the ship, shook
it, and dropped it. I hit the overhead." Thinking of the army's habit of
dropping sandbags on ships for practice, he thought, "'Oh, those army
planes are dropping really big sandbags on us.' But then the ship shuddered again, and I heard the general alarm and bolted for the door. I was
naked as a jaybird, but I went to my battle station on Number 5 port
5-inch 51-caliber gun." Richmond felt the battleship start to heel over to
port from three torpedo hits. "Then the lights went out."

John Murphy was waiting on *Vestal*. "We saw these planes coming in
low," he recalled. "One man said, 'Why is the army practicing on Sunday
morning?' Then the bombs began falling. I ran to the radio room and got
to work. One of the first messages I picked up was 'Air Raid Pearl Harbor.
This isn't a drill!' No kidding, I thought."

Vestal, being alongside *Arizona*, took two hits. "One bomb hit the
crew's mess and the other scored a hit where we stored the steel plate. If

The printed message received by John Murphy on *Vestal. John Murphy Collection*

that steel hadn't been there, the armor-piercing bomb would have gone right through the bottom of the ship."

At berth F-6, astern of *Oklahoma* at the very center of Battleship Row, was USS *West Virginia* (BB-48). Known with affection as the "Wee Vee" by her crew, her distinctive cage masts and those of the USS *Tennessee* (BB-43) stood out clearly against the blue early morning sky.

In *West Virginia*'s Quartermaster berth was Seaman 1/c Stuart Hedley of West Palm Beach, Florida. He related what happened. "I was in my dress blues and looking forward to going ashore to a picnic. Then the P.A. called out, 'Away all fire and rescue crews!' Then the bugler, that would have been Marine Corporal Richard Fisk, blew the General Alarm. I ran up five decks to my quarters to grab my hat, and a Bos'n's Mate kicked me in the seat of the pants and yelled, 'Get to your battle stations on the double! This is the real thing!'"

Upon reaching the main deck, Hedley saw planes coming in from all directions. "I saw torpedo planes going over us, and the pilot was laughing like anything."

The *West Virginia* takes a torpedo hit, *Tennessee* inboard, is being bombed. *Official U.S. Navy Photo*

The 33,500-ton battleship was hit by seven torpedoes, causing the ship to heave as Hedley climbed the ladder into the bottom of the Number 3 turret, just aft of the superstructure. On top of the turret was a catapult and two Vought Kingfisher floatplanes. "I climbed into the turret," recalled Hedley. "I was at the pointer station of the port 16-inch gun while my friend Crosslin was at the gun trainer's seat. There was a bulkhead between us and the starboard gun compartment. A small hatch down near the deck was dogged down tight."

Aboard the *Tennessee*, seventeen-year-old Seaman 2/c Jack Evans of Corcoran, California, was on duty. "On Friday we had been told we would be getting an inspection by Rear Admiral Isaac Kidd on Monday. So we polished all the brightwork and locked the ammunition for the deck guns away. I had just finished my cleaning station and was in the uniform of the day: white shorts, black socks and shoes, white pullover and cap. I was standing in our living space in the forward battle dressing station when General Quarters sounded. One of my mates said, 'This is

Stuart Hedley of the *West Virginia* and Jack Evans of the *Tennessee*.

a helluva time for the ship to hold a drill in port on Sunday morning.' Then a Bos'n's Mate said, 'This is no drill!' When I reached the main deck I saw Ford Island totally wrecked. Zeros were strafing the planes and a hangar had its door hanging off. I could see we were in trouble."

Nevada's crew scattered to their battle stations when the bombs and torpedoes came in. Down in her crew's quarters was Woodrow "Woody" Derby of South Dakota. "I was in my bunk, reading. A few minutes before 0800, the alarm sounded. I went to my battle station in the magazines for the broadside guns. We were all down there and on alert. I couldn't see a damn thing."

Two of the battleship's boilers were still on line. At just after 0805, a Kate dropped a torpedo that struck her port side, causing some flooding. "I felt the ship shuddering from the guns up on deck," said Derby. "There was one big lurch and we looked around, but none of us knew we'd been hit by a torpedo."

Jack Evans climbed the ladder on the outside of *Tennessee's* foremast. "There were about eight of us in the foretop," he said. "The foretop was

Battleship Row under attack. Note cage masts on *West Virginia* and *Tennessee*.
Official U.S. Navy Photo

like a metal bucket with a roof and a waist-high metal shield. We were
about 122 feet off the water and could see everything. My job was to
report aircraft to the fire control center phone talker. I saw plenty," Evans
chuckled. "I looked north towards the center of the island and watched
the smoke rising from Wheeler Field and Schofield Barracks. To the east
past the *West Virginia* and *Oklahoma,* a really big column of smoke was
rising over Hickam. I saw this one plane with fixed landing gear fly right
over our bow. The man in the rear seat looked at me. If I'd had a potato
I could have hit him."

    Oklahoma was listing far over on her port side, and *West Virginia's*
entire port side was a mass of smoke and boiling water from the torpedo
hits. The Kates and Vals continued their deadly dance. *Nevada's* captain
ordered the engine room to prepare to get underway. He wanted to clear
the harbor and have room to maneuver.

    In *Vestal's* radio room, John Murphy was busy intercepting and pass-
ing on the scores of frantic radio messages filling the airways. "Another
man came in and slammed the hatchway shut and dogged it tight. It was
on the side facing the *Arizona.*"

Arizona had been hit with one bomb on her aft deck, but worse was yet to come.

The pilot of a Kate bomber, flying at 12,000 feet, dropped an 800-kilogram armor-piercing bomb on *Arizona*'s starboard forecastle. What happened next was seen by virtually everybody in the area. The bomb impacted just forward of the second turret and plunged through several decks down to the space between Number 1 and Number 2 powder handling rooms. The delayed blast ignited propellant for the forward guns in an incandescent detonation that tore the heavy armored steel of the proud ship like tissue paper as it blew out her bottom.

Jack Evans was still in his lofty perch 120 feet over the water. "I was looking forward when the *Arizona* blew up. I hung on because the explosion made the mast whip back and forth in the hot blast, and I thought it would snap. When I looked back, the *Arizona* had been lifted about twenty feet out of the water. Then her keel broke in two and she sank."

A wave of water lifted *Tennessee*'s aft end several feet as an inferno of burning fuel oil enveloped her stern.

Vestal's John Murphy said, "Suddenly there was a huge roar outside, and our ship rolled way over. It sounded like the whole world had gone up. If that hatch hadn't been dogged down, everybody in the radio room would have been killed."

In *West Virginia*'s Number 3 turret, Hedley and Crosslin were listening to the sounds of battle. "Crosslin said, 'Stu, let's see what's happening out there,' and pulled the sight cap off the periscope. We both looked out and BAM! there went the *Arizona*. Over thirty bodies flew through the air. It was terrible to watch."

USS *Arizona* had turned into a twisted, blazing funeral pyre for 1,177 officers and men, including the division commander, Admiral Isaac Kidd.

Another bomb fell toward Hedley's turret. "It hit the wing of the OS2U floatplane on the catapult over the starboard gun. The admiral's plane next to it was blasted off the turret. The bomb came right through the five inches of steel into the starboard gun compartment. It didn't explode, but it hit the recoil cylinder on top of the gun. The burning fuel from the plane ignited the glycerin in the cylinder in a flash fire and killed eleven men."

The hatch between the two 16-inch guns was torn loose and flew past Hedley and Crosslin, slamming into the port bulkhead. "The blast threw us back eight feet into the elevating screw. Crosslin said, 'Stu, let's get the hell out of here!'"

By this time, *West Virginia* was listing at least 15 degrees to port. "We were on the port quarterdeck, and the water was up to my knees. We saw the *Oklahoma* capsize, and I was sure we were going to roll over."

Damage control officer Lieutenant C.V. Ricketts ordered the starboard voids between the battleship's armor belt and hull flooded. This saved the *West Virginia* from the fate of the *Oklahoma*.

She settled into the mud of the harbor bottom.

Jack Evans watched as a bomb struck the corner of *Tennessee*'s Number 2 turret. Splinters from the blast mortally wounded Captain Mervyn Bennion of the *West Virginia* as he directed the battle from his ship's flying bridge. Bennion died in the arms of Captain's Orderly Doris Miller, who would later be awarded the Navy Cross for heroism in defending the ship. Bennion's last words were, "Abandon ship!" He posthumously received the Medal of Honor.

Tennessee was hit again. "Another bomb hit Number 3 turret just at the hole where the gun comes through and killed about four men."

Meanwhile, Ray Richmond and his crewmates were struggling to climb out of the black prison of the *Oklahoma*, lying on her port side. She had initially been hit by three torpedoes, and two more struck as she rolled over. "I was feeling my way along in the dark and finally reached a room with a deck hatch," he said. "Sailors were being pulled up by hands reaching down through the hatch. I looked up and realized they were of Commander Kenworthy, the captain, and the executive officer Lieutenant Commander Hubbard. But I was too short to reach them, and they suggested I go out through the casemate of the nearest 5-inch gun."

Richmond found himself looking down at the water, twenty feet below. "The water between us and the *Maryland* was burning, filled with
bodies and swimming men. The *Oklahoma* was almost upside-down."
Richmond realized he would have to jump far out to clear the armor
blister at the waterline. He jumped as far as he could but hit hard on
his lower back against the riveted steel. "I felt a shock of intense pain. I
couldn't feel my legs and I had to use my arms to scoot down the hull. It
was like thick metal shingles," he recalled. "Then I slid into the oily water
and ducked under." The *Maryland* was about fifty feet from *Oklahoma*.
"As I swam I pushed bodies away from me, and when I came up for air, I
had to use my hands to clear a space of oil so I could get my head out and
breathe." More than four hundred men were trapped in *Oklahoma's* hull.
Richmond finally reached a rope ladder on the side of the battleship.
"There were a bunch of men trying to get up that ladder, and they kept
using my head for a step."

Near exhaustion, the sailor almost didn't make it onto the *Maryland's*
deck. "Then a man reached down and pulled me up by my hair."

Vestal's commander, Captain Cassin Young, had been blown over the
side into the water when the *Arizona* exploded. His executive officer, suddenly in nominal command, assessed the situation. The ship had taken
two bomb hits and was right up against the burning battleship. The water was on fire and hundreds of men were dead or dying. He ordered the
crew to abandon ship. John Murphy said, "Captain Young managed to
climb back up a ladder to the deck. He countermanded the abandon ship
order and got us underway and beached us on Area Landing."

On the *West Virginia*, Hedley and Crosslin reached the starboard rail
and looked at the spreading film of burning oil in the water between
themselves and the *Tennessee*. "We were going to shimmy over on one of
the hawsers like the other boys were doing," he said. "But then a Zero
flew right between the Wee Vee and the *Tennessee*, machine-gunning the
boys out on the hawsers."

Hedley spotted the extended barrel of one of the 5-inch guns. "I
asked Crosslin, 'Have you ever run down a railroad rail? You see those

5-inch guns? We're going to run across those barrels and jump down on the *Tennessee.*' So we did. When we got there, we were told to get to the beach. 'How?' I asked a chief petty officer. 'Swim, you idiot!' We stripped down and jumped into the water and swam underwater to the beach of Ford Island. Every time I came up to breathe, I inhaled hot, burning air."

At 0845, the second wave of bombers came in. Seventy Val dive bombers from *Akagi, Kaga, Hiryu,* and *Soryu* had been ordered to hit the American carriers but, with none in port, concentrated their bombs on the remaining ships around Ford Island and the navy base. Twenty-seven Kates led by Lieutenant Commander Shigekazu Shimazaki from *Shokaku* hit Kaneohe Bay Naval Air Station on the east end of Oahu. *Zuikaku's* Kates, under Lieutenant Commander Ichihara, returned to Hickam, Bellows Field, and Ewa Marine Air Station. "The dive bombers came in and put fourteen bombs in the water on *Tennessee's* starboard side," Evans said. "The Japs didn't hit the ship at all. But the bombs killed a lot of swimming men and destroyed all the ship's boats."

Nevada was underway and steering her way past the burning hulk of the *Arizona,* the sunken *West Virginia,* and the capsized *Oklahoma.*
Evans watched *Nevada* go by from *Tennessee's* foretop. "The only big ship moving was the *Nevada.* She was low in the water, and the bombers went after her."

The Vals of the second wave went after *Nevada.* Derby continued, "We were hit by three more bombs as we moved down towards the harbor mouth. I went on deck shortly after we got moving and just thought, 'Oh my god!' I was stunned about all those burning ships. The water was on fire, and the *Arizona* was just a big tower of fire and smoke. We were going to beach her at Hospital Point, but I guess it was not a good place to be, so the harbor tugs pulled us over to the opposite bank, and we settled into the shallow water."

After his escape from the *Oklahoma,* Ray Richmond got some clothing and then helped out at an anti-aircraft gun. He fought alongside them for two hours. "When it was all over, I collapsed in pain," he said. "I didn't learn until later that my back was broken."

Jack Evans also didn't escape the attack unharmed. "I didn't realize some fragments from that first bomb on turret Number 2 had hit my legs until after the attack was over," he said. "One of my buddies said, 'Hey Jack, you're hit.' I looked down and saw four tracks of dried blood running down both legs. I didn't want the Purple Heart, but I got it."

Stu Hedley went to the infirmary on Ford Island, and after being given clean clothes, began helping to care for wounded men.

By 0945, it was all over. The attackers headed back to their carriers and returned to Japan. In their wake, they left six battleships on the bottom, three more damaged, and several sunken and damaged cruisers, destroyers, and support ships. Hundreds of army, navy, and Marine Corps aircraft were burning on the runways across Oahu. And 3,690 Americans were dead. Over the next several days, holes were cut into the hull of the capsized *Oklahoma* to free 32 trapped sailors. Of her 1,398 officers and crew, 429 died. The hospitals were choked with the wounded and dying.

The sunken *California, Nevada, West Virginia, Cassin, Downes,* and *Oglala* were all salvaged, repaired, and returned to service. So were the damaged *Tennessee, Maryland, Pennsylvania, Helena, Raleigh, Honolulu, Detroit,* and many others. Only the *Arizona, Oklahoma,* and *Utah* were beyond salvage.

At first it appeared to be a decisive and crushing Japanese victory. In fact, the attack on Pearl Harbor was the biggest mistake the Japanese made in the war. They failed to destroy the dry docks, repair facilities, and fuel storage tanks. No American carriers were in port on December 7. The submarine base received only moderate damage. So the navy, long committed to a war of big guns against big guns, was forced to use the ships left to it—aircraft carriers and submarines. It was these ships that proved to be the most influential in the defeat of the Japanese Empire.

John Murphy remained on the *Vestal* during the Solomons, Gilberts, and Marshall Islands Campaigns until the summer of 1944, then went on to Anti-Submarine Warfare School.

Jack Evans served in the Pacific until ordered to do navy pilot training and later worked in the Pentagon under Admiral Arleigh Burke. He flew as a pilot for thirty years and retired as a full captain.

Oklahoma's Ray Richmond spent the next year in a body cast, learning to walk again. A gifted artist, he was sent to the Navy Recruiting Office in New York, where he created several posters and designed the famous "Sea Bee" emblem for the navy's construction battalions.

Woody Derby was still on the *Nevada* when the battleship was shelling Utah Beach in preparation for the Invasion of Normandy.

Stu Hedley was serving on the destroyer USS *Massey* (DD-778) when the Japanese surrendered in Tokyo Bay. He later became the chaplain of the Pearl Harbor Survivors Association. "You know what?" he asked. "Anchored in Tokyo Bay right by the USS *Missouri*, where the surrender documents were signed, was my ship, the *West Virginia*. She was almost the first American battleship to be sunk at Pearl Harbor, but she went on to be there for the end. I felt great knowing the Wee Vee was there. They didn't manage to sink her after all."

Pearl Harbor brought the United States into war with Japan but also Germany. Adolf Hitler rashly declared war on America four days after the

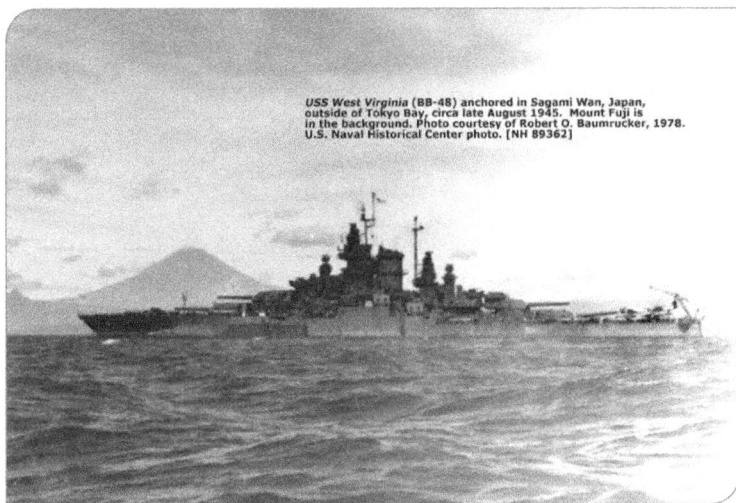

USS *West Virginia* (BB-48) anchored in Sagami Wan, Japan, outside of Tokyo Bay, circa late August 1945. Mount Fuji is in the background. Photo courtesy of Robert O. Baumrucker, 1978. U.S. Naval Historical Center photo. [NH 89362]

The "Wee Vee" in Tokyo Bay, September 2, 1945. *Official U.S. Navy Photo*

Japanese attack. He did this when his eastern armies were facing the bulk of Josef Stalin's Red Army and a Russian winter. At sea, Grossadmiral Erich Raeder's fast ships prowled the seas to attack Allied shipping. While his naval architects designed excellent ships, they were at risk from the new technologies of radar and long-range aircraft. The next essay tells the story of the Panzerschiffs—the newest class of surface raiders.

RAEDER'S RAIDERS: THE PANZERSCHIFFEN

A week before Hitler's attack on Poland, Germany was already preparing to initiate Grand Admiral Erich Raeder's Plan Z, the daring surface campaign to destroy Britain's military and commercial sea trade. Two ships, *Admiral Graf Spee* and *Deutschland*, were the vanguard of what Raeder hoped would eventually be dozens of fast and potent cruisers and battleships that would disrupt and destroy the Allies' sea lanes and starve England into surrender.

At the war's outset, Britain possessed about two thousand merchant ships and another thousand coastal vessels of less than 2,000 tons each. This added up to around four million tons of cargo capacity. Another three million tons came from countries conquered by Germany, while a further million tons were being launched each year. Great Britain required an annual fifty-five million imported tons of food, oil, cotton, wool, and other industrial products. Raeder aimed to sink more tonnage than Britain could replace and force capitulation. In essence, his raiders had to sink ships faster than Britain could replace them. As events proved, Raeder was doomed to fail before he even began.

Erich Raeder, who had risen to command the Kriegsmarine after a career that went back to being a junior officer aboard Kaiser Wilhelm II's yacht *Hohenzollern,* to the post of Chief of Staff for Admiral Franz von Hipper's battle cruiser force in the Great War, was a strong advocate of fast surface commerce raiders. They had proved successful during the war, even if their impact on the outcome was negligible. The most successful surface raider was the light cruiser SMS *Emden.* In three months in the Indian Ocean, *Emden* sank two Allied warships and captured or

sank sixteen merchant vessels totaling 70,000 tons. *Emden* undoubtedly inspired Raeder's vision of fast raiders running wild through Allied
shipping. But he failed to give much credibility to the U-boat campaign
of the First World War. Although U-boats were often hampered by the
diplomatic need to appease neutral nations who violently opposed unrestricted submarine warfare, in 51 months, U-boats sank 5,282 British,
Allied, and neutral merchant ships, totaling more than 11,000,000 tons.

Ignoring this persuasive statistic, Raeder convinced Adolf Hitler that
a surface fleet was essential to victory at sea. In January 1939, he proposed his Z Plan, envisioning a fleet of battleships, heavy cruisers, and
aircraft carriers that would roam and dominate the seas by 1948. Hitler
promised his fleet commander that there would be no war until at least
1943, giving Raeder a healthy margin of time to carry out his grand
building program.

But in the summer of 1939, Raeder learned of the planned invasion
of Poland. Even though there was little doubt that Britain would quickly
become involved, Hitler forged ahead, disrupting Raeder's carefully laid
plans to build a large surface fleet. Faced with a *fait accompli*, Raeder used
what few large surface warships he possessed to support Hitler's grand
campaigns.

But he was more a tactician than a strategist, a remnant of his time
with the battle cruisers under Hipper. He never developed a broad strategy, instead using his meager force in hit-and-run raids and attacks. Ad-
ditionally, Raeder gave little thought to U-boats as a viable means of
cutting the Allied sea lanes. But his greatest blunder was that he failed to
recognize the nearly two decades of advances in aviation, marine technology, and radar that made a surface fleet more of a target than a threat.
His shortsighted dogmas condemned the Kriegsmarine to defeat.

Erich Raeder was not only up against the powerful Royal Navy but
also the former First Lord of the Admiralty and Prime Minister Winston
Churchill, whose devotion to the navy was close to reverence. Churchill
gave the navy all the support it needed to ensure Britain's survival.

The last thing Churchill and the Admiralty wanted was for the distinctive shape of a huge German battleship to come out of the misty
horizon and open fire with its heavy guns on a helpless convoy of tankers

and transports. A salvo of heavy 8-inch or 11-inch high-explosive shells screaming out of the sky like angels of death could be devastating. The thin-skinned merchant ships could sink in minutes, leaving their crews to die in the freezing sea. Germany's powerful ships would be wolves in the fold, unstoppable and deadly.

Raeder lacked the strength and time to contribute significantly to the Third Reich's war aims, but he doggedly followed a radically shrunken version of his original raiding plan. His only advantage was that the Royal Navy was largely equipped with vessels launched during or shortly after the Great War. They were mostly older, slower battleships and battle cruisers with a leavening of light cruisers and destroyers.

However, Raeder's ships were all new, having been launched since 1931 and fitted with the latest naval technology and engines. They were, for the most part, fast, heavily armed, and armored equal to their larger British counterparts. But there were too few of them.

The numbers leave little doubt as to the inevitable outcome. Even in the shadow of its former glory, the British Home Fleet consisted of seven battleships, two battle cruisers, four aircraft carriers, twenty-one cruisers, more than fifty destroyers, and twenty submarines. The navies of Canada, New Zealand, and Australia added their own strength to this armada. Against this, Raeder never had more than ten powerful warships. Three were the so-called "pocket battleships": *Deutschland, Admiral Graf Spee,* and *Admiral Scheer.* In Germany, they were officially called *"Panzerschiffen,"* or "armored ships." They carried two triple turrets with six 11-inch guns. They were registered as 10,000 tons each but actually displaced over 12,000 tons. Three 14,500-ton *Admiral Hipper*-class cruisers—the *Hipper, Blucher,* and *Prinz Eugen*—each carried eight 8-inch guns in four turrets. Formidable in themselves, they were soon superseded by two larger vessels called heavy cruisers but were, in fact, battleships. *Scharnhorst* and *Gneisenau* were launched in 1936. They each carried nine 11-inch guns in three turrets. While officially registered as displacing 19,000 tons, their gross tonnage was closer to 32,000. This made them larger than any German warship ever constructed up to that time, but Raeder was not finished. His planned armada was only partially complete.

The zenith of Raeder's raider fleet was the huge new battleships *Bismarck* and *Tirpitz*, each of more than 50,000 tons and carrying eight 15-inch guns in four turrets. Launched in 1939 and 1940, the sisters were the largest and most heavily armed and armored warships ever built in Germany. But their very size and power made them the focus of the Royal Navy's attention even before they completed their sea trials. They were also the last capital ships ever built in Germany during the war.

In August 1939, Raeder initiated Plan Z by sending *Graf Spee* and *Deutschland* out to sea.

Since the saga of *Graf Spee* has already been related in detail, we will move on to her sister ship, *Deutschland*, which had a longer but far less successful career. Commanded by Captain Paul Veneker, *Deutschland* operated off southern Greenland and Nova Scotia to interdict British shipping. At first she was moderately successful, taking two ships, but then Veneker made an error that caused great embarrassment to the

The Panzerschiff *Deutschland* before being renamed *Lutzow* in 1939.

Third Reich—he captured the American steamer *City of Flint* less than twelve hundred miles from New York.

The ship was seized and the American crew taken prisoner. Evading prowling British warships, Veneker headed for Norway. This was a further outrage, as both America and Norway were still neutral. The United States sent a flood of protests to the Nazi government. Veneker tried to go to Murmansk, but the Soviets, still neutral, refused entry. This meant that *Deutschland* and her crew were, in effect, pirates and kidnappers. Returning to Norway, the *Deutschland* was boarded by Norwegian officials, and the Americans were set free. *Deutschland* returned to Germany for refit. To avoid any connection with the highly embarrassing incident, the ship was renamed *Lutzow*. This was the name of Admiral Franz Hipper's flagship in the Great War. The *Lutzow* was heavily damaged by gunfire and torpedoes during the invasion of Norway the following year and towed back to Germany. Her luck failed to improve when the ship was again torpedoed by a Bristol Beaufort of RAF Coastal Command in June 1941, a month after *Bismarck* was sunk. Repaired, the ship then went aground off the coast of Norway, thus missing the famous July 1942 attack that scattered convoy PQ-17. By 1944, *Lutzow* née *Deutschland* was supporting German troops retreating from the advancing Soviets on the Baltic coast. Then a RAF Lancaster bomber dropped a 12,000-pound Tallboy bomb on the deck, doing great internal damage. Repaired yet again, her ignominious career was ended when she was deliberately blown up four days after Hitler committed suicide.

Yet as ineffective as *Deutschland's* raids had been, she had managed to stretch the Royal Navy's assets to the breaking point. Dozens of cruisers and battleships were detailed to protect the convoys from German raids, both making things easier for Raeder's plans but also rendering his goals virtually impossible.

Worse was in store for Raeder's reputation. In November 1939, even before *Graf Spee's* death ride, the battleships *Scharnhorst* and *Gneisenau* found the armed merchant cruiser HMS *Rawalpindi* in the region between the Faroe Islands and the Denmark Strait. A small P & O liner of 16,700 tons, she was fitted with eight 6-inch and two 3-inch guns.

Under the command of Royal Navy Captain E.C. Kennedy, the *Rawal-pindi* savagely attacked the two German battleships. Even while the small liner sank from dozens of heavy shell hits, her guns continued to fire. The action forced the two German raiders to leave the area before a heavier Royal Navy force arrived.

Almost exactly a year later, another converted liner, the 14,000-ton SS *Jervis Bay* under Commander Edward Fegen, was escorting Convoy HX-84 from Bermuda to Britain. The *Admiral Scheer* found the convoy off the coast of Iceland, and Fegen charged at the German ship with her seven 6-inch and three 3-inch guns. *Jervis Bay* was sunk in twenty minutes. Fegen earned a posthumous Victoria Cross. The convoy escaped without loss.

Despite some victories, Raeder could not ignore that the German surface raiders needed fuel, ammunition, replacement parts, food, and other supplies as they roamed far and wide in their hunt for Allied ships. Tankers and freighters had to be stationed in neutral or friendly ports. The raiders could patrol no farther than a few thousand miles from a support vessel, limiting their range and effectiveness. Raeder recognized that it would become increasingly difficult for any raiders to evade the Royal Navy and patrol aircraft.

The other factor was geographical. Germany has only one coastline in the Baltic and North Seas. The major ports on the two seas were connected by the Kiel Canal, built in 1895 and expanded in 1913 to allow rapid deployment of ships, avoiding the long and often treacherous route around Denmark. But the fact was, Germany could only deploy any ships by passing England either via the North Sea or through the Channel. Raeder began to urge Hitler to invade Norway. This would provide dozens of fjords and harbors far up the North Sea from which to send his ships out to the Atlantic. Hitler, who had always considered the Norwegians a racially kindred nation with Germany and saw both strategic and tactical advantages to taking Norway, agreed. Raeder's ships and transports were used extensively in the campaign, which began in April 1940.

The heavy cruiser *Admiral Hipper* and four destroyers were escorting seventeen hundred troops to Trondheim when they were spotted and

attacked by the British destroyer HMS *Glowworm*. *Hipper's* captain first
fired on the *Glowworm* and then attempted to ram it, but the British ship
turned the tables by ramming the larger ship, tearing a 100-foot rent in the
hull. While *Glowworm* later exploded, *Hipper* needed extensive repairs.

Another invasion unit consisting of the newly named *Lutzow* and the
Hipper's sister, *Blucher*, were accompanied by the light cruiser *Emden*,
the namesake of the famous raider of World War One. They headed for
Oslo, which was guarded by forty-year-old 11-inch guns purchased by
the Norwegians from Krupp to defend the city. When the German ships
were almost near enough to "see the whites of their eyes," the heavy guns
began firing. *Blucher* was so heavily damaged that she was easily finished
off with torpedoes. More than a thousand German seamen went down
with her. As mentioned, *Lutzow* had also been damaged but escaped. The
big German surface ships had not played a major role in the Norwegian
campaign.

The Royal Navy sent the carriers HMS *Ark Royal* and HMS *Glorious*, which had recently arrived from the Mediterranean, to support the
defense of Norway. They were to recover the remaining RAF fighters and
bombers now stranded in Norway. The captain of the *Glorious*, a veteran
of the First World War, failed to have an air patrol watching for any attack as his ship landed the precious fighters and bombers. Then, vectored
in by Luftwaffe reconnaissance planes, the battleships *Scharnhorst* and
Gneisenau raced in and began firing their eighteen 11-inch guns at the
helpless carrier. Even with a smokescreen laid down by the escorting British destroyers, *Glorious* went to the bottom an hour later. This was the
only significant warship, other than HMS *Hood* the following year, to be
sunk by German surface raiders.

With the fall of Norway in June 1940, Raeder had his North Sea
sanctuaries for the raider fleet. Germany now controlled more than three
thousand miles of coastline from northern Norway to the Bay of Biscay,
ten times more coastline than before the war.

In the spring of 1941, Raeder examined the tonnage of ships sunk
by his raiders. *Graf Spee* had sunk sixteen ships, totaling 50,000 tons.
The *Admiral Sheer* did better in the less heavily patrolled Indian Ocean,

sinking seventeen ships totaling over 113,000 tons before sneaking back to Germany. *Scharnhorst* and *Gneisenau* managed to send 122,000 tons of ships to the bottom before being forced to run for a safe base in France. The totals were not nearly as high as Raeder had promised Hitler.

And things were only going to get worse. Using Radio Direction Finding (RDF) and brilliant cryptanalysis, the British Admiralty tracked the raiders with ever-increasing skill. Long-range patrol aircraft, such as the American-built PBY Catalina and its Canadian-built counterpart, the Canso, were scouring the Atlantic Ocean over the convoy routes. Added to this must be the work at Bletchley Park, where the German radio traffic was analyzed and distributed to the fleet. The Royal Navy could deduce the location and operational orders for Raeder's ships. Every tanker and supply ship that was found and sunk further limited Raeder's ability to find and attack the convoys. But his delusion that his few remaining ships could still do what he had envisioned in 1939 refused to die.

Raeder sent word to the newly operational *Bismarck* in April 1941 that she and her escort, the heavy cruiser *Prinz Eugen*, should move out of southern Norway and head to the Atlantic. His ultimate plan was to have the two ships join with the newer *Tirpitz* and the sisters *Scharnhorst* and *Gneisenau* to break into the Atlantic and hit the big convoys. His theory was that the two biggest warships could temporarily control and extend regions of the North Atlantic with their speed and heavy guns. *Bismarck*, the most dangerous, was to fight and distract the Royal Navy escort ships while the other German raiders sank the helpless merchant ships. Raeder's grand plan was never to materialize. *Tirpitz* was not yet fully operational, *Scharnhorst* was having her engines overhauled, and *Gneisenau* had been torpedoed in the harbor at Brest, France. All Raeder had left were the *Bismarck* and *Prinz Eugen*. No destroyer escorts could accompany them on their sortie as their range was too limited. There were no aircraft to provide long-range air cover. The Focke-Wulf Condor reconnaissance planes were hunting convoys for the U-boats and were not combat aircraft in any case. In addition, the Kriegsmarine and Luftwaffe were always at odds to curry Hitler's favor, and the bombastic Goering refused to provide any medium bombers to cover the raiders.

Raeder had little choice. The British convoys carried the weapons and troops for the invasion of Crete in the Mediterranean. They had to be destroyed or disrupted. This was pure folly on Raeder's part. The Royal Navy was well aware of *Bismarck*'s location and closely watching her. Norwegians, resisting their conquerors, reported any movement of German warships and planes to their British allies. With some justification in light of the *Rawalpindi* and *Jervis Bay*, Raeder assumed that the Royal Navy was defending convoys with as few as one warship or converted liner.

Yet the Royal Navy was more than willing to strip protection from other convoys to provide extra firepower to destroy *Bismarck*. In all, the British force consisted of six battleships, four battle cruisers, two carriers, thirteen cruisers, thirty-three destroyers, and dozens of patrol aircraft. This was, in fact, the largest force ever tasked with destroying a single ship.

Even without the additional support of three other large warships, the *Bismarck* was to sail in mid-May and wreak havoc on the convoys no matter what.

There is little need to detail the chase and sinking of *Bismarck* as it has been covered many times over the last seventy years. But it serves as an excellent example of bad planning, bad leadership, and bad judgment by both Raeder and the fleet commander, Admiral Günther Lütjens, who commanded *Bismarck* and *Prinz Eugen* on their ill-fated attempt to break out to the Atlantic. Lütjens made some poor decisions that not only sealed *Bismarck*'s fate but condemned nearly his entire crew to death without any hope of success.

By the summer of 1941, *Scharnhorst*, *Gneisenau*, *Admiral Scheer*, and *Admiral Hipper* were all being repaired or under constant air attack. They could not find a way to escape their French and Baltic Sea prisons. Then there was the last big raider, the *Tirpitz*. She was what Raeder called a "fleet in being," an Alfred Mahan-coined term for a single powerful ship dominating an entire region. That might have had some validity at the start of the war, but by late 1942, it was pure madness. But *Tirpitz*'s fearsome presence reaped some unexpected benefits for Raeder. When the

Soviet Union joined the Allied cause, Churchill promised Josef Stalin that he would begin sending convoys carrying vital war materiel to the arctic ports of Murmansk and Arkhangel. By the end of 1941, the first of these, designated PQ and JW, made it through to their destinations unscathed, but soon the Kriegsmarine would take action. More surface raiders and U-boats were sent to northern Norway, and long-range Condor planes were sent out to find convoys. Then the Royal Navy received word that the *Tirpitz*, the pocket battleship *Admiral Scheer*, and the cruiser *Prinz Eugen* were being sent to Norway. This was ominous news, as they could only have one objective: the Murmansk convoys.

Prinz Eugen was spotted and torpedoed, forcing her into a port for repairs.

In March 1942, *Tirpitz* was sent out to interdict PQ-12, but bad weather made finding the convoy impossible. The battleship returned to the safety of the Norwegian fjord. The Royal Navy conducted several air raids against the ship, but none could get close due to heavy anti-aircraft fire.

Convoy PQ-17 was assembled in Iceland. It consisted of thirty-five merchant ships, twenty-two of which were American. Their cargo was composed of hundreds of tanks, aircraft, and trucks, as well as fuel, ammunition, and supplies badly needed by the hard-pressed Red Army in its desperate battle to stop the German Army. The escort was six destroyers and a covering force of four cruisers, two British and two American. Three Royal Navy battleships were sent out in case *Tirpitz* emerged from her Norwegian redoubt.

On June 27, PQ-17 set a course into the Arctic Ocean, well aware of the threat that could come from the many fjords and harbors along the enemy coast. A Condor spotted the convoy on July 1, and the U-boats closed in to sink two ships. Then the Admiralty received word via Bletchley Park that *Tirpitz* was refueling in a northern Norway port. This could only mean one thing: She was going to attack PQ-17.

There was no way for the heavy battleships of the Royal Navy to get there in time to stop a bloodbath. Near panic ensued, and, in a series of badly conceived orders, the covering cruiser force was to head west, and the convoy was to scatter, each ship to make a run for Murmansk on its own. The last transmission from the convoy escort commander was, "Sorry to leave you like this. Good luck. Looks like bloody business." Convoy PQ-17 was now at the mercy of Doenitz's U-boats and the Luftwaffe. Day after day, they charged in with a savage fury. By the time the remains of PQ-17 reached Murmansk, only eleven of the original thirty-five ships were left. It was a costly debacle. It was also the German Navy's greatest single victory against an Allied convoy. The truth was, *Tirpitz* had never intended to attack the convoy but merely fuel and shift its berth. The scattering of PQ-17 served to show how much the Admiralty feared the power of heavy guns on a convoy. Yet neither *Tirpitz* nor any other surface raiders fired a single shot at the unprotected ships.

The turning point in the debate over the effectiveness of U-boats versus surface raiders was decided in favor of the former at the end of 1942. Early on, at Hitler's insistence, Raeder issued standing orders for the raider fleet. It stated that they engage at whatever cost, as long as they did not endanger or lose their ships. Even a casual reading of this order reveals its obvious contradiction. It ultimately led to Raeder's fall from power.

In December 1942, *Hipper*, *Lutzow*, and six destroyers left Norway to attack convoy JW-51B. The convoy consisted of fifteen ships moving through the Arctic Ocean to Kola. The force was heavily escorted by seven destroyers and two light cruisers in support. There were corvettes and air support from Murmansk at the ready. When the German ships hove into view on December 31, they attacked the outer escort screen, sinking one minesweeper and a destroyer. But it was apparent that many more British warships were coming, and further reinforcements had been called in. The German commander broke off the action. Raeder's order also made it plain that they were to disengage if the German force was confronted with ships of equal strength. Not one freighter had been sunk. Worse, *Hipper* received three hits from 8-inch shells. The BBC announced the incident, and Adolf Hitler, never one to accept or recognize his culpability, went into a rage and ordered all the remaining surface raiders scrapped, their guns turned into coastal fortifications, and their crews transferred to the U-boat fleet. In light of how poorly the surface raiders had served the Third Reich so far, this might have been a good tactical move. Raeder resigned on January 30, 1943. The new Grand Admiral of the fleet was Karl Doenitz. The U-boats finally had the high command's full support.

As for *Tirpitz*, she remained under heavy air and shore protection in Trondheim throughout much of the war, subjected to numerous and costly air attacks by Royal Navy torpedo planes and land-based bombers. The only time *Tirpitz*, the last and most powerful battleship in the Kriegsmarine, ever fired her guns at the enemy was a shore bombardment of a British weather station on the island of Spitzbergen in September 1943. Fuel shortages prevented her from further sorties, and the ship spent months sheltered in anti-aircraft and anti-torpedo defenses. More Royal Navy torpedo planes and land-based bombers attacked the *Tirpitz* through the summer and fall of 1944. The end finally came in November 1944 when Avro Lancasters of No. 617 Squadron, the same group that had bombed the Ruhr Valley dams in March 1943, attacked *Tirpitz* with heavy 12,000-pound Tallboy bombs. Even though most bombs missed, there were enough hits to ensure that the last German battleship would never leave port. In the end, the mighty *Tirpitz* rolled over and sank in Tromsø, Norway. No more surface raiders ever emerged from the Baltic or North Sea to threaten Allied shipping lanes.

After February 1943, the U-boats were the primary German naval weapon of the war. Altogether, U-boats sank 2,779 ships for a total of 14.1 million tons, or seventy percent of all allied shipping losses in all theatres of the war. The most successful year was 1942 when over six million tons of shipping were sunk in the Atlantic.

As for the surface raiders, the total tonnage sunk by their guns was just short of 800,000. Considering the expense and the number of men needed to operate them, the results were dismal. The irony is that Raeder, who oversaw all new construction, was undoubtedly aware that for the cost, materials, and manpower of building just one battleship like the *Bismarck*, the Kriegsmarine could have launched at least ten U-boats. If Raeder had turned the navy's efforts to constructing submarines as far back as 1935, there could have been as many as a hundred more U-boats manned and in service by 1940. Churchill had openly stated that the thing that most frightened him during the war was the U-boat menace. Fortunately for the Allies, Raeder followed his own doomed plan. Of all the German surface raiders put to sea in World War II, only one survived the war. The heavy cruiser *Prinz Eugen*, whose sole claim to fame was to accompany *Bismarck* on part of her death ride, was captured by the Allies and ended up in the Pacific. *Prinz Eugen* was made into a test ship in the Operation Crossroads atomic bomb tests at Bikini Atoll in July 1946. While *Prinz Eugen* survived two atomic bomb blasts, the sturdy cruiser was so totally irradiated that she had to be towed to Kwajalein and left as a derelict. She later turned over and sank. Her stern is still visible today. Thus was the final blow to Admiral Erich Raeder's raiders.

The next essay is more of an opinion piece, focusing on the third revolution in naval warfare. The parallel development of the submarine and aircraft carrier in the first three decades of the twentieth century set the stage for naval warfare for the rest of the century and beyond. Curiously, both concepts were beyond the pale to most traditional naval officers in Europe, the United States, and Japan. But the early prototypes of the sub and carrier showed enough promise that they soon found their way into their respective navies. Few nations, other than Germany, knew how to utilize the submarine, and only Japan led the world in the use of the aircraft carrier. As is often the case, the navy that led the way in the early years found itself unable to keep up when it counted the most.

THE THIRD REVOLUTION

There is little disagreement that the convoy system and the development of effective anti-submarine technology was the most important element in the Allied victory in the Battle of the Atlantic. But added to this was the coming of the long-range airplane. Flying from land bases, the four-engine bombers and twin-engine patrol planes covered most of the ocean between the New and Old Worlds. Carrier-based bombers and scouting planes scoured the seas around the convoys. Together with the convoy escorts and advanced anti-submarine warfare technology employed by the Allies, the U-boat threat was virtually eliminated by the summer of 1943.

Air power had, at last, changed the balance of naval power in place since the First World War. It was a Consolidated PBY Catalina flying boat that spotted the *Bismarck* after she had broken away from the shadowing British cruisers. From that point on, it was only a matter of time before the carrier HMS *Ark Royal* launched a flight of Fairey Swordfish torpedo bombers to attack the battleships. A single hit on *Bismarck's* rudder doomed the mighty warship. A day later she was a burning, sinking hulk from the shells of the Royal Navy's vengeful battleships. In the Pacific, it was a PBY that spotted the Japanese invasion force headed for Midway on the morning of June 4, 1942. While this battle did not involve surface combatants, the aircraft played the decisive role.

Aircraft were the bane of the big-gun warship. *Musashi* and *Yamato* were both sunk by American torpedoes and dive bombers. Land-based Japanese bombers found and sank the battleships HMS *Prince of Wales* and battle cruiser HMS *Repulse* near Singapore, further proving the doom of the big-gun ship.

Admiral Karl Doenitz, the commander of the Kriegsmarine U-boat fleet, summed up the folly of sending ships to sea without air cover. The subs were vulnerable from the moment they sailed from their French bases out to the Atlantic. In a diary entry dated May 24, 1943, just as two big convoys had escaped his U-boats, Doenitz wrote, "The enemy air forces played its decisive part. This can be attributed to the increased use of land-based and aircraft carriers, combined with the advantage of radar location." After the war, he stated that the problem was that Germany was waging a war at sea without an air arm. Truer words were never said.

A good measure of how seriously the Allies took the U-boat threat can be summed up in the early missions of the infant Eighth Air Force Bomber Command. From October 1942 to August 1943, when the Eighth Air Force was little more than a half-dozen heavy bombardment groups still learning how to fight a modern air war, it was tasked with the impossible job of destroying the impregnable U-boat pens along the Biscay coast in France. Bombs the United States used could not significantly damage these pens, which required almost as much reinforced concrete as Hoover Dam. More raids were focused on the ports of Bremen, Vegasack, and Wilhelmshaven, where U-boats were built. Dozens of costly raids by B-17 Flying Fortress bombers did nothing to blunt the U-boat menace. Even today, the hulking gray U-boat pens remain where they were built seven decades ago.

The role of the battleship had not yet changed and wouldn't until the middle of the Second World War. Even the largest and most powerful battleships had some major limitations. They were slow, burned immense amounts of fuel, and could only project their power as far as the range of their guns. In other words, a battleship's reach was only about twenty-five miles. It was impervious as long as an enemy nation remained inland, out of the battleship's reach.

Another factor was that battleships, in addition to being the most expensive of warships, required a minimum of thirty-nine months to construct. A carrier could be laid down and launched in half that time.

While the first flimsy wood and fabric biplanes of the 1920s promised nothing in the way of a threat to naval power, that day was coming.

General William Mitchell's demonstrations in 1921 proved that airplanes could sink warships. Mitchell was only interested in advancing U.S. Army airpower, specifically strategic bombing, yet he was ultimately responsible for the United States Navy's first aircraft carrier, USS *Langley*. A few far-sighted admirals saw the writing on the wall for surface warships and chose to add the arrow of naval aviation to its quiver. While it would take the better part of a decade to become apparent, the roles of the aircraft carrier and battleship had to be reversed. As late as 1929, when *Lexington* and *Saratoga* participated in naval fleet exercises, their role was to scout for the battle fleet. With the carriers proving to be more than floating airfields for reconnaissance planes, they evolved into a striking force. This resulted in new dive bomber and torpedo planes reaching the fleet by the mid-1930s. In contrast to what the Army Air Corps had yet to learn, the navy knew fighters were essential to protect the bombers to and from the target.

Naval warfare changed long before the United States and Japan came to blows in the Pacific. Japan was and is an old nation with a long warrior tradition, the code of *Bushido*. The ancient Samurai word literally translates as "to serve," as in fighting in the name of their master, the shogun,

The first U.S. aircraft carrier USS Langley in 1927. *Official U.S. Navy Photo*

or emperor. Their primary weapon, the superb Katana, was still carried by army officers in World War II. Even though it was little more than a symbol, its role closely paralleled the striking arm of the Japanese air forces and navy. The battleship was revered as the ultimate power in naval warfare. The Battle of Tsushima in 1904 cemented that belief as Japan entered the world's stage in the second decade of the twentieth century.

On the other side of the Pacific, the United States, which, from its earliest years, understood the power and reach of the gun, followed the British tradition of shipbuilding. As the century began, bigger, faster, and better-armed ships dominated the navy. In the years after the Great War, both nations assumed the big gun would decide any future war. For Japan, this led to the ultimate folly of constructing the biggest battleships in the world.

If we assume the first major revolution in naval warfare was the change from sail to steam and the second being the far faster evolution from wood to iron, then it is safe to say the invention and development of submarines and aircraft carriers are the third revolution. Their parallel evolution from birth to maturity took place in the first two decades of the twentieth century, entirely independent of one another. Other than the medium in which each called home, they had absolutely nothing in common except that the traditional surface fleet navy distrusted and scorned both. The history of the vessel that would become the submarine has its roots in the American Revolution when David Bushnell built the wooden *Turtle*, which unsuccessfully attacked the HMS *Eagle* in New York Harbor in 1776. The Confederacy built the *Hunley* in 1863, the first submersible craft to sink an enemy warship.

Irish-American inventor John Holland designed the first practical submarine in 1900, which was the basis for the subs of the First and Second World Wars.

As for aircraft, other than the limited use of seaplane tenders by the Royal Navy in the North Sea, the aircraft carrier did not come of age until the 1920s. Again it was a slow and uncertain progression to mate aircraft and ships. In the meantime, the big guns of the battle line held the lead role of sea power. Both Japan and the United States recognized what naval airpower could do. The Royal Navy made limited use of carriers in the Second World War, while Germany, with its limited coastline and access to the open sea, couldn't deploy a carrier fleet.

The United States, after altering the collier *Jupiter* into the *Langley* in 1922, then converted two battle cruisers into *Lexington* and *Saratoga* in 1927. The first purpose-built carrier was the USS *Ranger* in 1934. Each new ship advanced U.S. carrier doctrine as war approached. The *Yorktown*-class, which included *Enterprise, Wasp,* and *Hornet,* were to play major roles in the first years of the Pacific War. By 1943, the big and fast *Essex* class, the first of the ships to be launched from President Roosevelt's $5 billion 1940 Navy Bill, was re-writing the book on carrier warfare.

Across the Pacific, Japan was also building and launching carriers, beginning with HIJMS *Hosho* in 1921, a year before *Langley* was commissioned. She was followed by the *Akagi* and *Kaga* in 1925 and 1928. They formed the nucleus of the expanding Imperial Navy carrier fleet, which would grow to six divisions. *Hiryu, Soryu, Zuikaku,* and *Shokaku* joined the fleet by 1940.

Yet, in 1935, Japan was still developing its carrier doctrine. Their role was defensive air support for the battle fleet. Each fleet would have at least one carrier to give air cover. The Imperial Navy's general staff did not want too many carriers close together where they could be hit in one attack.

Commander Minoru Genda, who would become the primary planner of the Pearl Harbor attack, stubbornly opposed this doctrine because it discarded the carrier's greatest strength: long-range striking power. By 1939, Genda managed to change this policy by making the carrier the core of the Imperial Navy. Carriers were joined into two-ship divisions, and it would be the surface units, like cruisers and destroyers, that provided defense.

Genda was the father of modern aircraft carrier doctrine. He stressed that the role of the carrier was to "hit first, hit fast, and keep on hitting until the enemy is defeated." As for Genda's opinion of battleships, he had often said that the battleships are the "China Wall of Japan." He proposed scrapping them all and building more planes and carriers.

It can be said that the last time in history a fleet of big-gun warships made a momentous contribution to the outcome of a war was either at the Battle of Manila Bay in May of 1898 or at Tsushima in 1905. The Spanish-American War and the Russo-Japanese War ended rapidly with the destruction of the Spanish and Russian fleets.

For our purposes, the real moment that marked the end of the battleship's primacy of the seas was on that Sunday morning at Pearl Harbor in December 1941. Genda pushed for an initial torpedo attack on the carriers and battleships first, while dive bombers and fighters eliminated the airfields. But he also stressed the importance of destroying the navy yard, repair facilities, drydocks, tank farms, and submarine base.

Moored alongside Ford Island, as mentioned in a previous essay, was a large part of the United States Navy's battle fleet: three divisions of older but still-powerful battlewagons. When the Japanese strike force left Oahu behind, the *Arizona, Oklahoma, West Virginia, California, Nevada, Tennessee, Pennsylvania*, and *Maryland* were either sunk or severely damaged. It would be nearly two years before any of them would rejoin the fleet and fight again. While there is no argument that the attack on Pearl Harbor was devastating to the United States, in retrospect, it proved to be the biggest mistake the Imperial Japanese Navy ever made. In other words, it was a tactical win for Japan but led to a strategic victory for America. This resulted from two factors. First, due to poor timing, the prime targets of the strike, the carriers *Lexington* and *Enterprise*, were out of port that Sunday morning. Second, the third wave was never launched. Admiral Nagumo, fearing an American counterattack from the missing carriers or submarines, chose to stop the attack and return to Japan.

The navy began salvage and repair operations before the fires even died down. The fuel was there to replenish the ship, and nearly all the sunken vessels could be raised and put back into service. The submarine base could fuel, provision, and deploy the subs within days of the attack. The fuel tank farm, with its 140,000,000 gallons of oil, was left untouched. The most important result of the Pearl Harbor attack was how it welded the formerly antagonistic isolationist to the need to rebuild and fight back. Japan was no longer considered a backward nation incapable of threatening a mighty nation. The sleeping giant now turned its angry red eyes on Japan. In one stroke, Japan provoked and motivated the one Pacific nation it feared most.

The real benefit the United States gained from the attack was not so obvious. By attacking and removing, if only for a time, the backbone of the Pacific Fleet's capital warships, Japan forced the old guard of the navy, the "Big Gun Club," to make use of what ships were still available to them. The U.S. Pacific Fleet became a carrier and submarine navy. The navy had already learned, partially from Billy Mitchell's demonstrations in 1921, that battleships had to be protected against air attack. The three pre-war battleship classes, the *North Carolinas*, *South Dakotas*, and *Iowas*, had heavy deck armor and more anti-aircraft artillery than any battleship had ever carried. Their role would evolve into anti-aircraft artillery protection for the carriers and heavy bombardment for amphibious operations.

From the battles of Coral Sea, Midway, and Guadalcanal, and on to the Gilberts, Marshalls, Carolines, Philippines, and Marianas, the real power of the fleet was in the aircraft carriers.

At the same time, completely isolated from the surface navy, was the submarine force. When Admiral Chester W. Nimitz took command at Pearl Harbor on December 31, 1941, he ordered the sub force to conduct unrestricted undersea warfare on Japanese merchant and navy ships. More than two years would pass before enough submarines and effective torpedoes would be available to cut off the flow of vital shipping on which Japan depended. Any vessel, no matter how small, was worthy of attack.

Japanese subs were big, fast, and had incredible range and good torpedoes. Imperial Navy subs sank the *Yorktown*, *Wasp*, and *Indianapolis* and damaged the battleship *North Carolina,* but their overall effect on the war was negligible. The Imperial general staff, that tribe of old admirals who refused to consider pragmatism over tradition, ordered the submarines to seek out and sink American warships. In fact, their captains were told to ignore "soft" targets like transports, tankers, and troopships. They were not considered worthy of a samurai. Many ships were left alone while the subs hunted warships.

The two types of warships that the Japanese missed out on at Pearl Harbor soon eclipsed the battleships as the most important vessels in warfare. The big guns still had a role, but not in useless and costly ship-to-ship duels. The huge rifles pounded the beaches from Guadalcanal to Honshu, from Tarawa to Okinawa, and from Kwajalein to Iwo Jima.

For the rest of the war, the big gun was used to support amphibious landings and suppress enemy facilities.

Alongside them were the fighters and bombers of the carrier navy. The surface and air forces protected the transports that brought the soldiers and Marines to the beaches, after which they provided the support to keep them there. Under the surface were the submarines that kept the Japanese from reinforcing their island bases. The fact that Tokyo more often chose not to send ships and men to support their forces is silent testimony to the success of the United States Navy's submarine campaign.

The fleet that came to stay, eleven U. S. carriers in Ulithi Atoll. Summer 1944. *Official U.S. Navy Photo*

Above and below the waters of the Pacific, the ships of the Third Revolution changed the face and future of naval warfare. Even seventy years later, it requires little effort to see that the ships most advantageous to the modern United States Navy are the aircraft carrier and the submarine. The ships that once dominated the seas are now museums, and rightly so. Their role shouldn't be minimized or forgotten. After all, they were the foundation on which the modern navy was built.

The next essay, concerning an air wing at Midway, is an example of how new the United States Navy was at the art of carrier warfare in 1942. The learning curve was steep and brutally unforgiving. The Battle of Midway was certainly one of the turning points of the Pacific War, but the American victory could have been greater with less loss if two men had made different choices. This is the true story of Torpedo 8 and its parent, Air Wing 8, off the new carrier USS *Hornet* on June 4 at Midway.

WHICH WAY DID THEY GO?
AIR GROUP 8 AT MIDWAY

Published in *Flight Journal*, October 2018

In the broadest strokes, the Battle of Midway involved three American carriers and their small support fleet of cruisers and destroyers to intercept and attack Admiral Chuichi Nagumo's striking force of four carriers determined to neutralize the tiny island of Midway for invasion. The outnumbered American force was two hundred miles northeast of Midway, waiting for the moment to strike. They would be notified the moment the Midway PBY search planes spotted the Japanese strike force, expected around 0600 hours about 175 miles north-northwest of the island. In overall command was Rear Admiral Frank "Jack" Fletcher. He led Task Force 17 from the bridge of the carrier USS *Yorktown*. On the distant horizon were two more carriers, USS *Enterprise* and the new USS *Hornet* of Task Force 16 under Rear Admiral Ray Spruance. They planned to launch a powerful blow at the enemy as soon as it was sighted and within range of their planes, most of which had a combat radius of just under 300 miles. This wouldn't allow much time to search.

When reports came in of sighting the enemy carriers while launching their first strike on Midway, the three American carriers turned southwest to close the distance on the enemy ships. By 0700 hours, all three carriers had launched their fighters, bombers, and torpedo planes. All three air groups headed off on the same bearing, had the same information, and were ready to find and attack Nagumo's ships. When the battle reached its penultimate conclusion by 1030 hours, three of Nagumo's carriers, *Akagi*, *Kaga*, and *Soryu*, were burning hulks, and more than half of the Douglas TBD Devastator torpedo planes and their crews had been shot down. Several fighters and some dive bombers ditched at sea, unable to reach their carriers.

The dive bombers achieved an incredible victory, to quote Walter Lord. But only the dive bombers of *Yorktown* and *Enterprise* had found and attacked Nagumo's force. What happened to *Hornet*'s dive bombers and fighters? Not one found and attacked the enemy. For all they accomplished that morning, they might as well have stayed on board their ship. Only the fifteen Devastators of Torpedo 8, under the command of Lieutenant Commander John Waldron, found the enemy. All but one man died. Where were the thirty-four dive bombers?

Therein lies the mystery. Numerous official and unofficial explanations came down to simple bad luck. There is no denying that luck and chance played a major role at Midway. But in the case of *Hornet*'s Air Group 8, so did bad judgment, poor leadership, and arrogance. The truth lay buried in official reports for the better part of forty years. Even noted Pacific War historians Walter Lord, Edwin Palmer Hoyt, Edward L. Beach, Gordon W. Prange, and Samuel Eliot Morison never uncovered the real story.

A simple ten-dollar bill provided the missing clue to the mystery.

Bowen Weisheit was a Maryland native and trial lawyer. Before the war, he attended St. John's College in Annapolis and studied celestial aerial navigation under the legendary Commander P.B. Weems. One of his fraternity brothers was Markland Kelly Jr. Kelly was bound for a naval aviation career and soon joined *Hornet*'s Fighting 8 (VF-8) under Sam Mitchell. Kelly died at Midway. Weisheit, who joined the Marine Corps and served as a navigator, learned of his friend's death after the battle. Kelly's father established an educational foundation in his son's name and made Weisheit a trustee.

At one meeting, Weisheit spotted a framed ten-dollar bill on the wall. It was a "Short Snorter," traditionally given to the pilot of a rescue plane by a downed aviator. A Fighting 8 pilot had given the bill to PBY pilot Ensign Jerry Crawford on June 8, 1942. On the bill were latitude and longitude coordinates. The bill sparked Weisheit's curiosity. After making

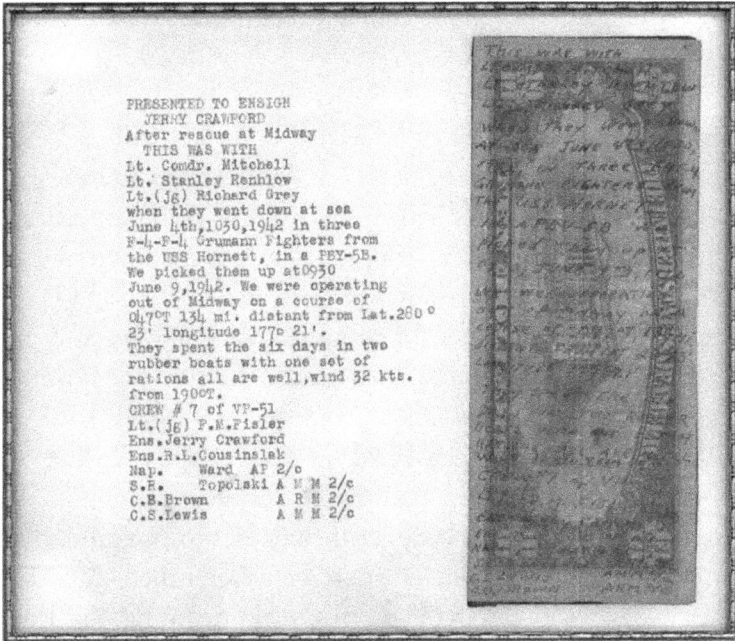

PRESENTED TO ENSIGN
JERRY CRAWFORD
After rescue at Midway
THIS WAS WITH
Lt. Comdr. Mitchell
Lt. Stanley Renhlow
Lt.(jg) Richard Grey
when they went down at sea
June 4th,1030,1942 in three
F-4,-F-4, Grumann Fighters from
the USS Hornett, in a PBY-5E.
We picked them up at0930
June 9,1942. We were operating
out of Midway on a course of
047°T 134 mi. distant from Lat.280°
23' longitude 177o 21'.
They spent the six days in two
rubber boats with one set of
rations all are well,wind 32 kts.
from 190°T.
CREW # 7 of VP-51
Lt.(jg) P.M.Fisler
Ens.Jerry Crawford
Ens.R.L.Cousinslek
Nap.   Ward AP 2/c
S.R.   Topolski A M M 2/c
C.B.Brown   A R M 2/c
C.S.Lewis   A M M 2/c

The ten-dollar "Short Snorter" found by Bowen Weisheit that revealed the truth about Air Wing 8 at Midway. *Photo courtesy C. Markland Kelly Jr. Foundation*

a copy of it, he went home and examined charts of the Pacific. After plotting the location where the VF-8 pilots had been found, he then read Walter Lord and Samuel Eliot Morison's accounts of the battle and realized the coordinates were more than 250 miles east of the location where VF-8 had supposedly been flying back to *Hornet*. So began his quest to find the truth.

All official reports had Air Group 8 taking off at the same time as the groups from *Enterprise* and *Yorktown*, flying a bearing of 240 degrees. In other words, all three air groups would have been going the same way. So what was VF-8 doing so far off course when they should have been taking the most direct route back to *Hornet* before running out of fuel? Dozens of interviews with surviving *Hornet* pilots convinced Weisheit there was no doubt the official report was wrong. He drew up a chart that reflected the true course of the four *Hornet* squadrons. Several noted naval historians examined Weisheit's findings and were in full agreement.

The mystery had at last been solved. He wrote the book *The Last Flight of Ensign C. Markland Kelly, Jr. USNR.*

This essay tells the true story, as related in Robert Mrazak's excellent book *A Dawn Like Thunder – The True Story of Torpedo Squadron 8.*

At 0530 hours, *Hornet's* squadrons were in their respective ready rooms waiting for orders from air operations. On the flight and hangar decks, the Wildcat fighters, Devastator torpedo bombers, and Dauntless dive bombers were being fueled and armed. At 0603, word came that two Japanese carriers had been sighted headed directly for Midway. Their position was more than 200 miles away. Another hour of fast steaming would bring the American carriers within range. All three carriers and their escorts turned to a heading of 240 degrees, almost directly southwest. While every mile brought them closer to Nagumo, they also brought the likelihood that the Japanese would spot the U.S. forces. *Enterprise* would send in thirty-three SBDs from Scouting and Bombing 6, fourteen TBDs of Torpedo 6, and ten F4Fs from Fighting 6, while

Grumman F4Fs of Lieutenant Commander Sam Mitchell's VF-8 launching from *Hornet* on the morning of June 4, 1942. *Official U.S. Navy Photo*

Yorktown contributed seventeen SBDs from Bombing 3, twelve TBDs of Torpedo 3, and six F4Fs from Fighting 3.

Hornet threw in everything she had: thirty-four SBDs from Bombing and Scouting 8, fifteen Devastators from Torpedo 8, and ten Wildcats from Fighting 8. Fletcher sent virtually every available plane to sink or at least cripple the enemy force.

Klaxons on *Hornet* sounded the call to General Quarters at 0610. "The enemy strike force is attempting to take Midway," said a voice over the loudspeakers. "All fighter and bomber pilots to the flight deck. Launch at 0700." On *Hornet*, Captain Marc "Pete" Mitscher called all his squadron commanders to the bridge. Mitscher had graduated at nearly the bottom of the Annapolis class of 1910. He became one of the first naval aviators. Historians have called him headstrong and even obstinate. Midway was his first combat command.

First to arrive was Lieutenant Commander Sam Mitchell of Fighting 8, whose F4F Wildcats were to protect the air group. Mitchell requested that his fighters stay with the slow and terribly vulnerable torpedo planes. But Mitscher, who apparently felt it was unlikely that the slow Devastators would even reach the Japanese force, ordered Mitchell's fighters to stay with the dive bombers. Mitchell protested but was again refused. Then the other squadron leaders arrived. First was Commander Stanhope C. Ring, the air group leader. He was followed by Lieutenant Commanders Walter Rodee of Scouting 8 and Robert Johnson of Bombing 8. Lieutenant Commander John Waldron, a popular and unconventional officer with a well-deserved reputation for being independent, sauntered in last. Mitscher detailed what they knew about Nagumo's position, then asked Ring what he planned for the attack. This was in character for Mitscher, who wanted to appear as though he listened to his subordinates. But he had likely told Ring what to say.

Ring was the epitome of the hard-driving, ambitious naval officer. Despite commanding *Hornet*'s air wing, he had never flown in combat. Now he wanted to make his mark. He followed the Mitscher script by confidently stating that the air group would head almost directly west at 265 degrees. This immediately raised some eyebrows, most notably Waldron's. He said that Nagumo's force had last been sighted at a bearing of

234 degrees, more than 30 degrees south of Ring's course. He suggested a course of 240 degrees, which took into account the likely possibility that Nagumo had turned north after launching his first strike. Ring flatly refused. The argument grew heated as the two assertive squadron commanders looked to Mitscher for support. Mitscher said, "The attack force will follow the course set by Commander Ring." That ended the matter as far as he and Ring were concerned. Only Waldron remained unconvinced. He was one-eighth Sioux Indian and relied on his intuition.

At 0700, orders came down from Mitscher. "Launch planes!" The Wildcats took off and climbed to 20,000 feet. One of the pilots was Markland Kelly Jr. Then Ring led the thirty-four SBDs up to 19,000 feet. Each Dauntless carried a 1,000-pound bomb. Waldron's TBDs clawed their way into the morning sky, each carrying a 2,200-pound Mark 13 torpedo. When Ring saw the TBDs form up, he signaled his air wing to head west. His compass read 265 degrees. The SBDs were formed into a giant "V" pointed west. Mitchell's Wildcats, inherently faster than the heavily loaded bombers, were forced to fly in "S" curves to stay with the formation. This used up fuel at a prodigious rate. Mitchell's planes couldn't waste fuel if they wanted to make it back to *Hornet*.

Enterprise's and *Yorktown*'s planes were soon lost to sight as they angled farther south on their bearing of 240 degrees. Soon the fifty-nine *Hornet* planes were alone. Yet Ring was determined to fly a course virtually guaranteed to miss Nagumo's carriers. This grated on John Waldron. Prior to takeoff, he had told his pilots, "Don't worry about navigating. Just follow me. Maybe it's the Sioux in me, but I have a hunch the Jap fleet will be in a different position than our reports have them." Then, in a chilling prophecy, he concluded, "If we find ourselves alone and outnumbered by the enemy planes, we'll keep boring in. If there is only one man left, I want that man to go in and get a hit."

At 0816, when they were about eighty miles out, Waldron broke the sacrosanct code of radio silence to announce that they were on the wrong course. His strong voice cut into the earphones of every pilot in the group. "I know where the damn Jap fleet is," he said firmly.

Ring, seething, said, "I'm leading this formation. You fly on us."

Fifteen minutes later, Waldron said, "To hell with you." Looking down, Ring and the other Dauntless crews saw the tiny shapes of the

Devastators bank slightly and turn southwest. Ahead of Ring and Mitchell, the sky and ocean remained completely empty of planes and ships. As the miles and minutes passed, their fuel gauges dropped lower and lower. They should have spotted the Japanese fleet.

At about 0915, Mitchell's Wildcats passed the point of no return. They had no choice but to turn back and leave the bombers to go it alone. One by one, the Grumman fighters banked and turned away. Ring and the other dive bomber crews did not see them go because their eyes were fixed on the empty sea, looking for enemy ships.

Admiral Nagumo, who had just learned of the presence of a U.S. carrier to the east, was almost ready to launch a counterattack. He was confident that his superb "Wild Eagles" could find and destroy the American carrier, and then he could resume his attack on Midway. Then lookouts spotted planes coming in low from the east. Waldron's well-known Sioux intuition had led him directly to Nagumo's ships. He called to Ring, "Johnny One to Stanhope. Enemy in sight." He made this call twice with no reply from Ring, even though some of the dive bomber pilots clearly heard it.

Seeing no other torpedo or dive bombers anywhere, Waldron signaled to his small force to begin their lone attack. Nagumo's Zeros were ready to take on the unprotected Devastators. One by one, Waldron and his men fell into the sea in fiery splashes until only Ensign George Gay was left alive. A few minutes later, Torpedo 6 attacked from the southeast with much the same result, then *Yorktown*'s torpedo bombers met the same fate. They had spotted the twisting white wakes of the carriers to the north of their course. In forty-five minutes, thirty-five planes had been shot down without a single hit on the carriers. Sixty-nine Americans had died. But their sacrifices had one positive outcome: Nagumo's force was wildly scattered. He had not been able to launch the strike against the American carrier. His flight decks were giant powder kegs of fuel and bombs waiting for a match.

Far to the north, Ring continued on, doggedly holding on 265 degrees. The commander of Bombing 8, Robert Johnson, had had enough and made a few calculations on his plotting board. He signaled his squadron to break off and head south-southwest, hoping to find the enemy fleet before they had to turn back. As his seventeen SBDs turned away, Walter Rodee glanced at Ring. The air wing commander signaled to Rodee to stay in formation and on course. By 0940 hours, Rodee, too, had reached his limit. Fuel was running dangerously low. He signaled to his squadron to turn 180 degrees and head back to *Hornet*. Over his shoulder Rodee saw Ring was still flying west. Alone.

At 1025 hours, just as the Japanese fleet was regrouping, Lieutenant Commanders Max Leslie, Wade McCluskey, and Dick Best arrived with fifty SBDs over Nagumo's carriers. Like the torpedo bombers, they, too, saw the enemy fleet to their north and turned to attack. Screaming down from 15,000 feet, the blue dive bombers rained death on the Japanese flattops. The heavy 500- and 1,000-pound bombs, driven by the SBD's 200-knot dives, slammed into the flight decks packed with the bombers and fighters being readied for an attack on the American carrier. Nagumo, in what has to be the worst decision in naval warfare, had chosen to change the waiting planes from a second land attack on Midway to a strike on the single U.S. carrier he knew of. Not all the bombs hit the carriers, but those that did exploded among bombs, torpedoes, and fuel, turning the wooden decks and hangar spaces into instant infernos. Five minutes later, three of Japan's best carriers were burning hulks. Commander Minoru Genda, the planner of the Pearl Harbor attack and Nagumo's air operations officer, looked at the destruction and spoke one word: "*Shimatta,*" meaning, "We goofed." But he was not the only one who goofed.

Flushed with victory, The *Enterprise* and *Yorktown* pilots headed east in triumph. None had any idea where the *Hornet's* dive bombers were.

At that moment they were desperately trying to find and land on *Hornet*. At 1040, Rodee was an hour closer to *Hornet*. He was thoroughly frustrated. Then he saw a lone SBD overtaking them at full speed, also headed back towards *Hornet*. It was Ring. It appeared he had every intention of reaching the ship first. Meanwhile, Fighting 8 was running out of fuel far from the ship. Mitchell had waited too long to turn back. One by one, the Wildcats lost power and fell into the empty sea. Mitchell was not overly concerned. He knew that once the battle was over, Midway would send out search planes. He prayed all his men would survive after such a botched mission.

Hornet's radar picked up a group of planes coming in from 260 degrees. Certain they were a victorious strike force, crewmen ran up to the flight deck to welcome the airmen. First to land was Commander Stanhope Ring, who climbed out of his cockpit, and without a word, ducked into a hatchway and disappeared. He went directly to his quarters and closed the door. Soon Rodee's SBDs landed and he was called to the bridge by Mitscher. *Hornet*'s captain demanded to know what had happened. The awful truth began to emerge. Air Group 8 had not bombed the enemy fleet. In fact, they never saw a single Japanese ship. Rodee described Waldron's departure and feared the worst. He said that Mitchell and the fighters had also turned back early. They had not returned to *Hornet*.

Northwest of Midway, Johnson's squadron of dive bombers was running out of time and fuel. He finally decided to try for Midway. Fortunately a Navy PBY appeared and led them in. But luck had run out. The

Ensign Bert Ernest's shot-rent TBF Avenger on Midway. This was the only one of the six new planes to come back from the attack on Nagumo's carriers. *Official U.S. Navy Photo*

SBDs lost power and ditched. The last *Hornet* planes in the air landed, almost out of fuel, on the smoking Eastern Island runway at 1130 hours.

The scope of the disaster was becoming apparent to Mitscher. He knew much of the blame would fall on his shoulders. But it was not over. Even when word of three burning Jap carriers arrived from *Enterprise* and *Yorktown*'s bombers, the gloom that settled over *Hornet*'s aviators was deep and painful. Waldron and the Devastators had failed to return, and from what the *Yorktown* and *Enterprise* TBD pilots were saying, Torpedo 8 was probably dead.

That afternoon, Walt Rodee wrote up his flight log. In it he noted the 265 degree heading they had taken. This was the only written account that mentioned the true attack course. But it was soon buried in the official reports.

The single surviving Japanese carrier, *Hiryu*, was still in the fight, but it too would soon rest on the ocean floor. It had wreaked revenge on Fletcher by launching a successful counterattack by twice crippling *Yorktown*. *Enterprise*, having recovered some of *Yorktown*'s planes, launched another attack on Nagumo. None of *Hornet*'s bombers played a role in that attack. The last strike mission of Air Group 8 was when reports came in of two Japanese battleships lingering to the northwest of Midway, perhaps searching for survivors or hoping to sink prowling American warships. Ring, desperate to redeem his wounded pride, led the attack. But they only found a single destroyer. Bombs rained down on the twisting ship but all missed. Even worse, Ring returned to the *Hornet* with his own 500-pound bomb still slung under the Dauntless. He bitterly complained to his plane captain that he had repeatedly hit the switch on his throttle to drop the bomb but nothing had happened. The other pilots who heard his tirade were shocked. Ring, the air group commander, the man who had led *Hornet*'s biggest air strike of the war, had not known that the button to release the bomb was located forward of the throttle. He had also been unaware that an emergency release lever was just under the control panel.

When the battle was over, the outnumbered and slapdash American fleet was victorious, but none of the victory could be attributed to *Hornet*. By any standards, it was a dismal performance, one likely to end careers.

But it did not. Mitscher decided he alone would write the After Action Report to the Commander-in-Chief of the Pacific Fleet, Admiral Chester Nimitz. Officially, each squadron commander was required to submit a report, but Mitscher took sole control. None of the squadron commanders ever saw it. His report stated, "The enemy force was calculated to be 155 miles out, bearing 239 degrees from this task force. The *Hornet* attack force followed this course." Then he added to the deception. "After searching the prescribed bearing, the squadrons turned south to search in the direction of the enemy advance." He included a map that showed the group's course from *Hornet* as 239 degrees. Mitscher knew that what he was writing was false and self-serving, but he desperately wanted another combat command.

Admiral Spruance personally held *Hornet*'s captain and air wing commander responsible for the debacle and told Nimitz as much. But Nimitz, not wanting to stir up a can of worms after such a victory, chose to ignore it and bury the truth.

Thus it was only after Bowen Weisheit found the short snorter bill that the real story merged. Even today, more than seventy years after the battle that changed the course of the war, many historians are unaware of the uncomfortable truth. None of the blame can be attributed to the pilots of Bombing and Scouting 8, Fighting, and especially Torpedo 8. The blame rests solely on the shoulders of Commander Stanhope Ring and Captain Marc Mitscher. While Mitscher did become a superb fast carrier task force commander, he had let a total victory at Midway slip through his fingers. If Ring had followed Waldron's instincts, *Hornet*'s bombers might well have sunk *Hiryu*, thereby saving *Yorktown*. But that did not happen. A final disgrace: Mitscher, wanting to salvage some honor from the debacle, submitted a request for a decoration to the man who was the worst choice for an air group commander—Stanhope Ring.

Ring did not deserve the Navy Cross, but he got it.

There are scores of books that tell the history of the big fast aircraft carriers, the flattops that won the war in the Pacific. But there was another class of carriers, the so-called *Jeep* or *Escort* carriers. Far smaller than the big *Essex*-class flattops, the CVEs (Carrier, Heavier than air, Escort) filled a vital role in both oceans. The next essay tells the story of one such ship, the USS *Kalinin Bay*, known to her crew as "The Lucky K."

LUCKY K: THE SAGA OF AN ESCORT CARRIER

The Battle of Samar on October 25, 1944, has gone down in history as the most remarkable David-and-Goliath sea epic ever. The six small and unarmored escort carriers of Taffy 3 fought a desperate and fierce battle against overwhelming odds. Two were lost, one being the only United States aircraft carrier to be sunk by naval gunfire. The escort carrier USS *Kalinin* Bay (CVE-68) was among the ships that churned the waters off Samar Island that morning. Named for a body of water on the southeastern coast of Alaska, *Kalinin Bay* was always known to her crew as "Lucky K."

Her war service is a saga of courage, audacity, and sheer good fortune.

The escort carriers, the brainchild of construction magnate Henry Kaiser, were an important but largely unheralded benefit to the U.S. Navy in the Atlantic and Pacific during the war. They effectively provided air cover for the vulnerable convoys that crossed the war zones daily. They obviated the need to divert big fast fleet carriers from major fleet operations. They carried replacement planes, bombs, rockets, and fuel to the big flattops involved in ongoing campaigns far from supply bases. The small carriers had earned a dubious reputation for being virtually defenseless and dubbed "Kaiser Coffins" or "Woolworth Flattops." While "CVE" stood for "Carrier, Heavier than air, Escort." It was derided as "Combustible, Vulnerable, and Expendable."

The fifty *Casablanca*-class escort carriers, type S4-S2-BB3, displaced 7,800 tons and were 512 feet long with a complement of 860 officers and men. Able to sail more than ten thousand miles at a maximum cruising speed of just over 20 knots meant they had little chance of evading fast surface ships. Since any surface combat action would certainly involve retreating from an enemy force, the ships mounted a single 5-inch gun on the fantail under the flight deck. For anti-aircraft defense, they carried twenty 20mm and sixteen 40mm batteries.

For a look at a typical CVE, find the 1973 Clint Eastwood Dirty Harry film, *Magnum Force*. At the end of the movie, Inspector Harry Callahan is fighting the rogue motorcycle cops. They are on the USS *Reboul* (CVE-121), and alongside her is the USS *Badoeng Strait* (CVE-116). Both of the later *Commencement Bay*-class, neither saw combat in the Second World War. It is worth seeing how small and tight the escort carriers were. Both ships seen in the film were scrapped shortly after the movie was made.

The keel of Hull No. 1105, authorized by Secretary of the Navy Frank Knox, was laid down on one of the twelve slipways at the vast Kaiser Shipyard on the Columbia River at Vancouver, Washington, on April 26, 1943. After being named on June 4, the new escort carrier was launched on October 15 and fitted out in six weeks, a remarkably

The damaged USS *Kalinin Bay* in San Diego, 1944. *Official U.S. Navy Photo*

short time. She was commissioned on November 27 at Naval Air Station Astoria. Her commander was Captain Charles R. Brown, United States Naval Reserve.

She was quickly dubbed the "Kay Bee" by her crew. On January 3, she headed for Pearl Harbor. Crowded onto her short flight deck were fifteen North American PBJ Mitchell twin-engine bombers, one short of the number carried on the USS *Hornet* for the Doolittle Raid almost two years earlier. However, the Mitchells wouldn't be flown off the ship but hoisted by crane onto the quay when the ship arrived in Hawaii. Yet this was not the most remarkable aviation cargo on *Kalinin Bay*. On her hangar deck were Grumman F6F hellcats, Curtiss Helldivers, and Grumman TBF Avengers. These, too, were offloaded at Pearl. The ship then took on the lead echelon of Marine Fighter Squadron 422 from Pearl Harbor to Tarawa, where they were to join the Marine air wing for Operation Flintlock, the invasion of the Marshall Islands. Twenty-four new Vought F4U-1D Corsairs were lowered into the hangar deck.

On the morning of January 16, *Kalinin Bay* and her destroyer escort USS *Fair* shaped a course to Tarawa in the Gilbert Islands, recently captured from the Japanese.

Accounts by the Marine pilots give a vivid description of what life was like aboard an escort carrier. Retired Colonel Robert "Curley" Lehnert said, "It wasn't much bigger than those paddle-wheelers I landed on at NAS Chicago." VMF-422's Corsairs were tied down on the aft hangar deck, wings folded. "They were really packed in there," said Lehnert. "You couldn't get a dime in between them. Those navy boys really knew their stuff."

Kalinin Bay was small, but her interior spaces were efficiently designed to make maximum use of the limited space. The Marines were berthed in the junior officer's quarters, cramped cubicles next to the forward engine room. The heat often became intolerable. Many chose to take their mattresses up to the flight deck and sleep under the wing of a plane. With the steady breeze from the bow, sleeping out in the open was much more pleasant.

When the ship was within twenty miles of Tarawa on January 24, the Marines launched from the single catapult to fly to Hawkins Field on

Betio. But for VMF-422, their destiny did not include a role in Operation Flintlock. The next day, during a routine ferry flight from Tarawa to Funafuti Atoll eight hundred miles to the south, they were savaged by a cyclone that cost the lives of a third of the pilots. To this day, it is known as the Flintlock Disaster.

Now in the War Zone, *Kalinin Bay* spent the next several weeks ferrying replacement planes, ordnance, and fuel to the task forces in the Marshalls. This was to be her primary role for most of the year. But her reputation for solid service, reliability, and luck soon made her a favorite to her crew and the navy.

During a rendezvous with Task Group 58.2, the ship launched ten Hellcats and two Avengers for the carriers *Essex*, *Intrepid*, and *Cabot*. Returning to Pearl on February 17, she was loaded with the most eclectic cargo of aircraft ever carried by a ship. Crammed into her hangar and on the flight deck were five Consolidated PBY-1 Catalinas, one PBY-5A, seven Lockheed PV-1 Venturas, six Curtiss SO3C Seamews, two Grumman J2F Ducks, and a single Curtiss SOC Seagull. The ship must have looked like a wartime version of Noah's ark as she left Pearl on February 19 and arrived at Naval Air Station Alameda five days later.

The squadrons assigned to the CVEs were designated VC, for "Heavier than air, Composite." Composed of torpedo bombers and fighters, they were a scaled-down version of the larger and more diverse air groups of the fleet carriers. Grumman Avengers proved versatile in strikes against land and ship targets with bombs, rockets, torpedoes, and depth charges against surface ships and submarines. In addition, they were excellent for long-range patrol and reconnaissance, as well as defense against air attack. The FM-2 Wildcats, the General Motors variant of the Grumman F4F, served as air cover for the ships and escort for the bombers.

At Alameda, *Kalinin Bay* was assigned her own air group, VC-3, under Lieutenant Commander William Keighley, consisting of 188 enlisted men, thirty-one officers, and an initial load of six TBM Avengers and eight FM-2 Wildcats. For the next few weeks, the airmen and crew conducted training off the southern California coast, ending on March 9. At San Diego she loaded a dozen more FM-2s and nine more Avengers. Forty Hellcats were loaded into the hangar deck as the ship headed west on April 9. After unloading the Hellcats, the carrier began conducting anti-submarine patrols as they sailed west for the Marshalls. Two of the TBMs were lost to accidents during patrols.

After joining her sister ship *Fanshawe Bay* and destroyers *Cabana, Elden, Harold C. Thomas*, and *Wileman, Kalinin Bay*, as part of TG 11.1 under Rear Admiral Gerald F. Bogan of Carrier Division 25, headed back to Pearl to prepare for Operation Forager, the invasion of the Marianas.

With the *Fanshaw Bay, Midway, White Plains*, and several destroyers, the ship was to be part of a vast naval campaign. It is worth noting that the USS *Midway* did not retain that name for long. The Navy Department decided that the Battle of Midway was too pivotal for a mere escort carrier. On October 10, 1944, she was re-commissioned as the USS *St. Lo*, the name of a recent land battle during the Normandy Invasion. This was considered bad luck, a belief that would prove justified.

On June 1, a Japanese submarine fired two torpedoes at *Kalinin Bay*. Even though they were spotted less than a hundred yards away, and the ship had virtually no time to evade, both torpedoes missed. The destroyer escorting the force hunted for the sub with no luck. The crew began calling *Kalinin Bay* "the Lucky K."

A week later, on June 7, an Avenger pilot came in for a landing. He was too low and the Landing Signal Officer (LSO) could not correct the approach. The Avenger skidded from port to starboard, ending up in the port 20mm gun tub. The damaged plane had to be jettisoned overboard, but the pilot and gunners were unhurt. What could have been a serious crash had resulted in minor damage. The ship's luck was holding.

Kalinin Bay stopped at Eniwetok to deliver fuel and aircraft parts to the Marine Corsair squadrons, one of which was VMF-422, the unit that had sailed with her from Pearl in January. He joined Task Group 52.1 for the invasion of Saipan. The Avengers proved their value against air attack on June 14, when a Mitsubishi G4M1 Type 1 "Betty" bomber approached *Kalinin Bay* only to be shot down by the Avenger flown by Lieutenant Patsy Capano and gunner Malcolm Gordon with their twin .50 caliber and single .30 caliber machine guns. That was a unique event, a torpedo bomber shooting down a medium bomber.

During the late afternoon and evening of June 17, the task group was attacked by an estimated seventy Japanese land planes carrying bombs and torpedoes. While being savaged by Wildcats launched from the CVEs *Fanshawe Bay*, *White Plains*, and *Kalinin Bay*, the enemy planes missed with their weapons.

Back at Eniwetok, *Kalinin Bay* launched eleven TBM Avengers, carrying thirty-nine fighter pilots as passengers to Stickel Field. These pilots manned the Avengers and Wildcats needed for TG 52.14 at Saipan. Without the carrier's timely arrival with the TBMs, Saipan would have been shorthanded.

On the night of June 28 came another air torpedo attack, followed by submarine-launched torpedoes. *Kalinin Bay* was again lucky to be missed. By this time, she was painted in Camouflage Measure 33, Design 10A. This gave her added security from detection by enemy aircraft. The task group was joined by *Gambier Bay* and *Kitkun Bay*, along with their escorts, forming Task Unit 52.14.

After supporting Operation Stevedore, the capture of Guam, *Kalinin Bay* returned to Eniwetok for re-provisioning for the August 28 assault on Purvis Bay in the Florida Islands near Guadalcanal, still under Japanese control. Launching air strikes from the carriers on Japanese positions led to the capture of the island on September 1.

The bloody assault by the First Marine Division on Peleliu in the Palaus required a full effort by the carriers of Rear Admiral George Henderson's Carrier Division 28, which consisted of *Kalinin Bay*, *Petrof Bay*, and *Saginaw Bay*. They escorted an assault force of transports and dock landing ships for Operation Stalemate II.

Kalinin Bay launched more than four hundred sorties and reconnaissance flights over the enemy positions during the pre-invasion phase of the operation. Her Avengers also flew anti-submarine patrols to protect the fleet from underwater attack. By September 25, her bunkers and ammo stores were depleted, and she was sent to a rear area for replenishment.

During this time, General Douglas MacArthur was preparing for his long-awaited return to the Philippines. Operation King II was to be the

USS *Kitkun Bay* of Taffy 3 launches F4Fs off Samar, October 25, 1944, while *White Planes* is straddled by shells from Japanese cruisers. *Official U.S. Navy Photo*

landings on the eastern shore of the island of Leyte from the wide gulf bordered by Negros, Dinagat, and Suluan.

Vice Admiral Thomas Kinkaid, Commander, Seventh Fleet, led a force that included TG 77.4, with a total of eighteen escort carriers consisting of TUs 77.4.1, 77.4.2, and 77.4.3, call signs Taffys 1, 2, and 3. They were to make history.

Rear Admiral Clifton Sprague, Carrier Division 25, hoisted his flag on *Fanshawe Bay* on October 12. Taffy 3's six escort carriers were to provide air support to the bombardment group of TG 77.2 under Rear Admiral Jesse Oldendorf.

On October 16, Taffy 3 moved east to provide air support for the 6th Ranger Battalion as they stormed ashore on Dinagat and Suluan Islands.

Kalinin Bay's aircraft flew 244 sorties against enemy positions on Negros, Samar, Leyte, Cebu, and Panay between October 16 and 24. A small celebration marked her 1,000th catapult shot with the launch of an Avenger flown by Ensign Jim Zeitvogel.

The Taffys continued to support the landings while the destroyers patrolled for submarines and defended against the kamikaze attacks.

Meanwhile, an alert went up the chain of command to the headquarters of the Japanese Combined Fleet and Admiral Soemu Toyoda. He issued the orders to launch the long-planned Operation Sho-Go to defend the Philippines. "*Sho*" is Japanese for "Victory." Two fleets of battleships, cruisers, and destroyers of the once-mighty Imperial Japanese Navy sortied to ambush and annihilate the American invasion forces.

At dawn on October 24, 140 ships and landing craft were off Red Beach on the eastern shore of Leyte. Starting at 0800 hours, the eighteen escort carriers of Taffys 1, 2, and 3 put up fighters to intercept Japanese attacks on the invasion fleet. Several of the landing ships and transports were hit while the FM2 wildcats tore into the Kamikazes.

The CVEs were screened by smoke from the destroyers to prevent being spotted by prowling enemy planes. At least twenty Japanese planes were downed in the gulf. The carriers recovered their planes and sent them out to defend the fleet and bomb enemy shore positions.

When the night of October 24 cloaked the fleet, the Taffys prepared for the next day's action. The orders were for more of the same. There was no indication that any substantial Japanese surface force was anywhere near Leyte Gulf.

Under cover of night, Admiral Takeo Kurita's mighty surface force was moving east into the San Bernardino Strait north of Leyte to attack the invasion fleet. Twenty-two warships were cruising in a single line under radio silence.

No one in the United States Navy knew they were there, least of all Admiral Kincaid. Like huge black mountains, they headed east under the light of a bright moon. Kurita's vessels included battleships *Yamato*, *Haruna*, *Kongo*, and *Nagato*, cruisers *Chikuma*, *Chōkai*, *Haguro*, *Kumano*, *Suzuya*, *Tone*, *Noshiro*, and *Yahagi*, and eleven destroyers.

The lightly armed CVEs and destroyers were all there was to stop them.

At 0645 on October 25, American lookouts spotted anti-aircraft artillery bursts to the northeast. The oncoming Japanese ships were shooting at a lone TBM Avenger from the Taffy 3 carrier *St. Lo* that had spotted them during the morning patrol. The TBM only carried depth charges, but the pilot released them in hopes that they would do some good.

Kurita was certain he had come upon six of Vice Admiral William Halsey's fleet carriers and ordered his big ships to close in and open fire.

At 0650, Sprague ordered an emergency course change to the south while the destroyers laid dense smoke screens to cover the retreat. The report of four battleships, six heavy cruisers, and a dozen destroyers at twenty miles, bearing 270 degrees, reached *Kalinin Bay*'s Captain Thomas Williamson at 0654 hours. When the formation turned south, *Kalinin Bay* became the trailing ship in the center column behind *Fanshawe Bay*, with *Gambier Bay* and *St. Lo* to her port and starboard. Consequently, she was the first to be taken under fire by the enemy cruisers. Captain Williamson called the engines to flank speed while the crew went to battle stations and all planes began launching. Japanese shells fell around them. Towering waterspouts from the cruisers' 8-inch guns exploded among the madly maneuvering CVEs and DDs.

Yet the Lucky K managed to launch all the ready planes ordered to attack the Japanese ships. In all, she launched two Avengers armed with ten 5-inch rockets and eight 500-pound general purpose bombs, six more TBM Avengers with eight rockets and six 100-pound bombs, and thirteen FM-2 Wildcats with full loads of .50 caliber ammunitions. The planes banked away and headed for the looming enemy ships. Since there was no way to recover and re-arm them after the strike, they were told to land at Tacloban Airfield on Leyte for re-arming.

"At this point," Sprague later said, "it did not appear that any of our ships could survive another five minutes of the heavy caliber fire being received. The task unit was surrounded by the ultimate of desperate circumstances."

When Kurita's ships were at a range of 33,000 yards, the destroyers *Johnston*, *Hoel*, *Heermann*, and the destroyer escort *Samuel B. Roberts* turned north in their courageous and suicidal charge at the enemy line. Even though this essay focuses on *Kalinin Bay* and the other CVEs, the courage of the men who served on and died that morning aboard those three destroyers warrants some attention.

The *Fletcher*-class destroyers and *Butler*-class destroyer escorts were tasked with protecting the six Taffy 3 carriers from enemy submarines and aircraft. With their 5-inch and anti-aircraft artillery guns, they were seemingly of little use against heavily armored warships. But they had one advantage—the Mark 37 Fire Control Director. As long as the Mark 37 had the enemy target on radar, all the guns automatically followed. This system had its baptism of fire during the desperate surface battles at Guadalcanal in late 1942.

The destroyers' smoke gave the American ships more than one advantage. While they screened the retreating carriers, they also made seeing the destroyers harder for the Japanese gunners, who did not have radar. In fact, with the rain squalls and smoke, the Japanese mistook the *Fletchers* for cruisers and the *Butlers* for full-size destroyers.

At 0700 hours, Commander Earnest Evans, on the USS *Johnston*'s bridge, saw huge towers of water bracketing the other ships. He told his gunnery officer to return fire on the nearest enemy ship. At that point, the leading cruiser turned its 8-inch guns on the *Johnston*. Evans ordered flank speed and hard left rudder. With foaming water under her stern, the destroyer leaped toward the Japanese line. Her 5-inch turrets caught the cruiser *Kumano* in their sights and inflicted several hits.

Now the *Johnston* was under the concentrated fire of several heavy guns, and her thin steel plating was not armored. She began taking fire and casualties.

At 0716, Sprague ordered Commander William D. Thomas, aboard the USS *Hoel*, to attack the oncoming enemy line. *Hoel*, *Heermann*, and *Samuel B. Roberts* made hard turns to port and drove at the big ships.

Johnston was still driving hard, making turns to throw off enemy fire. With her fire control radar, her guns never left their targets. At four miles range, she launched ten Mark 14 torpedoes. A few minutes later, at least three struck the *Kumano*, blowing off her bow. The battleship *Kongo* narrowly avoided four more of *Johnston*'s torpedoes, forcing her to pull away from the line. The heavy cruiser *Suzuya* had also been hit by 5-inch shells and slowed to assist *Kumano*.

Seeing that his daring dash had confused and damaged the enemy force, Evans turned away under her smoke screen. At 0730, the huge *Yamato*, seeing what was thought to be an American cruiser, fired and hit the *Johnston* with three 18.1-inch armor-piercing shells. The heavy shells tore through the small ship's port engine room. Badly damaged, *Johnston's* speed slackened. Three more 6.1-inch secondary armament shells from *Yamato* struck the destroyer's bridge, killing and wounding several men. With her decks red with blood, *Johnston* limped away from the fight.

Commodore Thomas called on the TBS (Talk Between Ships) for a torpedo attack. The *Hoel, Heermann*, and *Roberts* charged in while the damaged *Johnston* turned to add what support she could to cover the other three ships. Emerging from a rain squall, she was confronted by the *Haruna*, a 36,000-ton battleship. Firing forty 5-inch shells at the big ship, she scored fifteen hits on the bridge before turning away again. But *Johnston's* fight was not over. At 0830, she again hurled herself at the Japanese, firing at the *Hiro*, another cruiser. Ten minutes later, seven Japanese destroyers entered the fray, and *Johnston* turned to the new threat. Firing at the lead destroyer, Evans's guns forced it to turn away and then aimed at the second enemy ship. Incredibly, all seven Japanese destroyers turned away, launching their torpedoes at the distant carriers. At this point, the American and Japanese warships were hopelessly confused, churning the water in a wild melee of wakes and explosions.

The *Samuel B. Roberts* engaged the *Chikuma*, whose heavy turrets couldn't traverse fast enough to hit the wildly twisting destroyer escort. *Roberts* fired all her 5-inch ammunition at the cruiser, scoring several hits at close range.

Unknown to her crew, the *Heermann* was also firing at the cruiser, catching the big ship in a deadly crossfire.

Roberts was then taken under fire by the *Yamato, Nagato*, and *Haruna*. Three Goliaths on one darting David. Having fired all her torpedoes at close range, *Roberts* turned away but was hit by 8-inch cruiser shells, stopping her engines. She was sinking by 0900 hours.

The *Hoel*, having launched half of her torpedoes, was hit by several of *Yamato's* 6.1-inch shells on the superstructure, killing four and wounding Commander Thomas. Still under the smoke, *Hoel* used her radar to fire on the Japanese cruisers. But she was alone with the *Heermann* and *Roberts* fighting for their own lives.

Just as *Hoel* prepared to loose her second salvo of torpedoes, she was hit by forty large-caliber shells. Dead in the water, *Hoel* was sinking. But the forward gun crews remained at their stations and traded fire with two approaching cruisers. The fight only ended when the *Hoel* rolled over and sank at 0955.

All this time, the plucky *Johnston* had been fighting alone. She was an easy target for the enraged cruisers and destroyers. Instead of trying to hit the fleeing carriers, the big ships concentrated on the wallowing destroyer. She was hit so many times that some shells went through holes already torn into the hull. At 0945, Evans ordered the crew to abandon ship. She went to the bottom at 1010 hours with 183 of her crew. As the survivors struggled in the water, some of the destroyer's depth charges detonated, killing some of the swimmers. One Japanese destroyer passed close by, and some Americans saw officers saluting them. Evans was lost. He posthumously received the Medal of Honor.

Only the damaged *Heermann* remained afloat.

The charge of the destroyers was one of the most courageous ever seen in naval history. The doomed tin cans not only prevented the Japanese battleships and cruisers from savaging the carriers and invasion beaches, but they also managed to damage at least four ships severely, each weighing more than all the destroyers combined. Even with a vast superiority in heavy caliber guns, the only ships the Japanese managed to sink were the three destroyers and a single carrier, the *Gambier Bay*.

While their carriers ran for their lives, the fighters and bombers made aggressive runs at the Japanese ships, dropping their ordnance as they evaded the intense anti-aircraft artillery fire. Scores of 5-inch rockets trailing long fingers of gray smoke reached out to explode on the decks and superstructure, causing great damage and killing exposed gunners. Even when they ran out of bombs, the Avengers and Wildcats continued to make attack runs in order to distract the gunners from planes still carrying bombs.

The leading Japanese cruisers came almost abeam of the fleeing carriers and continued to fire. Tall multicolored waterspouts rose around the

CVEs. Sprague ordered Avengers from Taffy 2 to attack the cruisers. One air-dropped torpedo hit *Chikuma*, disabling her port screw and rudder. The ship fell out of formation for a time. At the same time, Lieutenant E. L. "Blue" Archer, who had gained a reputation for daring at Guam and Saipan, joined two Avengers to strafe the Japanese destroyers and looked for bigger game. They saw *Chikuma* and *Tone* turning to port and dived at them. Archer dropped his 500-pound bombs on one of the cruisers. He aimed his eight rockets at the superstructure. The missiles ripped apart the ship's bridge.

Taffy 3's dash to the south only postponed the inevitable. Starting at 0715, *Kalinin Bay* took the first of fifteen direct hits. One of the battleship *Haruna*'s 14-inch shells struck the starboard side of the hangar deck just aft the forward elevator on the hangar deck. The 14-inch armor-piercing shell was five feet long and weighed 1,400 pounds. Fortunately, that was the only hit by a battleship on the carrier.

Chikuma, *Tone*, and another cruiser closed within 18,000 yards and opened fire. *Kalinin Bay*'s gunners fired back with the single 5-inch gun on the stern fantail even as huge waterspouts erupted from the sea and drenched them. Guided by radar and good fire control, *Kalinin Bay* did better with a single gun than the cruisers. The 5-inch gun scored a direct hit on *Haguro*'s Number 2 turret. A plane immediately laid a bomb on the same spot, starting a fire. *Haguro* turned to port and away from the action.

The Japanese, still believing their targets were large fleet carriers, were firing armor-piercing shells. But the CVEs had nothing more substantial than splinter plating to protect the crew. The Japanese 8-inch armor-piercing round weighed 270 pounds. Some of the heavy shells tore through the thin steel without detonating. But *Gambier Bay* took a direct hit from one of *Yamato*'s huge 18.1-inch shells. She became the only American carrier ever sunk by naval gunfire.

Meanwhile, *White Plains* fired her single stern 5-inch gun at the cruiser *Shokai*, while the destroyer *Samuel B. Roberts*, during her heroic attack, fired at the same cruiser. A large explosion erupted from the *Shokai*, probably from her deck-mounted torpedoes being hit. The explosions damaged her engines, and she sheered out of line.

The remaining cruisers fired more salvoes, coming close to *Kitkun Bay*. The *Haguro* took *Chikuma*'s place in the line and, at 12,000 yards, straddled the carrier. At that point, she took several hits from 8-inch shells. *Kitkun Bay*'s radar and radio were destroyed while she slowed and tried to maintain course.

By 0850, nearly all the Japanese ships had suffered some damage from the air strikes and destroyer attacks. About sixty Avengers from TG 38.4 sank the destroyer *Noshiro*.

Farther to the south, Taffy 2 launched planes to attack the cruisers. An Avenger hit *Chikuma* with a torpedo, disabling her port screw and permanently removing her from the fight.

The light cruiser *Yahagi* and four destroyers got to within 14,000 yards of *Kalinin Bay* and opened fire. The carrier doggedly returned fire with her indispensable stern gun.

The Japanese launched at least twelve torpedoes at the Lucky K, all of which missed, the wakes easily spotted by her crew. *Haguro* resumed the attack and joined Tone from a range of 10,000 yards and fired twenty-eight armor-piercing shells at the beleaguered CVE. Ten more hits shook the ship. One shell detonated deep in the hull among the oil tanks and caused great damage. Responding quickly, the crew fought the fires. But for every enemy shell that exploded, at least one tore from port to starboard leaving only ragged holes in their wake. Some hit the smokestacks on the flight deck or damaged the elevator, but the plucky carrier fought on. The last 8-inch shell splintered the flight deck amidships, passed through the boiler uptakes, and came out the galley deck starboard. The Lucky K listed seven degrees to port, but this was slowly corrected. At 0910 hours, several torpedoes launched from the enemy destroyers ran at the twisting and damaged CVEs. One of *St. Lo*'s Avenger pilots, Lieutenant Leonard Waldrop, dived at a torpedo with his guns blazing and exploded it a hundred yards from *Kalinin Bay*'s stern. Remarkably, the 5-inch stern gun fired at an approaching torpedo and deflected it with a near miss. The ship's luck was stronger than ever.

Ten minutes later, under savage attack by planes and having lost the initiative, Admiral Kurita broke off the action and turned north. *Chikuma* was scuttled by torpedoes from Japanese destroyers. Kurita's force had managed to sink the *Hoel, Roberts, Johnston*, and *Gambier Bay*. The rest of Taffy 3, bloodied and crippled, was still on the surface. Among them was *Kalinin Bay*.

The carrier *St. Lo* is attacked by kamikaze planes at Samar, October 25, 1944.
Official U.S. Navy Photo

A measure of the American fighting spirit was personified by one of Sprague's crew on *Fanshawe Bay* when he yelled, "They're getting away!"

But the ordeal was not over. At 1050 hours, eight kamikazes came from the west and dived on the ships. *St. Lo* was sunk and *Kitkun Bay* damaged. Two of the A6M Zero suicide planes went for *Kalinin Bay*. Her anti-aircraft artillery batteries filled the sky with hot steel. The first Zero hit the starboard flight deck at a shallow angle and skidded into the sea in flames. The second came almost straight down. Hit by anti-aircraft artillery fire, it smashed into the port aft smokestack and catwalk before plunging into the sea. Two more were shot down by *Kalinin Bay* and the close escort. At last, the day's action was over.

Her exhausted gunners had fired 170 5-inch, 1,750 40mm, and 4,800 20mm rounds. The battle off Samar had lasted four hours and fifteen minutes. The battered *Kalinin Bay* recovered several of its own planes as well as nine from other carriers.

Nine of the crew had been killed and sixty wounded, a remarkably low number for such a horrific battle. Against all odds, three Japanese cruisers were sunk and three more heavily damaged.

The Battle of Samar was over. It had been a true David-and-Goliath struggle against the most incredible odds. Admiral Sprague wrote to

Chief Naval Officer Ernest J. King, "The high degree of skill, the un-flinching courage, the inspired determination to go down fighting, of the officers and men under my command cannot be too highly praised. The Japanese gunnery was good as to mean range, poor as to advance range, and with excellent patterns. It is believed they had an airborne spotter overhead. The fact that a large number of shells were armor-piercing, non-explosive, resulted in much less damage from hits received. In sum-mation, the failure of the enemy main body and encircling light forces to completely wipe out all vessels of this Task Unit can be attributed to our successful smoke screen, our torpedo counter-attack, continuous harassment of enemy by bomb, torpedo, and strafing air attacks, timely maneuvers, and the definite partiality of Almighty God."

A month later, Lucky K limped into San Diego, where the planes and pilots of the valiant VC-3 landed at Naval Air Station North Island. The ship headed north to San Pedro for extensive repairs.

Kalinin Bay resumed her duties of ferrying planes and crew to for-ward bases. Her crew knew she was special. On February 15, 1945, Cap-tain Williamson, who had received the Navy Cross, welcomed the new crewmen. "We hope that you will learn to love this ship and that you will share with us our pride in her. We who fought the ship against the best the enemy had to offer know that teamwork and devotion to duty can bring triumph in the face of tremendous odds."

Lucky K was decommissioned on May 15, 1946. She was sold for scrap in 1948. The winner of five battle stars and the Presidential Unit Citation no longer exists. In fact, not one of the feisty but unheralded CVEs are left. But they made history.

The next essay takes a great leap from surface warships to submarines. For the first two years after Pearl Harbor, American submarines, ordered to conduct unrestricted submarine warfare on Japan, were plagued with unreliable torpedoes. For every ninety torpedoes fired at enemy ships, only about fifteen resulted in a sinking. The problem had to be fixed, but first it had to be proven to exist. That was a harder task than it should have been. The next essay takes a hard look at when submarine technol-ogy and tactics ran up against hard-nosed bureaucracy.

THE MARK 14: FROM DUD TO DEADLY

Published in *World War II History*, 2022

In the first decade of the twentieth century, Britain's First Sea Lord, Admiral Sir John "Jacky" Fisher, the father of the modern Royal Navy, predicted that the submarine would one day be the "battleship of the future, and the torpedo the weapon of the future." It would take the better part of forty years before Fisher's prediction would be proven correct. Every nation, even Germany, suffered from problems with their torpedoes. The United States Navy was particularly afflicted just as it was entering the largest war in human history. The vaunted and highly sophisticated Mark 14 torpedo, a marvel of American technology, had a fifty percent failure rate.

Lieutenant Dan Daspit, captain of the U.S. submarine *Tinosa*, couldn't believe his luck. Framed neatly in the periscope eyepiece was a sitting duck. The 19,250-ton Japanese tanker *Tonan Maru No. 3* was all alone, dead in the water. *Tinosa* was on her second war patrol, having left Midway on July 7, 1943. For a week she had prowled along the Japanese sea routes between Borneo and Truk. On the afternoon of July 24, Daspit spotted a thin trail of gray funnel smoke on the horizon. Remaining submerged, he set up a textbook approach and fired four Mark 14 torpedoes at the ship, which was making only 10 knots. Every one of his "fish" ran true. Thirty seconds later, the sonarman heard the repeated "thumps" of the torpedoes striking the hull but no explosions. The tanker turned and increased speed.

Swearing, Daspit turned in pursuit. After a long nighttime chase, he was in position to try again. His torpedomen checked every fish to make sure it was working perfectly. Then, coming at the tanker from the starboard quarter, he fired two more torpedoes. Both hit and exploded. The muted rumble echoed through *Tinosa*'s hull. The crew cheered.

The *Tonan Maru* had been hit in the engine room and coasted to a stop. An experienced submarine commander, Daspit took his time approaching the ship's port side. He would fire one torpedo at a time from 1,000 yards, aiming to strike the tanker's hull at exactly 90 degrees. The 680 pounds of high-explosive Torpex would blast a huge hole in the hull. Two or three fish should send her to the bottom. The tanker couldn't run. *Tinosa* was going to hang the huge *Tonan Maru*'s scalp on her belt.

At 0930 hours, *Tinosa* fired her first torpedo. It ran straight and true. The wake was a long deadly white finger reaching out to touch the helpless ship. Then nothing happened. The torpedo had failed to explode. This was nothing new to the American submarine fleet, so Daspit fired again. No towering column of water erupted from the tanker's hull. No crushing roar echoed through the deep.

Gritting his teeth in frustration, the sub's skipper fired again. And again. Five, then six deadly Mark 14 torpedoes, the most advanced antiship weapon in the U.S. inventory, failed to explode. The fifth one appeared to raise a tall plume of white water as a tinny "Phwyinng!" noise came through the hull. Number 6 broached and leaped after striking the enemy's hull, then sank.

Then the tables turned. The *Tonan Maru* had radioed a distress call. A Japanese destroyer was coming with a bone in her teeth. *Tinosa* had to depart the area fast.

Daspit fired two more torpedoes at the tanker as they turned away. The sonarman reported that both weapons seemed to hit and then stop.

As his sub raced eastward, Daspit wrote of the frustrating hunt in his log. "I find it hard to convince myself that I saw this." He had no explanation for why the torpedoes failed to explode. Out of fifteen Mark 14s fired, only two had detonated, and those had been fired from an oblique angle. The others were so carefully set up as to be right out of the textbook. Yet not one had done its job.

He headed directly back to Pearl Harbor, doing what no American sub skipper ever wanted to do—return with an "empty bag." He was met at the sub pier by the new Commander, Submarines, Pacific (COMSUBPAC), Rear Admiral Charles Lockwood, a career submarine officer.

Lockwood was a hard-driving, conscientious officer who had a reputation for giving full support to his squadrons, his boats, his commanders, and their crews. He took Daspit up to his office, where the exasperated sub skipper related what had happened with the *Tonan Maru*.

Lockwood listened, nodding. He later wrote, "I expected a torrent of cuss words, damning me, the Bureau of Ordnance, the Newport Torpedo Station, and the base torpedo shop. I couldn't have blamed him. 19,000-ton tankers don't grow on trees. I think Dan was so furious as to be practically speechless."

But when the single torpedo *Tinosa* had brought back to Pearl was examined at the submarine base torpedo shop, it was found to be in perfect working order.

Lieutenant Commander Daspit's report was the most recent and extreme case of a growing problem within the U.S. submarine fleet since the beginning of the war. From the first patrols, after the Commander-in-Chief, U.S. Pacific Fleet (CINCPAC) Admiral Chester Nimitz had ordered unrestricted submarine warfare on all Japanese shipping, submarine commanders had complained of torpedoes that failed to work properly. On December 14, one week after Pearl Harbor, the USS *Seawolf* encountered a Japanese freighter near the Philippines and fired eight torpedoes. Seven missed, one hit. And failed to explode.

So began the litany of problems with the navy's technical marvel. In the first months of the war, American subs fired ninety-seven torpedoes at enemy shipping. Only three ships were sunk. Some torpedoes failed to explode, while others, even though aimed with care, seemed to miss or run under their target. Even worse, several had blown up before hitting the side of a Japanese ship.

Torpedoes were the first totally autonomous guided missile. The German Navy had sunk hundreds of Allied ships in the First World War with torpedoes; by 1925, the latest versions were highly complex machines. The Mark 14 was designed and developed to replace the older, shorter Mark 10 that had been in service during and after World War One.

Designed primarily by engineers at the Navy Bureau of Ordnance (BuOrd), the Mark 14 was built at the Newport Torpedo Station (NTS) in 1926. They were large and expensive weapons at 21 feet long, 21

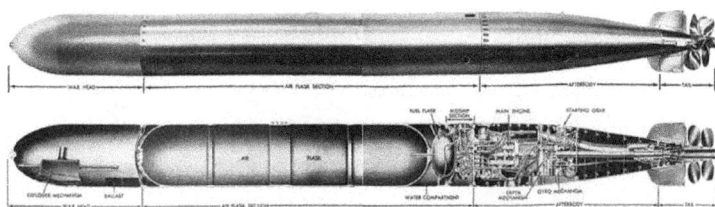

The Mark 14 torpedo, showing interior details.

inches in diameter, and weighing more than 3,000 pounds. Powered by steam, they could run for 9,000 yards (5.1 miles) at 26 knots. They were extremely complex and required the most meticulous machining and assembly work. By 1940, they cost upwards of $10,000 each, five times as much as a new automobile.

The most important component was the Mark 6 exploder mechanism, without which the torpedo would be useless. The way to sink a ship was to break its back at the keel. This often made a ship break in two. Obviously, this required a torpedo to explode directly under the hull. To this end, BuOrd had designed the new exploder based on the successful British Duplex and German magnetic mine designs. Its most radical feature was the magnetic influence exploder, Project G53. It was a closely guarded secret, so much so that even though a maintenance and operating manual had been written, it was never printed or distributed.

The influence of a steel hull triggered the magnetic exploder as it passed directly beneath a ship where there was no armor. For this reason, the first Mark 14s carried a moderate warhead. BuOrd was under a tight budget and wanted to avoid spending money on unnecessary testing. Only one test of the Mark 6 mechanism was conducted in May 1926. The target, ironically, was a derelict submarine. Two Mark 14s armed with the magnetic exploder were fired at the sub. One ran under the target and failed to detonate. The second one exploded and sank the sub. No further testing was done. So as the war drew closer, the submarine force would fight with torpedoes that only worked half the time.

In 1939, the navy demanded a larger warhead, and BuOrd authorized it to be increased to 680 pounds, enough to tear open the sturdiest

The only live-fire test of the Mark 14 torpedo before the war. Two were fired, only one worked. *Official U.S. Navy Photo*

hull. Several sub skippers fired at their targets only to witness premature detonation well before the torpedo was close enough to do serious damage. Often the enemy ship suffered little more than dented plates that were easily repaired.

The Mark 6 also had a contact exploder, consisting of a trigger, firing pin, and detonator. In essence, it was not much different from a gun's trigger, firing pin, and the primer in a cartridge. When the torpedo struck a ship's hull, the head was rammed backward, driving the firing pin into the detonator over the warhead, causing it to explode. The contact exploder was intended to provide a "backup" if the magnetic pistol failed to work. But it was useless since the warhead exploded even before contact with the hull.

By mid-1942, more than eight hundred torpedoes had been used in the Pacific war. Eighty percent had failed. But at Pearl Harbor, COM-SUBPAC Admiral Robert English consistently sided with BuOrd and blamed his sub skippers for their "lack of initiative."

But the man who would soon change everything, Rear Admiral Charles Lockwood, then Commander, Submarines, South West Pacific in Australia, was listening to his own submarine skippers. He undertook an unofficial test of the torpedoes in June 1942. He supervised firing torpedoes set to specific depths through a submerged net. This was the first real test of the Mark 14 since 1926. The holes in the net showed that the torpedoes ran far below the set depth, sometimes as much as ten to fifteen feet deeper than set. This was conclusive proof, but again, the sacred cows at BuOrd dismissed the findings and said the submarine commanders were not trimming the torpedoes properly.

Finally, under pressure from Admiral Nimitz, himself a former sub-mariner, BuOrd conducted their own tests in August 1942. The root of the depth setting problem had been the fault of BuOrd. When they increased the size of the warhead, which made the weapon heavier, they failed to change the mechanism that controlled depth.

Yet the erratic depth was only one of three major problems with the torpedoes. Dozens of torpedoes were exploding well before reaching the target. The cause was the hyper-sensitive magnetic exploder. It was being triggered by a combination of the Earth's magnetic field and the approach to a ship's hull. These problems should have been found and fixed long before the war began.

Rear Admiral Charles Lockwood was appointed COMSUBPAC in January 1943. When his captains turned in numerous reports of premature explosions, or duds, BuOrd steadfastly maintained that there was nothing wrong with the torpedoes. The problem was bad approaches and poor maintenance. This naturally started a furor among the submarine fleet. U.S. sub crews were risking their lives for nothing. The transports and warships of the Japanese Navy sailed on unmolested.

Lockwood requested permission to disconnect the magnetic exploder on the torpedoes, but BuOrd wouldn't allow it. The submarine crews were forbidden to do anything beyond regular maintenance to the torpedoes. They were not to touch the Mark 6 exploders. To prevent any unauthorized tampering, BuOrd ordered that the sub base torpedo shop apply dabs of paint to the screws that held the exploder mechanism to the torpedo body. Any attempt to remove or tamper with it would mar the paint. With the zeal that American military men sometimes take when going against orders, some torpedomen went into the shop and asked about the paint color. If someone said it was blue, crews found a

small can of blue paint to retouch the screw heads after they had personally worked on the exploders. In the event a torpedo was returned to the
shop, there was no way for anyone to know the mechanisms had been
touched.

To make matters worse, politics were involved. Rhode Island, traditionally a state with strong bonds between the electorate and legislature,
looked upon the NTS with protective eyes. One naval officer stated, "If
I had the temerity to fire an incompetent or insubordinate worker, the
secretary of the navy would be visited by both Rhode Island senators and
at least one congressman, demanding the man be reinstated."

This, of course, virtually guaranteed that American torpedoes would
be poorly designed and made. This became more evident by the spring
of 1943 when it was learned that the Japanese oxygen-fed torpedo had
a larger warhead, could travel eight miles at 60 knots, and rarely failed
to detonate on contact. The only good fortune for the United States was
that the Japanese submarine fleet was literally forbidden to attack unarmed ships such as transports, freighters, and tankers. They were told to
hunt down and find American warships, considered more worthy targets.
The ratio of transports to warships by 1943 was nearly five to one.

As the number of duds and premature explosions rose, there could be
no doubt something had to change. In the summer of 1943, Lockwood
flew to Washington, defended his skippers to BuOrd, and demanded
that something be done. Under pressure from the Chief of Naval Operations Admiral Ernest J. King, the order came down in June to disconnect
the magnetic exploder from all the torpedoes. This had been done when
the *Tinosa* left Midway on her second patrol. Lieutenant Commander
Daspit had every reason to believe his load of Mark 14s would do the
job. This proved to be a forlorn hope. While the *Tinosa*'s patrol was not
the incident that broke the camel's back, it was the most appalling. The
complaints continued to mount. Lockwood's staff began a systematic
examination of the problem.

Lockwood took personal action. In order to convince BuOrd that
the problem was not with his subs, skippers, or crews but with the torpedoes, he called in Commander Charles B. Momsen. "Swede" Momsen,
whose outspoken habit of going against the official grain had earned him

few friends in the Pentagon, was one of the most innovative submarine engineers in the navy. He had overseen the rescue of the crew of the USS *Squalus* after it sunk off Portsmouth, New Hampshire, in 1939. He was the inventor of the Momsen Lung, the portable breathing device that would save submariners from sunken subs. He was also the father of the Submarine Rescue Chamber, which had become part of the navy inventory in 1939. The modern submarine navy owes the lives of many of its men to Swede Momsen. He was in command of Submarine Squadron 2. Even after the BuOrd order, the reports of dud hits continued to pour in. He and Lockwood discussed the torpedo problem. Momsen, who had to endure the frustration of his skippers carrying useless torpedoes all the way to Japan for nothing, applied his engineer's mind to the solution.

The first step was to determine why the contact exploder did not work, even when fired under optimal conditions. He scoured charts of the waters around the Hawaiian Islands to find a place where sheer vertical cliffs went right down to deep water and a sandy bottom. There torpedoes could be recovered after firing. An area on the coast of the small island of Kahoolawe was perfect. Momsen, along with COMSUBPAC's gunnery and torpedo officer, Commander Art Taylor, supervised the live firings from the USS *Muskellunge* at the cliffs beginning on August 31.

The first two exploded. The third one did not. Momsen himself went into the water to examine the torpedo. It was broken in two, with the warhead split. Taking extreme care, the crew hoisted the unexploded torpedo onto a barge and took it back to Pearl Harbor. After disconnecting the warhead, Momsen and his crew found the reason for the failure. The contact exploder was a marvel of engineering, but it was both too ruggedly built and too delicate. This was further proven by sliding a torpedo warhead filled with sand and a live exploder down a cable from a 90-foot "cherry picker" onto a steel plate to simulate different angles and speeds of impact. Seventy percent of the hits failed to explode.

This confirmed what Momsen had suspected. Submarine commanders had been told that the best and most certain angle to fire a torpedo at a target was from exactly 90 degrees, or broadside on. Acute angles were less desirable. But as was shown by *Tinosa*'s experience, this was not true. Daspit had fired eight torpedoes at exactly 90-degree angles at his target and not one went off. Ironically, the first two he had fired that morning after the long chase both detonated, even though they struck the tanker's hull at an oblique angle.

Momsen and Taylor realized that the contact exploder's firing pin was being distorted in a head-on impact, and the deceleration forces slowed the pin's motion in its bearings. The spring failed to move it fast enough to set off the explosive charge. Examination of the primer showed hardly a dent, not nearly enough to ignite the warhead.

The drop test showed that a glancing impact allowed the firing pin to act properly. In other words, the best angle to fire was anything *other* than dead on.

Interestingly, BuOrd made a small attempt to find the root of the problem by consulting Albert Einstein at Princeton University. The distinguished physicist examined the Mark 6 blueprints and concluded that the impact was distorting the firing pin. He recommended a "void" between the outer shell and the firing mechanism to eliminate the problem. But BuOrd did not follow his suggestion. Momsen showed the test results to Lockwood, who then took them to Washington. Lockwood returned a few days later, as he said in his official war diary, "madder than hell." BuOrd finally admitted the exploder was at fault and would design a new one. But that would take a year or more. Then Momsen told Lockwood that it should be possible to rebuild the contact exploder with different materials. The exploder had to be both light and strong. Exotic alloys proved to be the key. The machine shop at the sub base obtained light alloys from, remarkably enough, the melted-down engine of a Japanese fighter that had been shot down during the Pearl Harbor attack. New firing pins, springs, and guide tracks were machined and assembled. The new designs were tested and performed exactly as hoped. Yet the project needed a lot more metal than one engine could provide, and another source was found at Hickam Army Airfield. Aircraft propellers had to be both light and strong. As one Army Air Force officer is alluded to have said after being asked for as many damaged propellers as he could find, "A better use for a busted prop couldn't be found anywhere."

Lockwood insisted on every single new exploder being perfect before allowing them to be installed in the torpedoes and loaded into his submarines. With every machine shop at the sub base working on it, by the late fall of 1943, the Pacific Fleet's submarines were finally armed with reliable weapons.

Underruns were still a concern. Taylor and Momsen again supervised firing torpedoes through a series of evenly spaced nets. The tests showed that not only were the Mark 14s running well below their set depth, but they also were not running flat. They appeared to wobble, like a sine wave, alternately deep and shallow. It was sheer luck on what part of the track a target happened to be. This was not something that could be fixed at Pearl Harbor. It would have to go right to BuOrd and the NTS. But at least Lockwood's skippers could make allowances for the erratic depth settings.

When the first reliable torpedoes were sent to sea, the war had been going on for twenty-one months. Of the fifty-three U.S. subs lost in the Second World War, twenty were sunk prior to October 1943. There can be no greater frustration than to die without having inflicted damage on the enemy. Dozens of patrols had been wasted, hundreds of American lives lost, and important enemy targets missed. At last the problem for the submarine commanders was what it should have been from the beginning: hitting the target. As Lockwood put it, "From that moment on, all major exploder problems suddenly disappeared."

By this time, the sub force had evolved. They had started the war with hardly any experience in undersea warfare. Submarines were intended to be scouts for the battle fleet, attacking any enemy ships that threatened the surface force and picking off any stragglers after a battle. The slapdash fleet of prewar subs skulked under the surface by day, then surfaced in the dark to recharge their batteries while hunting for enemy ships. While reducing the risk of detection, this cautious tactic cut in half the actual hunting time and reduced their patrol range. As more subs joined the fleet, they could cover more areas of the Pacific, reaching the Yellow Sea, East and South China Seas, and south to Australia. Midway and Brisbane became sub bases.

When Momsen and Lockwood finally fixed the torpedo problem, the men who had started the war with little experience had matured with a nucleus of aggressive, skilled, and innovative submarine commanders. Men like Dudley "Mush" Morton of *Wahoo*, Richard O'Kane of *Tang*, and Eugene Flucky of *Barb* were changing the tactics. They patrolled on the surface by day, keeping a sharp lookout for planes and scanning the seas with the new radar. This doubled the area they could patrol. With the reliable torpedoes virtually guaranteeing a kill, the men under Lockwood's command began sweeping the Pacific Ocean of Japanese ships. All they needed was good intelligence information, initiative, and luck. Lockwood told one new sub skipper, "If you're not lucky, I can't use you." It was still a dangerous game of cat and mouse, but now the fleet's subs were not unarmed. They were deadly sharks hunting for prey.

Momsen was promoted to captain and awarded the Legion of Merit for his work on finding and solving the torpedo problem. He had played a significant but little-remembered role in assuring that every U.S. submarine went to war against Japan with reliable torpedoes. By August 1945, 1,178 merchant vessels were sunk, totaling 5,053,491 tons. Of those, fifty-five percent were sent to the bottom by submarines. In fact, the United States sub fleet had done what Admirals von Holtzendorff and Doenitz had promised the Kaiser and Hitler that their U-boats would do but never achieved: the successful strangling of a nation by undersea warfare.

The role of the United States Navy's battleships was forged in the first year of the Pacific War. Once the power of the big gun was recognized to be better served to support amphibious operations instead of being wasted in ship-to-ship slugging matches, even the old guard of battleship admirals saw the light. The next essay tells the saga of a single battleship, the USS *South Dakota*, which could be considered a representative of the last of the big guns club. As BB-57, *South Dakota* was the lead ship of her class. Only seven more battleships would be launched in the United States, ending with the USS *Wisconsin* (BB-64) in 1944. At that time, an even larger class was being considered, the expanded *Iowas*, with the USS *Montana*, which would have four three-gun, 16-inch turrets. But by mid-1945, it was increasingly obvious that the *Montanas* wouldn't be needed.

South Dakota served in both the Atlantic and Pacific. Initially, she was considered an unlucky ship, having had some unfortunate accidents outside of combat. But she had one very lucky day off the coast of Okinawa in May 1945. The reader will again meet Captain Swede Momsen, commander of the *South Dakota* that day.

BATTLESHIP X: THE STORY OF THE
USS *SOUTH DAKOTA*

The United States Navy built sixty-four battleships during the twentieth century. We've all heard of the famous battleships like *Maine*, *Arizona*, and *Missouri*. Several have earned a place in the pantheon of great ships. But most have long since faded into obscurity to all but their crews. One such ship is the USS *South Dakota*. While she served from 1942 to the end of the war, *South Dakota*'s career never put her in the headlines of the American press.

So why write about a battleship most Americans have never heard of? Because *South Dakota* did her job, her sailors and officers did their duty, and together they brought victory closer.

Yet there is another reason.

Some ships have earned reputations, warranted or not, for being cursed, luckless, or, to use the vernacular of sailors, "hoodoo ships." Most sailors would admit to being superstitious, and serving on a ship plagued with accidents, unusually severe battle damage, or incompetent captains has been a constant in history. But a string of bad luck can turn around, changing a hard luck ship into one with a sterling reputation. Such it was with *South Dakota*.

Why did *South Dakota* seem to run into bad luck? Some of her crew believed the reason was that, in her case, a long-standing tradition was broken. Upon her commissioning, the governor of South Dakota, bound by tradition to present a handmade silver tea service to the captain, failed to come through. This was no small matter. Every United States battleship named for a state and all cruisers bearing the name of a city were presented with a silver platter or tea service upon commissioning.

The bad luck struck almost at once. During trials in the Chesapeake Bay, she went aground and her electrical system failed. A few weeks later, while conducting speed and gunnery exercises off the coast of Maine, the huge ship struck a whale, tearing the mammal in two. More repairs. Captain Thomas Gatch might have been court-martialed, but the incident never made the papers.

In 1936, upon hearing of Japan withdrawing from the terms of the 1931 Naval Limitation Treaty, the United States Navy decided to use the Expansion Clause in the treaty and design three new classes of battleships averaging 45,000 tons. This resulted in the *North Carolina*-class, the *South Dakota*-class, and the *Iowa*-class.

South Dakota, the lead ship in her class, was built at the New York Shipbuilding Corporation and launched on June 7, 1941. At 45,000 tons displacement fully loaded and 680 feet long, she was not the largest of the new battleships that saw service in the Second World War. Her main armament of nine 16-inch .45-caliber rifles in three turrets was formidable. She could fire nine tons of heavy shells at a target 37,000 yards away, far beyond the visible horizon. She was built for speed and long-distance hitting power.

Battleship *South Dakota*'s forward turrets, showing fire control radar. *Official U.S. Navy Photo*

South Dakota was fitted with SK air search and SD surface search radar, giving her a large advantage over the Japanese battleships, which did not yet have radar. In addition, she carried the Mark 3 fire control system for her main batteries and the Mark 4 for her secondary guns.

The new fast battleships were considered "a tremendous leap forward in technology, orders of magnitude over the old battleships, even those that had been modernized." In addition to their speed and modern fire control, they used a third less fuel than the pre-war battleships.

Chief of Naval Operations Admiral Ernest King ordered the new ship to the Pacific to support the navy and Marines on Guadalcanal on August 14, 1942. Rear Admiral Willis "Ching" Lee commanded Battleship Division 6 (BatDiv 6), which consisted of his flagship *South Dakota* and the USS *Washington*. In concert with the anti-aircraft light cruiser USS *Juneau*, *South Dakota* arrived at Tongatabu on the morning of September 6. Aboard *Juneau* were the five Sullivan brothers, whose deaths only two months later would make headlines across the nation. Bound for the Solomons, the ships weighed anchor and left port, passing the cruiser USS *Atlanta*, sister of *Juneau*, escorting the carrier USS *Saratoga*, damaged by the Japanese submarine *I-26* on August 31.

But the new battleship was back at Tongatabu in less than four hours, having suffered yet another of the humiliating accidents that were to plague the ship in her early career. Having to rely on outdated charts, Captain Gatch had run the battleship on a coral reef. The sharp hard fangs of coral had torn an 18-inch-wide gash the entire length of her underwater hull. She was ordered back to Pearl Harbor with the *Atlanta* and *Saratoga* for repairs in the drydock. It was a serious blow to the navy's plans for the fast battleships. Their role was critical in the Solomons campaign. Now *South Dakota* would be at least three weeks late for her baptism of fire.

She finally arrived off Guadalcanal in October. As part of Task Force 16 under Admiral William F. Halsey, *South Dakota*'s first fight against the Imperial Navy was at the savage Battle of Santa Cruz Island on October 26. While her main guns did not participate in this action, *South Dakota*'s dense forest of anti-aircraft guns dealt heavy losses to Japanese dive and torpedo bombers attacking the carrier *Enterprise*. *South Dakota* herself was targeted by Kate torpedo bombers, all of which she avoided. Another attack by Val dive bombers put one bomb on the ship's forward turret but failed to penetrate. Captain Gatch was wounded while directing the ship during the attack. The bomb tore deep gouges into two of the guns of Number 2 turret. The guns would be unusable until replaced. One Avenger from the *Hornet*, which was being savaged by Japanese bombers at that very moment, had ditched close to *South Dakota*. As the crew climbed out of the sinking bomber, some gunners mistook the big-bellied plane for a surfacing submarine and loosed some of the 5-inch turrets on it before the destroyer *Preston* moved in and picked up the downed flyers. Another destroyer, the *Smith*, was struck on her foredeck by a damaged Kate torpedo bomber, starting a huge blaze. The *Smith's* skipper, Lieutenant Commander Hunter Wood, directed his burning ship to the *South Dakota*, then moving at full speed toward the *Enterprise*. Wood got as close as possible to the boiling and foaming wake of the huge battleship. The spray washed over the small destroyer, dousing the flames.

After the battle, her anti-aircraft artillery gunners claimed twenty-six enemy planes, twice as many as had been shot down by the entire task force. Early claims by anti-aircraft artillery gunners tended to be high on ships that had just arrived in the war zone.

Enterprise was damaged in the attacks, but *Hornet* was a loss and had to be sunk by a U.S. submarine. *South Dakota* withdrew with the rest of TF 16, but in yet another debacle, collided with the destroyer *Mahan*, named for the prophet of naval warfare, Captain Alfred Thayer Mahan.

While *Mahan's* bow was crushed back to the forward turret, the battleship reached Nouméa for repairs. The repair ship *Vestal's* crew induced a list in *South Dakota* in order to expose the damaged hull plates. The work was completed on November 6. *Vestal* had been tied up alongside USS *Arizona* at Pearl Harbor on December 7.

With *Enterprise* the only carrier in the southwest Pacific, Halsey ordered *South Dakota* to join *Washington*, the heavy cruiser *Northampton*, and nine destroyers to stay with the carrier. They headed to Guadalcanal to head off a predicted bombardment of Henderson Field on the island. Rear Admiral Willis Lee was going to face Admiral Nobutake Kondo's force of the battleships *Kirishima*, two heavy cruisers, and a destroyer screen. For once, luck came to *South Dakota*'s aid. Japanese search planes spotted the task group but identified them as cruisers and destroyers. Kondo, who was expecting battleships, was confused.

The two fleets discovered each other that night off Savo Island.

Washington and *South Dakota* had little experience with their main batteries and almost no training for night fighting. The Japanese had a great advantage in this, except for having no fire control radar. *Washington* fired at 2317 hours on November 14, using her fire control radar. *South Dakota* followed suit, targeting two of Kondo's destroyers. The battleship's gunners claimed to have sunk both enemy ships, but neither was seriously hit. In the early part of the action, *South Dakota* was hampered because two of her forward guns were still out of commission.

At 2330, her luck took a turn for the worst. A short in her main electrical panel cut off the radar and most of her fire control, leaving her virtually blind in the battle. She was silhouetted by two burning American destroyers, making her easily visible to Kondo's heavy ships.

At 2340 hours, she fired her aft turret main guns at two of Kondo's destroyers. The first three-gun salvo set fire to the Kingfisher search planes on the quarterdeck. The second salvo blew the blazing planes overboard.

Again her electrical system was disabled by shock, leaving her gunners blind for five minutes. Just before midnight, the repaired radar picked up the approaching *Kirishima* and two cruisers.

Following Japanese night doctrine, Kondo fired several torpedoes at the battleship, but they all missed. At this point, *South Dakota* was closely engaged with the Japanese, only 5,000 yards away. She received twenty-six hits from the cruiser's 8-inch guns and one 14-inch hit from *Kirishima*. Most of the damage was on the superstructure.

While *South Dakota* acted as Kondo's whipping boy, *Washington* was left unmolested. She could concentrate her full salvos on *Kirishima*. *South Dakota*, despite having only part of her main battery functioning and a balky radar, managed to hit one Japanese cruiser and hit *Kirishima*.

Kirishima was fatally damaged by the 16-inch shells, and Kondo withdrew after firing more torpedoes. Lee ordered Gatch to leave the area at high speed. The battleship had sustained heavy damage above and below the waterline. Forty of her crew were dead, and 140 were wounded, including Calvin Graham, who was twelve years old. He had lied about his age to get into the navy and was the youngest American serviceman of the Second World War. *South Dakota* received the Navy Unit Commendation for her role in the Second Battle of Guadalcanal. Japanese destroyers later sunk *Kirishima*.

At Nouméa, *South Dakota* tied up alongside the repair ship *Prometheus*, which restored some of her ailing systems. But she wouldn't return to the Solomons. By November 29, she was bound for the Panama Canal and New York for an Atlantic deployment.

At the Brooklyn Navy Yard, she went into drydock for repairs and refit. Despite her less-than-stellar performance, she was lauded in the press as the ship that won the naval battle of Guadalcanal. This was when she was given the code name "Battleship X" as a security measure.

In early 1943, Captain Gatch was relieved by Captain Lyndee McCormick. *South Dakota* was sent to the North Atlantic along with her newer sister, *Alabama*, and the carrier *Ranger* as part of a screening force to protect the arctic convoys queueing up for runs to Murmansk.

The main threat was the German battleship *Tirpitz*, sister of the *Bismarck*, and the heavy cruiser *Scharnhorst*. The two German warships likely would come out of their Norwegian fjords and wreak havoc among the convoys. Considering the excellent German gunnery, it was fortunate that the unlucky *South Dakota* never encountered the powerful raiders.

For three months, in concert with Royal Navy warships, *South Dakota* provided escort for the Murmansk convoys. In August, she returned to Norfolk. As part of Battleship Division 9 under Admiral Edward Hanson, *South Dakota* again sailed for the Pacific, arriving at Fiji in November. She was to be part of the pre-invasion bombardment of Tarawa in the Gilbert Islands for Operation Galvanic. After Tarawa fell to the Americans, *South Dakota* and BatDiv 9 was again under Admiral Willis Lee. With four other battleships, she bombarded Nauru, which fell with little opposition. Then it was on to the Marshall Islands for Operation Flintlock, the largest combined amphibious, naval, and air assault in history.

The United States' Fifth and Third Fleets under Admiral Raymond Spruance boasted four task groups consisting of twelve fleet and light carriers, eight battleships, twenty cruisers, one hundred destroyers, almost a thousand planes, one Marine division, and one army division. The objectives were the islands of Kwajalein, Roi-Namur, Majuro, Enewetak, Jaluit, and Mili.

South Dakota was at last part of a major campaign, and her crew was determined to put the bad luck behind them.

The huge Japanese anchorage at Truk Lagoon in the Carolines was the next target of the U.S. Navy. Battleships and naval aviation bombarded the islands and ships at Truk (now known as Chuuk Lagoon), sinking and damaging a large portion of the Imperial Army and Navy support fleet. *South Dakota* and two other battleships under Admiral Lee were tasked with bombarding the island of Pohnpei in the Carolines at the end of April while the carriers continued to hammer Truk. The Japanese Navy and merchant fleet were on the defensive, with little time or room to consolidate their rapidly diminishing forces. The fast battleship was at last showing its value in the war. Now part of a task group of nine battleships and four heavy cruisers, *South Dakota* escorted the carriers during Operation Forager, the invasion of the Marianas.

By this time, the old battleships, including the ones repaired after Pearl Harbor, were adding their firepower to the Pacific. While *South Dakota, North Carolina,* and the other new ships worked in concert with the carriers to provide anti-aircraft artillery and radar support, the older ships, not as fast, were tasked with pre-assault bombardment.

After Admirals Willis Lee and Marc Mitscher, who commanded the carrier task force, conferred, they had the battleships stay with the carriers and add their radar and anti-aircraft artillery support to protect against expected air attack. On June 19, Lee's battleships were circling in an area of the Philippine Sea, awaiting an air strike from the First Mobile Force, a slapdash fleet intended to sink the American carriers. *South Dakota's* air search radar was the first to spot the incoming force of dive and torpedo bombers. She received one hit on the deck from a bomb, tearing a twelve-foot hole in the steel. More attacks came in and the sky was black with anti-aircraft artillery bursts and burning planes. Through the next day, Lee's ships handled the air attacks while Mitscher's carrier planes mauled the First Mobile Force.

On it went, from raids on Formosa to Okinawa, until at last *South Dakota* was part of Task Force 34 under Rear Admiral Forrest Sherman. In what would be called the Battle of Leyte Gulf, as related in Chapter 17, the fleet was deployed to support the landings on Leyte in the Philippines and to intercept the approaching Japanese fleet. Operation Sho Go had assembled every available carrier, battleship, cruiser, and destroyer in the Imperial Navy. Three task forces were to attack the amphibious fleet at Leyte, while a northern force, under Admiral Ozawa, was to use the carriers as bait to draw Halsey north. Three other task forces would pass through the Surigao and San Bernardino Straits from the west to encircle the U.S. invasion fleet.

Admiral Takeo Kurita's force was found by search planes, and a large air strike was launched to intercept them in the Sibuyan Sea. The battleship *Musashi* was sunk and Kurita turned west. But not for long. He still had *Yamato*, several battleships, heavy and light cruisers, and a score of destroyers.

The decoy worked and Halsey sent Mitscher north to hunt down and destroy Ozawa's carriers. *South Dakota*, five other battleships, seven cruisers, and eighteen destroyers of TF 34 were sent north with Mitscher. Sherman insisted that TF 34 remain with the invasion fleet, but Halsey, in the decision that would plague him for the rest of his life, discounted the risk to the landings and ordered TF 34 north to precede Mitscher and give him anti-aircraft artillery support on the attack. The irony is that Ozawa's four carriers had less than a hundred planes in all and were incapable of defending their ships, much less attacking the United States fleet. Mitscher launched six air strikes at Ozawa's carriers, sinking and damaging them.

During the night of October 24, Kurita had turned back through the San Bernardino Strait and resumed his plan to attack the landing fleet. He then encountered the escort carriers and destroyers of Taffy 3 off Samar Island. When word of the surprise re-emergence of Kurita's battleships and cruisers reached Halsey, he held off making a decision. An hour later, he ordered TF 34 south to find Kurita's ships. But this was delayed as *South Dakota* had to slow and refuel the thirsty destroyers. The delays added two hours to the time it would take for TF 34 to reach the battle area. By then, Kurita had withdrawn with heavy losses from the destroyers and escort carriers.

South Dakota, through no fault of her officers or crew, had missed out on the chance to use her advanced fire control system to destroy the remainder of the Imperial Navy, including *Yamato*, who would re-emerge as a threat five months later at Okinawa. It was not bad luck, but it rankled nonetheless.

The ship went back to Leyte to provide fire for the troops on the ground on November 4. She provided more support on Luzon over the next week. While most of her non-combat time was spent refueling destroyers, more was in store for Battleship X. When Spruance took command of the Fifth Fleet, the fast carriers and battleships still under Admiral Lee were designated Task Force 58.

During the landings on Iwo Jima, the battleships were sent north to bombard Tokyo. More bombardments were planned on Kobe and Nagoya, coincidentally the targets of the Doolittle Raid of 1942. But bad weather canceled the latter operations. *South Dakota* supported more strikes and bombardments on southern Kyushu and the huge naval base at Kure, destroying airfields and ships. It was a clear portent of an invasion of the Japanese Home Islands later in the year.

South Dakota and the other battleships refueled at Ulithi and sortied to begin the first bombardments of Okinawa for the landings in late April. While she was at Ulithi, the Japanese submarine *I-58*, under Lieutenant Commander Mochitsura Hashimoto, was one of the subs being sent by the naval general staff to launch the Kaiten suicide manned torpedoes to enter the anchorage and sink capital ships. But the attack was recalled. Only three months later, Hashimoto would sink the heavy cruiser *Indianapolis* between Tinian and Leyte. It was a slight brush with disaster that the *South Dakota* had managed to avoid.

The war was creeping ever closer to Japan. *South Dakota*'s run of bad luck seemed to have been left behind.

There is, of course, no such thing as an invincible warship. Since the days of Henry VIII's *Mary Rose* and well into our own time, both mighty and small warships have fallen prey to enemy action, storms, accidents, and bad luck. The ocean floor is strewn with the rusting carcasses of such ships, each sent to their graves by forces both profound and prosaic.

But to the crew of a fighting ship, nothing can equal the terror of ammunition magazines exploding. To have an entire ship erupt into a cataclysmic fireball, leaving only burning debris and floating bodies in its wake, is the most terrible event that can strike a warship. In essence, there was little fundamental difference between the early dreadnoughts and the sleek new battleships that entered service in 1944 and 1945. Besides the addition of radar and sophisticated fire control systems, the way battleships loaded and fired their main batteries was not much different than what a World War One gun crew would have used.

As for the *South Dakota*, there would be little argument that her career during the Pacific War had more than its share of bad luck. Groundings, collisions, electrical and fire control breakdowns, and a lot of unusual battle damage seemed to plague her. But luck can change. It did on a day in May 1945.

Readers of the essay on torpedoes will recall Captain Charles Bowers Momsen. Known as "Swede" throughout the navy, Momsen was best known not as a battleship officer but as a submarine driver. Despite his technical and operational successes, Momsen had made few friends in the navy's bureaus of ships, ordnance, and repair, each of which considered him a thorn in their collective hides. Momsen's restless drive and high visibility in the navy eventually brought him a special command, USS *South Dakota*.

During the Okinawa campaign, she was cycling from bombardment assignments on southern Okinawa and replenishment far offshore out of range of Japanese air attack. On May 6, Momsen watched from his bridge while the warship's nine 16-inch rifles rained heavy shells on the Japanese defenders on the beaches and hills. But soon, the ammunition was low, and he ordered the ship offshore to replenish powder and shells. He waited as the ammunition ship *Rangle* tied up alongside and began hoisting the heavy shells and powder canisters into the chutes that led deep into the ship's magazines. All was going well when suddenly a cloud of dirty yellow smoke erupted from the vents at the base of Turret Number 2 on the foredeck. Momsen was looking down on the forward turrets from the navigation bridge as more smoke seemed to stream out from every seam and vent. Suddenly there was a deep, rumbling roar and a single muffled boom, then the huge ship shuddered as if hit by a torpedo. The *South Dakota*'s 45,000-ton hull shook with each detonation.

Momsen realized that a battleship captain's worst nightmare was coming true—the magazines were exploding. Hundreds of tons of high-explosive cordite were in danger of turning his ship and crew into an instant crematorium.

Without a moment's pause, he slapped the 1/MC intercom to the damage control station. "Flood the magazines for number two turret!" he ordered into the microphone.

All he could do was wait. He then saw his ship was virtually alone. The ammunition ship had dropped its lines and was moving away rapidly with a boiling wake under her counter. Every other vessel nearby was also running as far as possible from the doomed battlewagon. If she blew up, the blast would destroy anything nearby.

The ship shuddered again as a second explosion shook her sturdy hull, followed by three more. It was terrifying to feel the heavy battleship rock violently with each muffled boom deep in the hull.

Just then, Rear Admiral Willis Lee, the division commander, came on the bridge, his eyes wide. "For Christ's sake, Swede," he roared. "What in the hell is happening?"

A quartermaster at his post at the helm recalled the exchange. Momsen did not take his eyes off the clouds of yellow smoke pulsing from the fore turret as he replied, "Admiral, I believe the forward magazines are exploding."

No stranger to danger in combat, Lee stared at the tall captain. "Good God, man, what are you doing about it?"

"I have ordered the magazines flooded." Momsen's voice was calm, level, and clear.

"Well, is it being done?" Lee was also not one to panic. He had been through the naval campaign at Guadalcanal and fighting battleships throughout the war. But he couldn't understand how Momsen could be so calm.

South Dakota's captain never stopped looking at the hulking turret. "I hope so, Admiral. But I'm not going to call them now to find out. Anyway, we'll know soon enough." Then he looked up and pointed his finger to the sky. "If they are not, that's where we will be in about thirty seconds."

Deep in her steel hull, to over a thousand men, from cooks to gunner's mates, from signalmen to Marines, from officers to mess stewards, the shaking and reverberating booms echoing through the ship would have been obvious. The big battleship was about to explode. They would all die in the blink of an eye. It was a testament to their discipline, devotion to duty, and courage that none of the crew panicked or jumped overboard. They remained at their posts, awaiting annihilation and extinction.

Then, several minutes after the first explosion, the rumblings and shaking subsided. The battleship stopped shuddering. A collective sigh went through the crew. It appeared that the magazines had been flooded and a catastrophe narrowly avoided. Icy beads of sweat on upper lips and foreheads were wiped away, and a nervous relief coursed through the crew. The ship would not be torn apart in a massive blast after all. Soon the normal routine of running the ship took over again. But it had been so close.

When all was again quiet, Momsen was already pondering the cause. How could the routine loading of ammunition lead to the annihilation of a powerful battleship? The damage control officer called the bridge and reported that the magazines for turret Number 2 had been flooded. The doors that prevented fire or water from spreading were closed. Three men were dead, and eight more fatally wounded from fire and severe concussion. Another twenty-four men were also injured but would survive. They were taken up to Sick Bay and treated for smoke inhalation and burns. Momsen visited his men and found one gunner's mate who had witnessed the initial explosion.

He was headed for the heavy doorway to the handling room of turret Number 2. Two men were passing the steel canisters that contained the silk bags containing the nitrocellulose cordite propellant. Suddenly a searing white tongue of flame speared out from the end of one canister. The handling room quickly became an incandescent hell. Fortunately for him, the heavy steel door closed toward him. The sudden blast pressure slammed the door shut, sealing the explosion in the far room. The initial detonation rocked the ship as alarm klaxons clanged and men began running and shouting. Some ran for the ladder; others grabbed fire extinguishers and hoses. Over the next few minutes, a second explosion rocked the ship, followed by a third.

Flooding the magazine brought hundreds of tons of cold seawater roaring into the lower rooms. After one more violent detonation, the worst was over. After the water was pumped out, the damage control party checked the handling room. It was a black, seared charnel house of torn, burned bodies and badly burned men. The wounded were evacuated. The remains of five steel canisters littered the ankle-deep water on the deck. Farther inside the handling room, the stacks of stored canisters remained intact, but the truth was obvious. If Momsen had not ordered flooding the magazine, the *South Dakota* would have been blown apart by the more than 100 tons of highly volatile propellant.

Momsen, with his intuitive engineer's mind, examined the possible causes. He was aware that nitrocellulose propellant was susceptible to ignition by spark. But the silk bags that tightly bound the cordite were supposedly immune from generating a spark. He wondered about the stainless steel canisters. They were sixteen inches in diameter, a foot long, and contained one propellant bag. Normally used only for transporting the propellant, they were opened and discarded when the powder bags were sent up the hoist to the turret.

One possibility entered Momsen's mind. The silk bags could shift inside the canisters, making them easier to remove before putting them on the hoist. Momsen was also an experienced chemist, having worked with exotic gases during his trials with the early breathing and diving tests. Heat and friction could generate a static charge. This seemed plausible as he wrote up his report and opinions on the accident. He theorized that the transport of the canisters from man to man shifted the silk bags, creating friction and generating static electricity. But how to prove it? Momsen knew he had a hard fight ahead of him to convince the Navy Department, and specifically the BuOrd, that the fleet of United States battleships were floating powder kegs waiting for a spark.

Now, armed with this evidence, Momsen inquired about other incidents of accidental explosions on other battleships. He did not concern himself with destroyers or cruisers since, in most cases, they utilized shells with a large brass cartridge rather than silk powder bags of nitrocellulose cordite propellant. He was determined to find out how it happened and, more importantly, how to prevent it from happening again.

In late May, Rear Admiral Lee was sent to the east coast to head up an investigation to find and test defenses against kamikaze attacks. Momsen waited until a reply arrived from BuOrd. They had considered his theories and flatly refuted them. Thousands of powder bags had been used in the fleet for years, and it was impossible for a spark to be generated and it certainly couldn't ignite an explosion. In short, Momsen was out of his mind. Undeterred, Swede pressed on. He gathered support from sympathetic officers and forced BuOrd to take the matter seriously. He was on familiar ground. This was not the first time he had encountered BuOrd's intransigence. The Mark 14 torpedo problem was only the first. It had been Momsen's tenacity and brilliance that tipped the tables in Lockwood's favor, but it had earned him no friends at BuOrd. Now, eighteen months later, the audacious former submariner was again backing BuOrd into a corner. There is little doubt that they were still smarting from the Mark 14 debacle, and having the unconventional Momsen come up with a "crackpot" theory of the tried and true silk powder bags exploding from friction and static electricity was absurd and insulting.

But true to his nature, the redoubtable Momsen did not give up. He gathered enough clout, in the form of Chief of Naval Operations Admiral Ernest J. King, to force BuOrd to conduct a month-long series of tests to find out if his theory had any validity. At the Pearl Harbor Ammunition Depot, officers and engineers ran several tests in which the metal canisters containing the silk powder bags were moved and transported. Days and weeks went by, and with each test, no spark was created. The smug smiles on the faces of the BuOrd officials widened. Then, on the very last day, when it appeared Momsen had been wrong, one canister was being moved in accordance with conditions in a battleship's magazine. A spark suddenly ignited the test powder. It happened exactly as Swede Momsen predicted.

BuOrd had no choice but to accept the truth. It was determined that the friction between the metal canister and the bag could generate a charge of static electricity strong enough to cause the powder to burn.

The temptation to say "I told you so" had to have boiled in Momsen, but that was not in his nature. Having helped avert more deaths and potential disasters, he resumed his duties.

There were, of course, more explosions on American battleships, the most famous being the April 1989 explosion in USS *Iowa's* Number 2 turret during training exercises. While the navy originally claimed that a disgruntled sailor deliberately set the explosion, a second independent investigation showed that poor training of the turret crews and old powder from the 1930s was the culprit. The old bags had been improperly stored and were highly volatile. It is likely that Swede Momsen, had he been alive, would have recognized the cause far earlier than the first investigative board.

As for USS *South Dakota*, her narrow brush with annihilation required her to sail to Ulithi Atoll for repairs. She entered the Auxiliary Floating Drydock ABSD-3 for inspection, which revealed that her propellor shafts and screws were pitted and required replacement or repair. This was done by May 27, and she was sent for assignment for anti-aircraft training and, surprisingly, an anti-submarine drill with two destroyers. After this, she returned to Leyte Gulf as part of Task Group 38.1 as the flagship of Rear Admiral John F. Shafroth. The anti-aircraft artillery training was in anticipation of what was sure to be relentless kamikaze attacks during the planned November invasion of Kyushu, the southernmost Home Island of Japan.

South Dakota, along with *Indiana, Massachusetts*, two heavy cruisers, and nine destroyers, were to shell the Kamaishi Steel Works on Kyushu. The task group then provided anti-aircraft artillery support for the carriers launching air strikes on Honshu and Hokkaido. During late July, she worked in concert with Royal Navy ships, including the old warhorse HMS *King George V*, to shell Tokyo, sinking several warships and other craft.

This duty continued until August 15, when she was recalled upon hearing of the Japanese surrender. Entering Tokyo Bay on August 27, she hosted Admirals William Halsey and Chester Nimitz. As Commander-in-Chief, Pacific Fleet, Nimitz remained aboard until the morning of September 2, 1945, when he took a launch over to the USS *Missouri* for the surrender ceremonies. *South Dakota*, the hard-luck battleship, was there to see the end of the war. Halsey made the ship his flagship while he worked with Douglas MacArthur to oversee the dissolution of the remains of the Imperial Japanese Navy.

South Dakota sailed in company with scores of warships to Okinawa, then on to Pearl Harbor, arriving in San Francisco on October 27, Navy Day. Governor Earl Warren boarded the ship for the double celebration. After transiting the Panama Canal, *South Dakota* arrived at the Philadelphia Navy Yard on January 20, 1946. For just under a year, she was the flagship of the short-lived Fourth Fleet, a reserve unit. On January 30, she was decommissioned and laid up in the Atlantic Reserve Fleet. For the next fifteen years, the battleship was under consideration for modernization to carry Talos guided missiles. But the renovation of *South Dakota* and her sisters was deemed too costly, and she was ignominiously struck from the Navy Roll in February 1962.

In November, she was towed to New Jersey for breaking up. Almost exactly twenty years after fighting her first battle at Guadalcanal, USS *South Dakota* was no more.

On a personal note, I have often wondered about the men who operate the cutting torches and haul the steel away for melting down. Do they ever think about the ship they are dismantling? Sure, it's only a ship, not a living thing, but every ship has an identity, a history, even a memory. Every bulkhead, hull plate, turret, and room has been through the war and bears scars and evidence of battle. It is a sad thing for a ship to die, but to end up as razor blades and carbeuretors is an insult. The worst decision the United States Navy ever made was allowing the scrapping of the carrier *Enterprise*, clearly the icon of the gallant struggle of the Pacific War. But the Big E, *South Dakota*, and thousands of others are gone forever. Ironically, the only ones that still exist, except for the favored few preserved as museums, are the valiant ships that lie on the bottom of the sea with their honored dead.

South Dakota's anchor and bell were retained by the Sioux Falls, South Dakota, Chamber of Commerce for a memorial. A low concrete wall outlines the full-scale shape of the ship, with mockups of her super-structure and a forward turret on display.

While the *South Dakota* might not have been one of the outstanding battleships of the Second World War, she did her duty, through bad luck and good. She and her crew deserve to be honored.

The final essay concerns Japan's second biggest blunder during the Second World War. The first was the attack on Pearl Harbor. While that was more a serious underestimation of American reactions and poor tim-ing, the second mistake was literally a *big* one. The concept, design, con-struction, and deployment of the super-battleships *Yamato* and *Musashi*, along with the uncompleted *Shinano*, never should have been attempted. No Imperial Japanese naval officer could ever conceive that these three huge steel monsters, each displacing 63,000 tons and carrying nine 18-inch guns, could be anything but successful in naval combat. But they were total failures.

JAPAN'S GRAND DELUSION: HIJMS *YAMATO*

Published in *World War II Quarterly*, 2022

The Imperial Japanese Navy reigned supreme in the western Pacific from 1941 until the spring of 1943. While it once outnumbered the United States Navy's Pacific Fleet, its true value to the navy was primarily that of pride and faith. Once the big fast carriers, the most effective striking arm, had been decimated, all Japan had left to fight the increasing might of the U.S. Navy was its big-gun surface warships. Yet these had long since become outdated anachronisms in naval combat. His Imperial Japanese Majesty's Ship *Yamato*, the greatest of all the Imperial Navy's warships, was, in reality, a grand illusion.

Japan still believed in the battleship as the supreme weapon for any seagoing nation. This was a holdover from the long-standing warrior tradition. The samurai sword was used to defeat an enemy at close range, face to face. At Tsushima in 1904, the Japanese fought the Czarist Russian fleet with battleships. It was the last time in history that the big gun played a significant role in deciding the outcome of a war. After the Treaty of Versailles was signed in 1919, Japan began early plans to "liberate" mainland China from the oppressive western nations. When Japan invaded Manchuria in 1931, the Chinese failed to recognize the island nation's claim of altruism. A war in the Pacific was inevitable, and the most likely enemies would be the United States, Great Britain, and the Netherlands.

As for the British, their economy had been ruined by the costly naval building program before and during the Great War. For no other navy to be stronger than the Royal Navy, Britain proposed a Naval Arms

Limitation Treaty in 1922 in London. The terms were simple. Japan would be allowed to construct three capital ships for every five launched by the U.S. and Great Britain. It was no surprise that the Japanese naval officers left the signing table with a bad taste in their mouths. The second treaty, signed in Washington in 1931, further inflamed the hotheads in the Imperial Navy. Japan needed a powerful fleet of battleships to protect its colonial ambitions. Japan chose to abandon its commitment to the naval treaties in 1934.

The coming of the aircraft carrier and submarine changed the equation of naval power, albeit slowly. Great Britain, the United States, and Japan were still wedded to their battleships in the interwar years.

Several members of the Japanese naval general staff had once served as naval attachés in Washington and had a grudging respect for the power of the United States Navy's ships, if not its leadership. Having studied American naval doctrine in the 1920s, these officers were certain that their American counterparts would fight a naval war with the battleship. But at that time, the U.S. Navy did not possess a two-ocean navy and, in the event of war in the Pacific, would have to move its fleet through the Panama Canal.

Japan's leading naval architects were told to design a class of super-battleship larger than anything the United States or Great Britain could build. The limiting factor for those navies was the size of the Panama Canal locks, which were 1,000 feet long and 110 feet wide. Japan, having no designs on the Atlantic, was not limited by the canal's locks. The new battleships would be far larger than the canal could handle and, consequently, bigger than the other nations' ships.

At Yokohama Naval Test Center in 1937, the first elements of the new super battleship were laid out and developed. But it had been a long and frustrating series of discarded ideas, concepts, and blueprints to reach this point. The new design had been changed twenty-three times since first considered in October 1934. Secrecy was paramount, which, in retrospect, led to some of *Yamato*'s worst flaws. With only a few hand-picked naval architects in on the program, they were denied the experience of other designers.

The final design displaced 71,600 tons with three main turrets. *Yamato*'s keel was laid down in a huge Kure Naval Base drydock concealed by high bamboo walls in 1937. Her sister, *Musashi*, began construction a year later in the Mitsubishi yard in Nagasaki on the island of Kyushu.

Musashi was followed by *Shinano* at Yokosuka. Two more of the giant ships were planned. Their sole reason for being was to destroy the United States Pacific Fleet.

Yamato was commissioned just after the attack on Pearl Harbor. Secrecy was still maintained, even to the point that no reports appeared in the newspapers. With supreme irony, she entered service with the Imperial Navy at the very moment that the battleship was rendered obsolete for surface warfare. The aircraft carrier and submarine would soon dominate the seas.

Her proud namesake was *Yamato*, literally the "Soul of the Japan people," also the name of the district around the ancient city of Mara, the first permanent capital of Japan. Battleships were traditionally named for cities and prefectures.

Yamato was the largest ship ever launched in Japan. At 863 feet, the endless teak deck stretched from her graceful flared bow with the

Yamato fitting out prior to commissioning in 1941.

Chrysanthemum Seal to the broad flat expanse of the stern aircraft cata-
pults. Despite her staggering size, she was undoubtedly a beautiful, even
graceful, ship. For two decades Japanese capital ships had been ungainly
with tall, awkward pagoda masts and ugly smokestacks. *Yamato* was designed to be the pride of the Imperial Navy.

She displaced nearly 70,000 tons. So much steel was needed that
Japan's steel industry, which depended heavily on foreign iron ore, had to
shift its entire production to steel armor plate. She had 6,150,030 rivets
in her hull.

The six-deck-high armored steel citadel of the command tower was
eighty feet above the main deck. Aft of the superstructure was the single
funnel, raked back at an angle of 25 degrees, followed by the tall tripod
of the mainmast with its forest of antennae and halyards. Dozens of gun
tubs bristling with anti-aircraft artillery guns surrounded the superstructure like terraced walls. At the broad stern was a crane and hangar deck
that could hold and maintain seven Nakajima E8N floatplanes while two
more were ready for use. Under the 8-inch armor of the long, graceful
weather deck was a labyrinth of five decks, miles of corridors, and 1,147
watertight compartments. It usually took her eight division heads an entire day to inspect their departments. Eighty cooks prepared three meals
a day and battle rations for the crew. Along and below the waterline, the
outer hull was sheathed in 16-inch steel that would presumably stop
any torpedo. This heavy belt tapered to less than four inches twenty feet
below the waterline. The bottom of the hull, 32 feet down, was built in
three layers under the magazines. Even the funnel was armored in 2-inch
thick steel with a perforated steel casing of 15 inches to prevent a bomb
from penetrating to the boilers.

Yet it was *Yamato*'s armament that most impressed those who saw her,
particularly from the water. Three massive barbettes and turrets dominated the immaculate teak deck, each mounting three immense 18.1-
inch guns, the largest ever mounted on a ship. Each turret and barbette
weighed 2,700 tons, as much as a light cruiser. The heavy rifles could
fire 3,200-pound shells a maximum of 26 miles, well beyond the visible
horizon. Their blast was so powerful that boats couldn't be hung from davits in the open. They had to be kept in the hangar. Exposed anti-aircraft

artillery gunners would likely be scorched from the immense flash when the big guns were used. Two more turrets with triple 6.1-inch secondary guns were mounted behind the big batteries. Originally two more of the triple mount turrets had been fitted amidships, but more anti-aircraft artillery mounts replaced them. Clustered protectively around the superstructure were twenty-four dual-purpose 5-inch guns and thirty-one triple mounts of 1.5mm rifles. Another 162 25mm rapid-fire guns were fitted later in the war. Being tightly concentrated around the superstructure, they were highly vulnerable to direct fire from large-caliber naval guns or aerial bombs.

Deep in the hull were twelve Campon oil boilers which could provide 15,000 shaft horsepower to each of the Campon steam turbines driving the four bronze propellers to move the huge ship at a maximum speed of 27 knots for 7,000 miles.

Yamato was, without a doubt, the world's biggest and most powerful warship. However, the steel leviathan was not all that she appeared. She was, in fact, vulnerable and dangerously flawed. A double longitudinal bulkhead from bow to stern contained a complex pumping system that could counteract a list by pumping the water from flooded compartments into empty torpedo blisters outside the armor belt. Some of the older British and American battleships had this bulkhead, but it was abandoned in favor of greater stability. In the case of the three ships of the *Yamato* class, a breach in the hull would cause the ship to list unless the pumping system was used, and that was only if power remained and a crew was trained to handle it.

Another attempt to give the battleship greater survivability was also, in fact, a major weakness. An armored "box" enclosed the magazines, fuel tanks, boilers, and engines. While this addition was another layer of armor protection, it made the hull too rigid. No large ship can be totally rigid. It must have some flexibility as the hull rolls and pitches through swells and waves. The designers made her more vulnerable by taking away *Yamato*'s ability to flex.

The command plot, the domain of the admiral, was located behind the bridge. One side of the plot held the consoles for the Type 13 surface search and Type 22 air search radar. Capable of identifying ships at a range of twenty-two miles, the Type 13 was a large "bedstead" at the top of the tower next to the 30-meter optical rangefinder. The newer Type 22 could detect aircraft at closer range, but unlike the Mark 37 Fire Control Director in common use on American warships, the Type 22 couldn't direct the anti-aircraft guns. Four years into the Pacific War, Japan still lagged far behind in radar technology, even for the Pride of the Imperial Navy.

Once she had been commissioned just after Pearl Harbor, *Yamato* became the flagship of the Commander-in-Chief of the Combined Fleet, Admiral Isoroku Yamamoto. Her first major campaign was the attack on Midway in June 1942. However, her only service was to intercept American radio transmissions. When Admiral Chuichi Nagumo lost all four of his front-line carriers, Yamamoto was urged by his staff to use the battleship's huge guns to shell Midway. He refused, stating it was "folly to bombard shore bases from ships." The brilliant admiral failed to foresee the only future left to battleships.

In the end, *Yamato* turned west, her mighty guns silent.

Shinano's construction was halted just after Midway, later to be converted into an aircraft carrier support ship. This was a measure of how desperate Japan had become. Instead of a 70,000-ton aircraft carrier, *Shinano* would have tanks for fuel oil and aviation gasoline. So much space was dedicated to this that she could only carry forty-seven planes for her own defense.

As for the other two proposed ships of the class, they were canceled along with two immense battle cruisers. Aircraft carriers were cheaper to build and more needed.

There was a reason *Yamato* was not included in the fleet that Yamamoto assembled to destroy the American landings and navy vessels at Guadalcanal in late 1942. She couldn't keep up with the Imperial Navy's fast aircraft carriers, each of which could make 32 knots. *Yamato*'s lack of 5 knots made her a liability in the battles of the Solomons. The *Kirishima* and *Ie* were less well-armored but could make 33 knots. Both were lost in fights with the U.S. Navy.

By late 1943, the naval general staff began appreciating that *Yamato* was a white elephant. She burned huge amounts of fuel oil, was too slow to keep up with the fast ships, and had little use in a navy on the defensive. Reduced to making supply runs or ferrying troops to isolated bases, *Yamato* was torpedoed by the submarine *Skate* on Christmas Day in 1943. A single Mark 14 penetrated the very armor intended to stop such weapons, causing severe flooding. Repairs took months.

Yamato had become a joke in Japan, being called a "floating hotel for useless admirals." It was said that the "three most useless things ever built were the Great Wall of China, the Pyramids, and *Yamato*."

She finally sortied to attack the landings at Leyte Gulf in October 1944. As the flagship of Admiral Takeo Kurita's powerful Center Force, *Yamato* and *Musashi* led the other battleships, cruisers, and destroyers to attack the U.S. amphibious force. Even before Kurita's force reached the strait, *Musashi* was attacked by Admiral Marc Mitscher's carrier planes. She was hit by at least fifteen bombs and nineteen air-dropped and submarine torpedoes in the Sibuyan Sea. The second of the super battleships went to the bottom of the Philippine Sea without even reaching her goal. *Yamato* was hit by two bombs dropped by Curtiss Helldivers from USS *Essex*, causing minor damage but allowing more than 3,000 tons of seawater to flood the hull.

At the same time, Vice Admiral Shoji Nishimura's Southern Force was mauled by a sustained night attack from PT boats, destroyers, and battleships in the Surigao Strait. In fact, the action was the last battleship-to-battleship engagement in history.

When *Yamato* and the other ships burst out of the San Bernardino Strait early on the morning of October 25, they encountered the six escort carriers and fifteen destroyers of Taffy 3, which had been left to fend for itself when Admiral William Halsey diverted Task Force 38 to attack Vice Admiral Jisaburo Ozawa's decoy force of carriers.

But even with the awesome advantage afforded by the Japanese battlewagons, they failed to stop the invasion. As for the mighty *Yamato*, this was the only time her big guns were used against other ships. At least one of her shells hit the escort carrier USS *Gambier Bay*, the only American carrier ever to be sunk by naval gunfire. *Yamato* also hit the destroyer *Johnston* with three of her big shells, dooming the brave ship. Then a spread of torpedoes fired by the destroyers forced *Yamato* to veer away, putting her out of the rest of the battle. After having three cruisers sunk and three others heavily damaged, Admiral Kurita chose to withdraw to the west. So ended *Yamato*'s only naval engagement with enemy ships, and her role was embarrassingly insignificant.

Worse was in store for the Imperial Navy. In November, *Shinano* was being moved from Yokosuka to Kure for final fitting when the submarine *Archerfish* fired six Mark 18 electric torpedoes at her. The ship's crew could not work the complex pumping system, and *Shinano* capsized in seven hours. It was a bad omen for *Yamato* but a good one for the United States Navy. In her hold were fifty Ohka kamikaze flying bombs.

Japan was now living off its shrinking hump. The few raw materials that slipped past the American submarine cordon were not enough to sustain the country. Now down to a few weeks' worth of bunker oil, the Imperial Navy experimented with soybean oil run in by submarine from Korea and Manchuria for the destroyers fleet.

But what to do with the battleship? Some admirals said she should be anchored in Kure as a permanent anti-aircraft island. But none of her guns were of any use against the high-flying B-29s. There was little doubt her heavy armor would protect the ship from submarine, surface, and air attack, but in fact, *Yamato*'s damaged control department could not cope with serious combat damage. She neither carried life rafts nor life jackets. Her medical department was better equipped to deal with colds and minor shipboard injuries than battle casualties. The wounded crew were expendable. Yet this was fully accepted by the 3,332 men and officers who considered service aboard the huge flagship a supreme honor. As a mark of loyalty to the emperor, many anti-aircraft artillery gun crews refused to wear helmets or flak vests during battle.

Despite her less-than-glorious war career, *Yamato* was the pride of the Imperial Navy. Her officers and crew were constantly at work, keeping the great ship looking her best. But appearances were just that. Nearly a third of her crew had never gone to sea. It had been three months since the last training rotation. Most of her turret and anti-aircraft artillery gunners had never fired a shot at an enemy.

Deep within the dimly lit steel catacombs, damage control teams checked their equipment and areas of responsibility. Inside each of the three massive turret barbettes, the 150 men who loaded, trained, and fired the huge rifles checked the ammunition hoists, communication lines, and electrical circuits. Hundreds of rounds of armor-piercing shells, each weighing over a ton and a half, were nestled in the heavily armored magazines at the bottom of the hull. Six hundred tons of highly combustible powder bags were kept in separate compartments behind thick automatic blast doors. She was armed with a revolutionary type of shell called the *Sanshiki*, or "Beehive." These 18.1-inch projectiles weighed 2,900 pounds and were essentially giant shotgun shells containing 600 steel darts and 1,200 incendiary explosives. They would be deadly against aircraft and lightly armored ships. The detonation of these shells was described by a Grumman Avenger pilot at Leyte Gulf as a spectacular blossom of pyrotechnics, leaving a shimmering circle a hundred yards across like a burning ring of tin foil. Sanshikis made up a full third of *Yamato*'s load of ammunition.

The spring of 1945 heralded the last gasp of the Imperial Japanese Navy. At her anchorage in Kure Naval Base on the morning of March 28, the battleship was tethered to Buoy Number 26, specifically for the use of a flagship. Vice Admiral Seiichi Ito, commander of the Second Fleet, oversaw his small fleet from *Yamato*'s Number 1 bridge forty feet above the main deck. Sitting at the table in the command plot, Ito read over the operational orders issued by the commander of the combined fleet, Admiral Soemu Toyoda. Ito had been on Admiral Yamamoto's staff the month before the Pearl Harbor attack, so he was no stranger to audacious schemes. But unlike the carefully planned raid on Oahu, the order he was reading was desperate. In fact, it was intended to be suicidal.

Ito had not been in favor of a war with the United States. He, like his former commander Yamamoto, knew that America might be a nation of money-hungry *Gaijin*, but they had an industrial capacity thirty times that of Japan. The American people were strange but not to be underestimated. Now Ito read over the orders he knew would doom him, his ship, and probably Japan. The orders were simple. *Yamato*, the antiaircraft cruiser *Yahagi*, and eight destroyers were to be part of a combined kamikaze assault named Operation Heaven One.

The reason for the desperate sortie of Japan's last warships was the invasion of Okinawa. The U.S. Fifth Fleet's Task Force 58 consisted of twenty-four aircraft carriers, a dozen battleships, dozens of heavy and light cruisers, and scores of destroyers and support ships. Task Force 58 was already massing for the pre-invasion bombardment before landing more than 100,000 Marines and army troops on the beaches. Okinawa was only 330 miles southeast of the southernmost island of Kyushu.

After Kure was attacked by carrier-based aircraft on March 19, it was obvious that unless the Imperial Navy acted, every one of its ten remaining ships would be sunk at anchor.

For this reason, Admiral Toyoda decided to use the superbattleship for one all-out, make-or-break sortie to destroy the Okinawa invasion force and reclaim the honor of the navy. After three years of hide-and-seek with the U.S. Navy, *Yamato* would have her chance for glory. It was a daring and impossible scheme inspired by kamikaze special attack units in the Philippines under Admiral Takijiro Onishi. *Yamato* would be the ultimate kamikaze, along with her crew of 3,332 men.

There was little to do but follow orders. Ito called in Rear Admiral Kosaku Ariga, *Yamato*'s commander, and Captain Jiro Nomura, the executive officer, and explained the orders. Though stunned, both officers nodded and made preparations. All wooden furniture, paneling, drapery, and even the carpeting and linoleum flooring on the interior decks were removed. In fact, anything on board that could cause or feed a blaze was taken off the ship. The only wooden object left on board was the teak case holding the sacred portrait of Emperor Hirohito. All but two of *Yamato*'s planes would remain in Japan to end up as kamikazes, while the others would fly one anti-submarine patrol at the start of the operation. There was no point in having them along. The slow planes would be helpless against American Hellcats and would be a fire hazard if left on board. The only reason *Yamato* had them in the first place was to act as long-range spotters in the absence of radar.

The engineering, damage control, communications, gunnery, and radar departments were told only what they needed to know, but it was obvious to many in *Yamato*'s crew that something big was in the wind.

Then, just as the ship prepared to cast off, executive officer Jiro Nomura, standing on the armored roof of the Number 1 turret, faced *Yamato*'s entire off-watch crew as they stood at attention on the broad foredeck. In an eerie echo of Horatio Nelson's famous flag signal at Trafalgar, Nomura read a directive from Admiral Ito: "This operation will be the turning point of the war. The future of the Empire rests on our efforts. Every man will do his utmost for the glory of the navy and of Japan."

Then all was ready. On Ito's order, the huge turbines had been warmed up, the crew ashore rounded up, and the anchor raised. Accompanied by two minesweepers to scour the harbor and route to the fueling depot, *Yamato* steamed out of Kure for the last time.

At the sheltered anchorage of Tokuyama Oil Depot in the Inland Sea, *Yamato* and her escorts began fueling. Once containing more than three million tons of fuel for the fleet, Tokuyama had little more than 15,000 tons left in the nearly empty tanks. The special attack force received only enough fuel to support a one-way dash to Okinawa. *Yamato* normally carried 6,300 tons of fuel oil, sufficient for 7,000 miles of steaming. The orders from Kure stipulated only 2,000 tons total would be dispensed for the battleship and screening force. The officers at Tokuyama, angered at such insanity, went against orders and scrounged 8,000 tons of oil for the force to give it a fighting chance but with little conviction that it would do any good.

The ten Japanese warships would have to cover more than 300 miles of open sea in the dark, past prowling American subs and patrol planes and into the sensitive radar umbrella over the Fifth Fleet. Admiral Matome Ugaki was the commander of the Fifth Air Fleet. He had inherited the land-based kamikaze units of Operation Floating Chrysanthemum. They were to keep the American carriers from launching attacks on the approaching Japanese warships. Ugaki had a mixed force of Zeros, old Val dive bombers, and twin-engine land bombers for this purpose. Few pilots had more than a hundred hours of flight training, barely enough to find their destination, let alone make a coordinated strike.

After *Yamato* had torn through the American fleet, she was to beach her hull on the shores of Okinawa, where her massive guns and anti-aircraft artillery batteries would serve as a steel citadel to erase the invasion force. All the crew not involved with the guns were to go ashore and join the infantry fighting. There was no explanation of how *Yamato* would maintain power to the turrets after being beached.

At 2345 hours on April 5, the officers on *Yamato*'s bridge learned that the emperor's brother, Prince Takamatshu, himself a naval academy graduate, had gone to the navy shrine to pray for the success of Heaven One. There were plenty of prayers at the ship's Shinto Shrine and in private.

Yamato and her escorts were in Kagoshima Bay, coincidentally the very place the torpedo bombers that attacked the American fleet at Pearl Harbor had trained. The discussion among the junior officers was about how close they would get to the American ships.

"Without air cover, we'll never see the American fleet," Ensign Mitsuo Watanabe said bitterly. "But you remember the Grummans at Leyte Gulf? We'll see plenty of them."

A new ensign asked, "But won't our Sanshiki shells bring them down?"

"Are you kidding?" Watanabe said and left to go outside. The air was cold, the wind making an eerie sound through the halyards. Watanabe's station was at the TBS on the main bridge, where he would be the link between *Yamato* and the rest of the force.

When *Yamato* cast off her moorings and headed for the Bungo Strait between Kyushu and Shikoku, she was already marked for attack. Two American submarines, *Threadfin* and *Hackleback*, had been alerted from Pearl Harbor. But Operation Heaven One was lucky. Japanese anti-submarine patrols kept them at bay until it was too late. The night and low clouds cloaked the ten ships of Heaven One as they left the coast of Kyushu behind.

Yamato's captain, the bulldog-like Rear Admiral Kosaku Ariga, was certain Heaven One would end in failure, but like a loyal Japanese citizen, he followed orders. Ariga had never conned anything larger than a destroyer, but his bravery was unquestioned. Now on his first time in command of the flagship, Ariga sat on the wooden stool in the bridge, giving orders through speaking tubes to the helmsman in an armored cubicle. The officers had luminescent letters on the back of their caps to be distinguished in the dark. As the ship picked up speed, her small escort of the cruiser *Yahagi* and the eight war-weary destroyers formed a protected screen. They were steaming at 22 knots in a zig-zag pattern with the destroyers in an arrowhead pattern forward to either beam of the flagship. But already, the noose was tightening around Admiral Ito's fleet. Four American long-range Martin Mariner flying boats had the Japanese force on radar and reported its position to Task Force 58.

Three hundred miles to the south, Admiral Marc Mitscher, whom many readers may recall from the *Hornet*'s poor performance at Midway, was pacing Flag Plot aboard his flagship carrier USS *Bunker Hill*. It was just after midnight on April 7. He was determined that air power be the death of the Japanese battleship. Even though naval aviation had sunk *Musashi* six months before, U.S. submarines had also had a hand in that victory. Mitscher wanted a clean sweep by his bombers. With his Chief of Staff Arleigh Burke, he worked out what to do when dawn broke over the East China Sea. Commander of the Fifth Fleet Admiral Raymond Spruance, who was by experience and training a cruiser commander, wanted a constant air patrol maintained over the invasion fleet. Mitscher and Burke tried to find a way to divert part of the carrier force to intercept *Yamato* and keep enough fighters over the invasion fleet to protect them from suicide attacks.

Mitscher had four carrier task groups. TG 58.3, under Admiral Ted Sherman, and Admiral Joe "Jocko" Clark's TG 58.1 were in position 70 miles east of Okinawa, while Admiral Arthur Radford's TG 58.4 was refueling and would be ready in the morning. The last, TG 58.2, under Admiral Ralph Davison, was headed for the refueling rendezvous. Even if Mitscher pulled Task Groups 1, 3, and 4, that left twelve fleet and light carriers with 985 aircraft to provide air cover over the fleet. He made his decision quickly, ordering the three task groups to be ready for air strikes by dawn. He did not inform Spruance, wanting to have the opportunity to sink *Yamato* and her consorts before any submarines could arrive. They were already converging on the projected course of the Japanese ships. One was *Lionfish*, commanded by the son of Admiral Spruance.

Burke, a superb tactician, was certain that once the *Yamato* force emerged from the rain squalls into the dawn, they would feint to the east to divert American search planes away from their intended objective. Mitscher agreed. This was, in fact, exactly what Admiral Ito had planned to do. Once he could be certain that the U.S. Navy had been decoyed to the east, he would order a straight speed run to the Okinawa beachhead.

For Mitscher, the gamble was in moving north enough to allow a large air strike with fighters and bombers while still being slow enough to react in case they were needed. There was little margin for error. He had to be close enough to *Yamato* to allow his planes, which had a combat radius of about 300 miles, enough time over the target.

He was also concerned with communication. The aircraft radio sets were only good for about a hundred miles, so several planes would patrol at between 70 and 100 miles north to provide radio links between the attack force and the carriers. At 0200 hours, Mitscher retired to his cabin behind Flag Plot to get some sleep. But all he could do was lay awake, reading a mystery novel.

Aboard *Yamato*, Admiral Ito was pacing his bridge. The coming of dawn would be the last and most important day in the Imperial Japanese Navy.

When the sky to the east turned from purple to pink, Mitscher, clad in khakis and his long-billed red baseball cap, was out on the admiral's bridge, tasting the cold, wet, salt-tinged air blowing from the bow. Far out to the east and west were the three task groups, more than seventy-five ships covering an area of 150 square miles. They were indistinguishable in the gloom as the admiral sipped his first mug of hot coffee. He began chain-smoking the first of the cigarettes he would consume that day.

At dawn, three divisions of Grumman Hellcats, carrying extra fuel, took off and fanned out to cover the area between 335 and 56 degrees. Somewhere within that 81-degree arc, they expected to find *Yamato*. On they flew, straining their eyes into the low clouds and squalls. At 0755 hours, one division spotted the pride of the Imperial Japanese Navy coming out from under the low clouds.

It was a magnificent sight. The early morning sun turned *Yamato*'s tall superstructure and funnel gold, and a long shadow spread out from her starboard side. A large Japanese battle flag streamed out from her mainmast. Around the battleship were a cruiser and eight destroyers, like attentive chicks with their mother. Every ship had a white bone in her teeth as they drove southwest at 22 knots.

The call went out and reached TG 58.1 via the radio link planes.

By 0820 hours, *Yamato* was plotted at 325 miles from the carriers on a heading of 240 degrees, nearly southwest. Burke had been right. The Japanese force was headed for Okinawa. While the weather was not ideal, with nearly solid cumulus clouds as low as 3,500 feet, the fighters reported no enemy air cover. That was good news. The air strike would have to deal with the anti-aircraft artillery but no fighters.

Another fifteen Hellcats were launched to relieve the ones watching the enemy fleet.

At 0830 hours, Admiral Mitscher was about to make the most critical decision of his career, possibly even more than the one he had chosen on June 4, 1942. Glancing at the bulkhead-mounted chronometer, he knew it would be another ninety minutes before the air group could launch and still have a good chance to make it back to the carriers. Until then, all he and his staff could do was watch the loading of the planes and wait.

"Order the air strike for a launch at 1000 hours," he told Burke. "Heading 344 degrees, range, 238 miles."

In the squadron ready rooms aboard the carriers, fighter and bomber pilots drank coffee and watched the ticker tape chattering out of the tele-type machines for any new information. They were advised they would only have about twenty minutes over the targets. Men in multicolored shirts armed, fueled, and spotted the blue planes on the flight and hangar decks.

At last, it was time. On the flight decks of the carriers, *San Jacinto, Belleau Wood, Hornet,* and *Bennington* got their Hellcats, Helldivers, and Avengers off first. Then Mitscher's own *Bunker Hill* launched at 1025, followed by *Essex, Cabot, Bataan,* and *Hancock.* The first wave numbered 132 F6F Hellcat fighters, 50 SB2C Helldiver dive bombers, and 98 TBM Avenger torpedo bombers. They turned north and disappeared under the cloudy horizon. Another 158 planes launched from TG 58.4 at 1045 hours. Mitscher was eager to ensure that naval airpower alone would sink the remnants of the Imperial Navy.

At 1105 hours, another 106 planes launched from *Intrepid, Yorktown*, and *Langley*, the latter two named for earlier carriers. Naval aviation had come full circle.

Aboard *Yamato*, the radar was already sweeping the seas and skies for approaching ships and aircraft. The six-deck-high armored steel citadel of the command tower, eighty feet above the main deck, was a maze of ladders, platforms, bulwarks, and bulletproof windows, which were never closed during battle. It was part of the samurai ethos that officers could hardly hide behind armored glass while their subordinates fought in the open. The bridge, the domain of Admiral Ariga and his staff, had an elevator in the center and bridge wings to port and starboard. The forward bridge was festooned with high-powered binoculars, a magnetic compass, and a bewildering array of indicators showing engine performance, propellor revolutions, and the large glass inclinometer. The VHF phone and the TBS were mounted on the elevator next to a large chart table, safe with the code books. As morning rose, the officers manned every station, delivering information to the admiral and awaiting his orders. Every moment brought reports from engineering, fire control, radar, and the communications room. *Yamato* was at battle stations.

As soon as the last plane was gone, Admiral Mitscher turned to Burke. "Send a message to Spruance. I propose to attack the *Yamato* group at 1200 hours unless otherwise directed. Will you take them or shall I?"

He was presenting Spruance with a *fait accompli*. A short time later, a message arrived from what had to be a surprised Fifth Fleet commander. The three-word message, which Mitscher read with a grin, simply said, "You take them."

It was all in the hands of the pilots and fate.

Back at Okinawa, the battleship admirals were upset that they wouldn't get the chance to duel with the mighty *Yamato*. But Spruance had decided to keep his biggest guns and concentrated anti-aircraft artillery batteries with the fleet.

Lieutenant Commander Hugh Wood of *Bennington*'s air group had eleven Helldivers, each carrying a 1,000-pound bomb and eight rockets. He was in the lead of the first 280 planes. Around his Curtiss Helldiver were Grumman Hellcat fighters carrying two 500-pound bombs, extra fuel, and 5-inch rockets. The Helldivers each carried either a 1,000-pound armor-piercing bomb or a larger semi-armor-piercing bomb. The Grumman Avengers were loaded with bombs or a single Mark 13 Mod 9 aerial torpedo. These were set for a depth of ten feet for the destroyers, or from eighteen to twenty feet to strike below *Yamato*'s armor belt.

The Marines were also on the strike. Dozens of Vought F4U corsairs, the "bent wing wonder," could carry a ton of bombs and rockets for a distance of a thousand miles. The Marines would add their weight to the attack.

USS *Hornet* sent the order, "Sink the big bastard!" From the start, the air groups faced a serious problem. Every pilot wanted to hang *Yamato*'s scalp on their belts. But there were nine other ships to attack, and they all had to be sunk. Wood and the other air group commanders had to spread the strike out to hit the Japanese force from all sides.

Finally the weather cleared and the ship, which boasted the most powerful concentration of anti-aircraft artillery afloat, was spotted by Wood's Helldivers at a range of eight miles.

From the Japanese ships, the approaching swarm of blue planes looked like a black cloud that scattered and spread out to port and starboard. Admiral Ariga looked through his binoculars. "Torpedo planes, bombers, and fighters. Those Yankee bastards have everything." He turned to Ito. "Have we?"

Ito shrugged. "We have all we can expect."

Ariga picked up the microphone and spoke into the ship's PA system. "This is the commanding officer. Prepare to repel air attack."

At 1217 hours, the two air strikes stayed close to the clouds as they circled the Japanese ships. Then, one by one, the squadrons were ordered to turn in and move in for torpedo and bomb attacks.

The mighty battleship looked much less formidable from the air as she raced at her maximum speed of 27 knots. Her gunnery officers had no way of knowing from where the first attack would come. The anti-aircraft cruiser *Yahagi* shot forward and left *Yamato* behind, while the destroyer *Akashimo* was far in the rear, apparently with engine trouble.

Some order emerged from chaos. The Hellcats, with their six .50 caliber machine guns and rockets, were ordered to strafe the destroyers while the bombers concentrated on *Yahagi* and *Yamato*.

Bennington's bombers drew first blood at 1235 hours. Almost immediately, three of Wood's Helldivers hit the battleship on her aft superstructure, causing extensive damage. The exposed anti-aircraft artillery gunners were mauled by hot steel and explosions.

After three years of carrier warfare, the United States Navy had developed a coordinated attack profile. The dive bombers streaked down from 10,000 feet on all four quarters of their target while the Avengers came in low from port and starboard. The torpedoes had to be released to hit even with *Yamato* turning to avoid them. At a range of 1,200 yards, at least two of every four torpedoes were certain to hit. *Yahagi* was hit by both bombs and torpedoes, cutting her speed.

The Japanese gunners fired back with everything they had. The entire superstructure looked like a fireworks display with red and orange flashes of anti-aircraft artillery fire and streaks of tracers reaching out to the planes. A few fighters and bombers were hit, causing them to break off, while others trailed leaking fuel and hydraulic fluid as they struggled to return to their carriers. Few Americans were killed in the attack, but about a third of the airmen were wounded.

The massive 18.1-inch rifles swiveled ponderously around to aim at approaching planes. "It was like looking into a volcano," one *Belleau Wood* Hellcat pilot commented. The Sanshiki shells bloomed out like fireworks, creating huge rings of smoke and silver shrapnel. But they rarely scored a direct hit. It was easy enough to steer clear in the few seconds one of the Sanshiki took to reach the planes. Pilots saw at least seventy strange cone-shaped purple clouds of anti-aircraft artillery fire at their altitude, but they seemed harmless. It was another example of how the Imperial Navy overestimated the lethality of its weapons.

Yet the gunners did not falter in their spirited defense. When a plane was hit or shot down, the anti-aircraft artillery crews cheered.

By 1259, the first wave departed. Admirals Ito and Ariga watched the last blue plane disappear. They were certain it was not over. How long the respite would last was anyone's guess. The radar was not functioning. *Yahagi* was falling behind, almost dead in the water. Her decks and superstructure looked as if a giant had gone over the cruiser with a battle axe. *Yamato* was still moving but had been hit hard by bombs and torpedoes. Executive officer Jiro Nomura was at the damage control panel, deciding what had to be fixed first.

Ito ordered the Z flag hoisted on the starboard halyard. During the historic battle of Tsushima in 1904, Admiral Heihachiro Togo hoisted the flag, with its intersecting red, yellow, blue, and black triangles, just as the Russian fleet had been spotted. The flag had come to represent the same call to duty as Nelson had at Trafalgar. "Do your duty."

Five minutes later, the second wave from *Bunker Hill, Essex, Cabot,* and *Bataan* took over and moved in. Due to a communications and navigational error, *Hancock's* planes never found the enemy force. Her pilots had to jettison their ordnance and return to the carrier, grinding their teeth in frustration.

One Helldiver released a 1,000-pound semi-armor-piercing bomb which glanced off *Yamato's* aft fire control station, obliterating two 25mm gun mounts and exploding two decks below in the port aft damage control room, killing every man inside.

Black smoke boiled out of the radar room and split open like a melon. The ladders to the bridge were bent and twisted into black fingers.

One Marine pilot, Lieutenant Ken Huntington, flew his Corsair at *Yahagi*. With the skill demanded of naval aviators, he drove in close among the web of hot anti-aircraft artillery fire and planted his 1,000-pound bomb on the forward turret. "One Marine, one bomb, one Navy Cross," was the phrase that would stay with Huntington for the rest of his life.

Again Ito and Ariga coordinated the defense. They had no way of knowing that another 106 planes were on the way after this wave. *Yamato* was damaged with large fires blazing out of huge bomb holes. For the next forty minutes, the second wave hammered the ship as her ineffective damage control crews tried to keep her moving forward. At least six torpedoes had already torn into the behemoth's armored hull. Thousands of tons of seawater flooded in, causing a severe list to port. It was obvious to Ito and Ariga that *Yamato* would never reach her impossible goal.

Nomura ordered 2,000 tons of seawater to be pumped into the starboard blisters to counteract the port flooding. But as *Yamato* listed farther to port, the pumps lost suction, and the blisters were only partially flooded.

The radio room, four decks below the main deck, was flooding. The men inside were drowning at their stations.

By 1342 hours, the second wave had finished their attacks and returned to their carriers.

Lieutenant Commander W. Raleigh of TG 58.4 had finally arrived at his destination. The third attack wave had the longest distance to travel from the launch point. The low rain clouds forced the planes to fly at 500 feet, making visual spotting difficult.

A torrent of bombs finished off *Yahagi*, which finally sank around 1350 hours. Avengers from *Yorktown* and *Langley* and bombers and fighters from *Intrepid* jostled for attack positions.

Ariga would not give up. While he had to have known that Operation Heaven One would fail, he ordered the forward turrets to fire shells into the sea directly in front of another wave of incoming Avengers. It was an ironic move, the obsolete battleship using its main guns to swat down the future of naval warfare. Huge waterspouts blasted into the sky, but only one Avenger fell into the sea. More torpedoes streaked toward the battleship. The chief quartermaster, the old salt Koyama, twisted the wheel at Ariga's orders, hoping to reduce the ship's cross-section to the attack.

It almost worked. Two torpedoes missed, passing the bow and stern, but two struck midships, one below the bridge, causing a deluge of dirty yellow water to crash down on the anti-aircraft artillery gunners.

Bombs fell from the Hellcats and Helldivers, blasting great holes in the superstructure and deck. Two anti-aircraft artillery gun tubs were blown overboard with their crews. Most bombs missed, exploding in the water. But these loosened rivets and allowed more water to pour into the hull. The ship's list had reached 15 degrees. Nomura saw the inclinometer on the bridge increasing to 22 degrees. He informed Ariga, who told him to flood the starboard outer engine room. This would hopefully right the list, but it would drown about three hundred men. It was done, and the list slackened off. But now *Yamato*, running on a single propellor, slowed to 8 knots. This made her an easy target. At that speed, it would take a full twenty-four hours to reach Okinawa. By now, no one believed they would ever reach their goal.

Gray clouds of smoke and floating debris drifted in their wake as bombs and bullets shredded the decks. Few of the anti-aircraft artillery guns were still in action. Nomura desperately worked at the damage control panel, seeing a galaxy of red and yellow lights. Behind him, Koyama tried to steer the ship from the orders shouted at him from Ariga. Every turn had to be arrested or increased as more bombers and torpedoes streaked at his ship. The hull shuddered under more hits. Belowdecks, fires threatened to ignite the magazines of the 5-inch guns. At that point, *Yamato*'s flawed design became apparent. The huge "armored box" that protected the engines, boilers, magazines, and fuel was stressed by internal damage. Hull plates and bulkheads twisted and sheared off thousands of rivets, allowing water to spread throughout the ship. Nomura tried to counterflood, but the same gremlin that doomed *Shinano* five months before now crippled *Yamato*.

The commander of one of *Yorktown*'s torpedo divisions, Lieutenant Tom Stetson, took four Avengers, along with two others under Lieutenant (jg) William Gibson, in low at *Yamato*'s starboard side. This angle would hit the exposed red-painted underbelly of the ship as she listed far to port and steamed in a broad circle. Stetson knew that torpedo hits so far under the hull would tear the bottom open. There was no danger of anti-aircraft artillery fire since the gunners couldn't depress their fire low enough. Driving in at 300 knots, Stetson and Gibson's planes released only a hundred yards from *Yamato* before pulling away. It isn't certain how many hit, but the powerful Mark 13s tore huge holes into the plating.

It was the death blow, and in a way, revenge for the first *Yorktown*, lost at Midway. All over the ship, men fell into the sea from the violence of the explosions. *Yamato*'s decks were a twisted mass of torn steel, flames, and shredded bodies. When the list to port caused men and equipment to fall into the churning sea, Admiral Ito retired to his quarters to await the end.

Admiral Ariga tied himself to the compass binnacle, determined to go down with his ship. He ordered Jiro Nomura to save himself. "Someone must survive to tell our story." Like a steel mountain, the superstructure leaned far out to port. The shredded battle flag and the Z flag soon touched the waters teeming with dead and dying men. Several were killed as they were sucked into the black maw of the smokestack. In moments, the ship was lying on her side as water poured into hundreds of holes and open hatches. The final moments were utter chaos and misery. As the hull rolled ponderously, the survivors crawled up along the red-painted plates, thick with undersea growth. One of the massive bronze propellors gleamed in the cold sunlight, still turning slowly. Then *Yamato* slipped into the cold sea. Moments later, a titanic eruption boiled out of the waves, creating a 1,000-foot-high mushroom of orange fire. Several others followed, killing hundreds of men in the water. A looming black cloud rose to more than 10,000 feet, visible as far away as Kyushu. The world's greatest battleship had died after 102 minutes of battle.

Yamato sank at 1420 hours, still 240 miles from her goal, taking nearly three thousand of her crew with her. Her hull fell 450 fathoms to the bottom of the East China Sea. *Yahagi* and four of the destroyers were also sunk.

In all, at least eleven torpedoes and eight heavy bombs hit the battleship. Survivors put the number closer to sixteen torpedoes and an equal number of bombs.

The three titans cost Japan more than 250 million yen. To put them on the bottom required thirty-six torpedoes costing $10,000 each and eighteen bombs averaging $1,000 apiece, a total of $378,000.

The survivors numbered 269 officers and men. The count of dead was 3,063, including Admirals Ito and Ariga. Another 1,864 men died on the escort ships. Twelve American airmen died and ten planes were shot down to destroy the last ships of the Imperial Japanese Navy.

When Imperial Naval Minister Admiral Mitsumasa Yonai reported to Emperor Hirohito on April 8, he stated that Operation Heaven One had failed and that *Yamato* and four escorts were sunk. The emperor's eyes widened in shock. "The fleet," he said hoarsely. "What of the fleet."

Yonai sighed, tears streaming down his face. "There is no fleet, Imperial Highness. The Imperial Japanese Navy no longer exists."

CONCLUSION

In the 169 years between 1776 and 1945, the very nature of naval warfare went through several remarkable changes. From sail to steam, from wood to iron, it has become apparent that the only constant was and is change. But humanity has used the oceans of the world for commerce, exploration, and war. That isn't likely to change. We are now in an age where navies are smaller in numbers but greater in capability. Submarines and carriers dominate where battleships once reigned. Satellites and GPS now take the place of men with sextants and charts. Sonar, radar, computers, and missiles have superseded the big gun and the torpedo. One thing is certain; naval history is far from being completely written.

Mark Carlson, CL, ACS
San Marcos California
August 2022

ACKNOWLEDGMENTS

I owe so much to my family, friends and associates for their help and support in this an all my other works. Being blind, I have been blessed to know so many wonderful people who have willingly and even insistingly given much of their time and effort to me.

My friends in the Distinguished Flying Cross Society, Pearl Harbor Survivors, Order of Daedelians, Lions Club of San Marcos, the Thursday Knights of Hope United Methodist Church, the Rancho Bernardo Writers' Group and many other community organizations have long since become a foundation on which I was able to work and write my articles and books.

They are far too numerous to list, but a few deserve particular mention.

Rob Wood, Linda Stull, Tom Christopherson, Brian Radder, Carol Gendel, Kate Rogelstad, Jen and John Zingg, John Missoni, John and Geneva Tolbert, Wanda and Gene Elmore, Barry Stemler, Alan Cutsinger, Vicki Moen, Mike Dralle, Dave Piontek, Dave Barnett, Don Ramm, John Tittle, Captain Vic Vizcarra, Captain Royce Williams, Commander Dean Laird, Admiral James D. Ramage, Colonel Walter Boyne, General Robert Cardenas, Captain Wallace Griffin, Colonel Steve Pisanos, and Pearl Harbor Survivors John Finn, Woody Derby, Ray Richmond, Ray Chavez, John Murphy, Stu Hedley, and Jack Evans. Unfortunately many of them are gone but will never be forgotten.

My good friend and kindred spirit, Tom Christofferson, a devoted student of military history and war movies, has been an avid fan of my writing and work. Through Linda Stull, I met Tom, who owns a business that created amazing and detailed models and dioramas of virtually any event in the history of warfare. His creations, done both by hand and with 3-D printers are displayed in many museums and private collections around the world. He made small dioramas of Taffy 3 at Samar, the *Hornet* launching Doolittle's planes, and a magnificent model of the battleship *Missouri* worthy of the Museum of the Pacific. It is among my most treasured posessions. I will always be grateful to Tom for his friendship and devotion to re-creating history's most pivotal moments in wood and plastic.

To Lawrence Knorr, my publisher at Sunbury Press for his enthusiasm, and to my editor, Sarah Peachey, for doing such a great job of making my words readable and perfect.

To them and many others, I offer my deepest gratitude.

And to my Lord and Savior, my eternal love and devotion.

BIBLIOGRAPHY

Ballantyne, Iain. *The Deadly Deep, The Definitive History Submarine Warfare.* New York, NY: Pegasus Books, 2018.

De Kay, James. *A Rage for Glory: The Life of Commodore Stephen Decatur.* New York, NY: Free Press – Simon & Schuster, 2007.

Foreman, Laura and Ellen Blue Phillips. *Napoleon's Lost Fleet: Bonaparte, Nelson, and the Battle of the Nile.* New York, NY: Random House, 1999.

Fuller, J. F. C. *A Military History of the Western World: Vol. II.* New York, NY: Plenham Publishing, 1955.

Fuller, J. S. C. *A Military History of the Western World, Vol. III.* New York, NY: Plenham Publishing, 1956.

Hornfischer, James D. *Neptune's Inferno: The U.S. Navy at Guadalcanal.* New York, NY: Random House, 2011.

Hornfisher, James D. *The Last Stand of the Tin Can Sailors: The Extraordinary World War II Story of the U.S. Navy's Finest Hour.* New York, NY: Random House, 2004.

Hoyt, Edwin P. *How They Won the War in the Pacific: Nimitz and His Admirals.* Gilford, CT: Globe Peacock Press, 2000.

Hoyt, E. P. *The Battle of Leyte Gulf: The Death Knell of the Japanese Fleet.* New York, NY: Pinnacle Books, 1972.

Keegan, John. *Intelligence in War: Knowledge of the Enemy from Napoleon to Al-Qaeda.* New York, NY: Alfred Knopf, Random House, 2003.

Labaree, Benjamin W. *America and the Sea: A Maritime History.* Mystic, CT: Mystic Seaport Press, 1998.

Lang, A. *American Ship.* New York, NY: American Heritage Press, 1971.

Lord, Walter. *Day of Infamy: The Moment-by-Moment Story of Pearl Harbor, December 7, 1941.* New York, NY: Bantam Doubleday Dell, 1957.

Maas, Peter. *The Terrible Hours: The Greatest Submarine Rescue in History*. New York, NY: HarperCollins, 1999.

Mahan, Alfred T. *The Influence of Sea Power Upon History*. New York: Little, Brown and Co., 1890.

Massie, Robert K. *Castles of Steel: Britain, Germany, and the Winning of the Great War at Sea*. New York, NY: Ballantine Books, 2003.

McSherry, P. *Voyage of the Oregon*. Naval Institute Proceedings.

Mrazak, Robert J. *A Dawn Like Thunder: The True Story of Torpedo Squadron Eight*. New York, NY: Little, Brown and Co, 2008.

Nelson, James L. *George Washington's Great Gamble, and the Sea Battle that Won the American Revolution*. New York, NY: McGraw-Hill, 2010.

Offley, Ed. *The Burning Shore: How Hitler's U-Boats Brought War to America*. New York, NY: Perseus Group, 2014.

Parkin , Robert Sinclair. *Blood on the Sea, American Destroyers Lost in World War II*. Da Capo Press, 2007.

Prange, Gordon W. *At Dawn We Slept: The Untold Story of Pearl Harbor*. New York, NY: McGraw-Hill, 1982.

Prange, Gordon W. *December 7, 1941: The Day the Japanese Attacked Pearl Harbor*. New York, NY: McGraw-Hill, 1983.

Sloan, Bill. *The Ultimate Battle: Okinawa 1945: The Last Epic Sturggle of World War II*. New York, NY: Simon & Schuster, 2007.

Snow, Richard. *Iron Dawn: The Monitor, the Merrimack, and the Civil War Sea Battle That Changed History*. New York, NY: Simon & Schuster, 2016.

Spur, Russell. *A Glorious Way to Die: The Kamikaze Mission of the Battleship Yamato*. New York, NY: New Market Press (HarperCollins) 1981.

Toll, Ian W. *Pacific Crucible: War at Sea in the Pacific, 1941 to 1942*. New York, NY: W. W. Norton, 2012.

ABOUT THE AUTHOR

MARK CARLSON is a lifetime student and writer of military history. He has written more than two hundred articles and essays on world military history from ancient times to the Gulf War, specializing in naval and air combat. As an honorary member of several veteran and aviation groups, he has become friends with some notable veterans of the Second World, Korean, and Vietnam Wars.

Totally blind, he works with software that makes it possible to do research and write his articles and books. His first book, *Confessions of a Guide Dog, the Blonde Leading the Blind*, about his first guide dog, Musket, was released in 2011.

As a past president of a local Toastmasters club, since 2009 he has been a popular public speaker for adult education programs, schools, colleges and universities, including Yale and Stanford. He has spoken at the National Museum of the Air Force and several prestigious naval and aviation museums and organizations across the country.

While primarily a writer of nonfiction history, he does enjoy writing novels. His first published novel series, "The Vengeance of the Last Roman Legion" was released by Sunbury Press in 2022.

His last nonfiction book, also by Sunbury Press, was *The Marines' Lost Squadron, The Odyssey of VMF-422*, which won several awards and has been praised by aviation historians. Prior to that, he wrote *Flying on Film, A Century of Aviation in the Movies 1912 to 2012.*

War at Sea is his latest nonfiction work, and he is currently working on *When Yamamoto Ran Wild*, the definitive history of the first six months of the Pacific War, which Sunbury Press will be publishing later in 2023.

Carlson lives in San Marcos, California.

OTHER BOOKS BY MARK CARLSON

Vengeance of the Last Roman Legion series, Sunbury Press
Out of the Darkness, April 2022
Legionary, May 2022
Hunters & Hunted, September 2022
Vindicta, December 2022

Confessions of a Labradiva: Another Blonde Leading the Blind
Iuniverse, July 2021
Companion to: *Confessions of a Guide Dog:*
The Blonde Leading the Blind
Iuniverse, November 2011

The Marines' Lost Squadron: The Odyssey of VMF-422
Sunbury Press, November 2017
Audio: Beacon Audio Books, March 2022

Flying on Film: A Century of Aviation in the Movies 1912-2012
BearManor Media, July 2019

Chicken Soup for the Soul: The Dog Did What?
Story #48 "Musket"
Simon & Schuster, August 2014

After the Pandemic: Visions of Life Post COVID-19
Chapter 2: Plagues in History
Sunbury Press, May 2020